DISCARDED

UNDERGROUND ECONOMIES IN TRANSITION

Underground Economies in Transition
Unrecorded activity, tax evasion, corruption and organized crime

Edited by
EDGAR L. FEIGE
KATARINA OTT

Ashgate
Aldershot • Brookfield USA • Singapore • Sydney

© Edgar L. Feige and Katarina Ott 1999

All rights reserved. No part of this publication may be reproduced, stored in a retrieval system, or transmitted in any form or by any means, electronic, mechanical, photocopying, recording or otherwise without the prior permission of the publisher.

Published by
Ashgate Publishing Ltd
Gower House
Croft Road
Aldershot
Hants GU11 3HR
England

Ashgate Publishing Company
Old Post Road
Brookfield
Vermont 05036
USA

Ashgate website: http://www.ashgate.com

British Library Cataloguing in Publication Data
Underground economies in transition : unrecorded activity,
 tax evasion, corruption and organized crime
  1.Informal sector (Economics) 2.Europe, Eastern - Economic
  conditions - 1989- 3.Europe, Central - Economic conditions
  - 20th century 4.Former Soviet republics - Economic
  conditions - 20th century
  I.Feige, Edgar L. II.Ott, Katarina
  330.9'43

Library of Congress Catalog Card Number: 99-73166

ISBN 1 84014 960 4

Printed and bound by Athenaeum Press, Ltd.,
Gateshead, Tyne & Wear.

Contents

Acknowledgements   vii

Introduction
Edgar L. Feige & Katarina Ott   1

PART I: GENERAL ISSUES

1 Underground Economies in Transition: Noncompliance and Institutional Change
 Edgar L. Feige   11

2 Economic Policy and the Underground Economy in Transition
 Katarina Ott   29

3 Between Opportunism and Distrust: Socio-Cultural Aspects of the Underground Economy in Croatia
 Aleksandar Štulhofer   43

PART II: POLICY ISSUES

4 Tax Policy, Tax Evasion and Corruption in Economies in Transition
 Roger A. Bowles   67

5 Policies Dealing with Tax Evasion
 Cedric Sandford   87

6 Russia's Underground Economy During the Transition
 Svetlana Glinkina   101

7 Political Economy of the Unofficial Economy: the State and Regulation
 Vojmir Franičević   117

PART III: MEASUREMENT ISSUES

8   Electricity Intensity and the Unrecorded Economy in Post-Socialist Countries
    Mária Lackó — 141

9   Measuring the Underground Economy by the System of National Accounts
    Sanja Madžarević & Davor Mikulić — 167

10 Assessment of the Underground Economy in Agriculture, Industry and Trade
    Davor Mikulić & Saša Madžarević — 191

11 Measuring Employment in the Unofficial Economy by Using Labor Market Data
    Sanja Crnković-Pozaić — 211

12 Hidden Labor in Poland
    Małgorzata Kałaska & Janusz Witkowski — 245

13 The Spatial Distribution of Informal Marketplaces and Informal Foreign Traders in Contemporary Hungary
    Endre Sik — 275

Subject Index — 307
Author Index — 313

Acknowledgements

This book is an outgrowth of the International Conference on the Importance of the Unofficial Economy in Economic Transition held in Zagreb, Croatia in May 1997. The conference itself was the culmination of a research project on the unofficial economy in Croatia, undertaken by the Institute of Public Finance – Zagreb for the Ministry of Finance of the Republic of Croatia.

The success of the conference was due to the intellectual contributions of the participants, the organizational skills of its co-organizers Ivo Bićanić and Katarina Ott, the administrative support of the capable staff of the Institute of Public Finance and the financial support of the Ministry of Science and Technology of the Republic of Croatia, the British Know How Fund, Friedrich Ebert Stiftung and the Open Society Institute Croatia. Our special thanks are due to Saša Ivanišević for computer support, to Mirela Mikić for library and reference assistance and Natalija Špehar for administrative and secretarial support. USAID supported Professor Feige's conference participation and a Fulbright Research Grant supported his subsequent research in Croatia.

Edgar L. Feige
Katarina Ott

Introduction
EDGAR L. FEIGE & KATARINA OTT

The underground or 'second' economy was a critical component of the pre-transformation planned systems of Central and Eastern Europe (CEE) and of the Former Soviet Union (FSU). Consisting of prohibited economic activities involving arbitrage, speculation, and private production and distribution employing public resources, the second economy functioned in a salutary manner to circumvent many of the inefficiencies and incentive incompatibilities that plagued centrally planned economies. It was thought that liberalization and privatization would eventually legitimate and absorb most of these economic activities into the official market system of the emerging post-transition states.

It is now apparent that underground or unofficial economic activities continue to play an essential, albeit, transformed role in many post transition economies. Unrecorded economic activity, tax evasion, corruption and organized crime represent forms of non-compliant behavior that have important and primarily negative consequences for many of the transition countries. Many newly legalized economic activities continue to seek invisibility in order to evade explicit taxation and regulation, just as illegal corrupt and coercive activities substitute for the enforcement and property adjudication services that were traditionally provided by agencies of the state. What exactly are the roles and consequences of these underground activities in transition economies? How do they effect the transitions and how, in turn, have the transitions affected the nature of underground activities? These are among the issues addressed by this volume.

Although interest in underground economic activities has spanned developed and developing countries, the process of transition focused a special renewed interest on the topic. In Croatia, a group of young economists associated with the Institute of Public Finance in Zagreb became concerned with the economic, political and social aspects of various types of unofficial activity. Croatia was faced with the difficulties attendant on the establishment of an independent nation; recovery from a devastating war and a radical transformation from socialism toward a market economy. Casual observation revealed that markets were flooded with goods smuggled in from neighboring countries, workers were unregistered, employers were not paying contributions or taxes, foreign exchange dealers were found at every corner, and politically well connected individuals suddenly appeared to be displaying new found wealth. In short, there appeared to be a flourishing underground economy comprising a variety of unofficial economic activities. As a first step, Croatian researchers attempted to assess the magnitude of this underground economy. Employing rough measurement methods that had been used in other countries, (Section 3 of this volume) they concluded that at least 25% of overall economic activity was unrecorded in the newly established Croatian National Income and Product Accounts. This stimulated a number of other scholars to examine both the causes and implications of underground activities during transitions. These findings, along with comparable studies from other transition countries, were presented at an International Conference on Unofficial Economies in Transition in May 1997 in Zagreb. The present volume is an offshoot of that conference. Among the themes raised in this volume, perhaps the most important is the concern that underground activity on a large scale can fundamentally undermine the success of the transition process.

The first set of papers place underground economic activity in the broader context of institutional economics and examine the complex causal interrelationships between noncompliant behavior and the economic transition to a market economy. The papers question whether unofficial activities are the natural legacy of pre-transition behavior or a phenomenon largely resulting from the uncertainty and institutional disintegration of the transition itself. The second set of papers examines both the theory and practice of economic policy in the context of transition as well as the consequences of policy failures. The final section is concerned with the difficult problems of measuring the size and growth of underground activity.

As developed in the first set of essays on general issues, the causes and consequences of post-transition unofficial economic activities can best be understood in the context of the New Institutional Economics (NIE). The NIE is concerned with the costs and benefits that accrue to individuals and societies from the establishment of rules, both formal and informal, that constrain behavior. Underground economics, (UE) is concerned with the costs and benefits that accrue to individuals and societies when rules are evaded, avoided, circumscribed, or corrupted, in short, with the consequences of noncompliance with institutional rules. These two analytic frameworks are entirely complementary, opposite sides of the same intellectual coin. Institutional economics examines the consequences of compliance with institutional rules - underground economics analyses the consequences of noncompliance with those rules.

Both institutional economics and underground economics have taken on a new importance in our efforts to understand the historic transition taking place in CEE and the FSU. A decade has passed since the world witnessed the extraordinary collapse of the socialist/communist experiment. As these countries began their unprecedented efforts to transform their economies from central planing to market mechanisms, few correctly anticipated the extraordinary importance that institutions, and institutional failures, would play in the process. Western economists, whose training and experience focused on solving incremental problems, suddenly encountered regime shifts involving fundamental changes in political, social and economic institutions and processes. The very institutions, which were taken as given in most previous economic inquiry, suddenly became the salient variables in the analysis. Policy prescriptions that called for stabilization, liberalization and privatization required implementation in a context of radical institutional change accompanied by massive uncertainty. Institutions were increasingly confronted with noncompliance, evasion, avoidance, abuse, corruption and criminality. Underground economic activities flourished, obfuscating true economic performance, undermining government revenue sources and hence the quantity and quality of government services, redistributing income and wealth, and unraveling the rule of law.

Just as institutional economics addresses the issue of what types of institutions are required to reduce transaction costs and thereby improve economic development and performance, underground economics must distinguish between various types of noncompliant behavior in order to analyze their short and long-term consequences for efficiency, equity, and stability. As economic activities move underground, firms and individuals increasingly seek to conceal their behavior. Concealment increases transaction costs and monitoring costs. Noncompliance with reporting conventions increases the relative growth of the unrecorded or unofficial sector of the economy, making it increasingly difficult to observe and monitor the true macroeconomic course of the transition. Some countries appear to have made great strides toward a successful transition to a market economy, while others appear to suffer from massive unemployment, declines in output and the collapse of their social capital. Assessing the actual progress of each economy during the transition requires measures of the size, growth and composition of its unrecorded economy.

Noncompliance with fiscal codes takes the form of failure to report income and evasion of taxes. Tax evasion places great strains on government revenues in many transition countries. Revenue shortfalls create budget deficits as governments struggle to maintain levels of social expenditures. Budget deficits, in turn, are met with reduced expenditures and/or inflationary finance. These measures tend to increase uncertainty, public dissatisfaction with government and further tax evasion, thereby sparking a vicious cycle. Investment from abroad is discouraged, economic performance suffers and the deteriorating situation increases incentives for even greater shifts to the underground economy with resulting dynamic instability.

The shifts toward underground activities during transition are qualitative as well as quantitative. Pre-transition second economy activities often involved survival strategies that circumvented inefficient rules and regulations, that is, 'bad rules'. The circumvention of high transaction costs and other inefficiencies not only served as survival mechanisms for individuals, they actually enhanced the overall efficiency of resource allocation under socialism (Grossman, 1977). However, during transition, when legalization, liberalization and stabilization attempt to improve the institutional framework, evasion and noncompliance with the new 'better rules', renders them ineffective. As old institutions crumble and new institutions encounter noncompliance, uncertainty increases, property rights become more fragile, and the rule of law becomes more tenuous. Without the rule of law, privatization efforts that attempt to transform limited value, de facto use and income rights into more valuable de jure alienable rights fail to capture potential public gains. In countries where a weakened state loses its ability to enforce property rights or adjudicate property right disputes, these critical functions are usurped by criminal elements willing and able to employ coercion for their own ends. Resources previously devoted to the creation of new wealth are reallocated to efforts to redistribute the existing stock of wealth. And as the interface between public and private resources grows, so do the opportunities for corruption and criminalization.

Edgar Feige's introductory paper adopts the framework of the NIE (North, 1990) to emphasize that a nation's limited resources must be allocated between activities involving production, protection or predation. During radical transition with weakened institutions, the incentive structure becomes skewed toward protective and predatory activity at the expense of production. Noncompliant behavior creates conflicts between formal and informal rules, suggesting that 'path dependence' may be the result of the pervasive noncompliant behavior that defined informal norms in some pre-transition economies. Feige identifies the legacy of distrust and noncompliance that was inherited from the pre-transition Soviet regime as a major source of the failure of reforms in the present FSU.

The papers of **Katarina Ott** and **Aleksandar Štulhofer** take issue with the view that unofficial activity in transitions is the result of path dependence. Citing the important differences that exist among pre-transition countries, they claim that for countries like Croatia, it is the economic policy of the state and the uncertainty brought on by radical transition that is the major source of underground activity. They focus on the detrimental aspects of the noncompliance and opportunism that not only threaten the success of reforms, but the very stability of the social, political and economic system. Ott focuses attention on the nexus between economic policy and underground activity, and argues the case that credible economic policy requires informed policy makers, transparency and the equitable application of the rules. Štulhofer's empirical findings reinforce Ott's concerns, and reveal that it is the younger survey respondents in Croatia who admit to the greatest tolerance for tax evasion, bribery and opportunism and exhibit the greatest distrust of institutions. Both authors stress the dynamic danger that corruption and opportunism represent to the success of the transition process.

The paper by **Roger A. Bowles** formalizes some of these concerns by extending the typical model of tax evasion to incorporate administrative corruption on the part of the tax collector. The transition creates both uncertainties and opportunities that can be exploited by the unscrupulous. The institutions in charge of collecting taxes are given strong power and the temptation for bureaucrats and politicians to abuse these powers for personal gain may be very great. This is potentially a very destabilizing force because abuse on the part of those inside the system may well lead citizens to become disenchanted with the activities of the state and weaken their own will to support it and pay the taxes on which it depends. By modeling the propensity of the taxpayer to evade and the tax official to behave corruptly, Bowles demonstrates the linkages between administrative corruption, the choice of tax policy and the citizen's decisions about tax evasion. By investigating the interactions between tax rates, the penalty structure, social attitudes and efforts by the tax administration to control corruption, the model demonstrates that a policy that appears to be tough on corruption may not be particularly effective and can even be counterproductive.

In a similar vein, **Cedric Sandford** analyses the problem of tax evasion from the perspective of the design of tax policy. First, policy makers must decide on the appropriate amount of resources to devote to tax administration. They must also determine how tax evasion can be minimized for any given level of administrative resources. Sandford describes the practical steps required to minimize evasion by creating a simplified and honest administrative structure and the perception of tax equity and nonwasteful public expenditures.

Svetlana Glinkina's paper graphically describes how the criminalization of Russia's economy poses a national crisis with international ramifications. With the collapse of the state, and the absence of the rule of law, criminal organizations have taken on the role of contract enforcement and adjudication of disputes about property rights. Given the huge share of property that remains in the public domain, Russia offers broad opportunities to acquire wealth by influencing redistribution, as all claims to property and income are now contestable. The society loses the resources used in attempts to influence the distribution of income, resources that could have been used in productive activity to add to national income. The rent-seeking society experiences lower growth. Rather than accumulating capital, it dissipates resources in contesting and defending redistribution.

Vojmir Franičević's contribution focuses on the political economy of underground activities, namely the role of the state and regulation. Basing his analysis on the Croatian experience, Franičević identifies the state itself as a significant source of underground activity due to its size, inefficiency and inclination to paternalism. He therefore stresses the importance of institutional reforms including the professionalization of state services, judicial independence, greater transparency of regulations and procedures, improved public access and public sector services. His analysis suggests that while underground activity will remain a permanent feature of the Croatian economy, its dynamics will depend both on the character of the developing regulatory regime, on the character of the state itself and on its capability to increase the credibility of its sanctions.

The third set of papers deals with the complex issues of measuring the underground economy and determining its composition. It is widely understood that any effort to access the macroeconomic implications of the transition requires estimates of the size and growth of unreported income. However, all attempts to quantify the magnitude of underground activity are constrained by serious methodological issues. Most important among these is the effort to observe activities that economic agents have a strong incentive to conceal. It is therefore unlikely that direct observation or reliable self-reporting is an option. Typically, measurement requires a variety of indirect approaches. Attempts to use popular monetary approaches for measuring the underground economy were precluded by the short time-span of the transition and the radical changes in financial institutions. The most common indirect measurement approach therefore relied upon changing patterns in electrical consumption as a proxy for changes in overall production.

Mária Lackó's paper addresses the electrical consumption approach and points out its shortcomings. Lacko demonstrates that the variations of electricity intensity in transition countries are not necessarily reflections of the growth of the underground economy. Statistical and econometric analysis of data for eighteen transition countries reveals that measured and registered structural changes are sufficient to explain the differences in the changes of electricity intensity. Her work suggests that using aggregate electricity consumption data and the assumption of constant electricity intensity is not the proper way to calculate the size or growth of unrecorded income in either mature market economies or in transition countries. Other indices such as residential electricity consumption and other assumptions appear to lead to more satisfactory estimates

Three papers attempt to estimate the amount of unrecorded income in Croatia using different approaches. **Sanja Madžarević** and **Davor Mikulić** undertake the difficult task of measuring the size and growth of unrecorded income in Croatia by employing the national accounting discrepancy method between income and expenditures. To the extent that households are more likely to falsely understate their true incomes than their true expenditures, the discrepancy between GDP as measured by the income approach as compared with the expenditure approach yields a lower bound estimate of unreported income. Madžarević and Mikulić find that total GDP expenditures are indeed higher than total GDP income. The difference between the two is the basis for estimating the size of unrecorded income. Since their calculations require various assumptions, the authors carefully provide a sensitivity analysis, which provides a range of lower bound estimates rather than a single estimate of underground activity In a similar manner **Saša Madžarević** and **Davor Mikulić** examine all available sectoral data to estimate the amount of unreported income arising specifically in the agriculture, industry and trade sectors of the Croatian economy.

Sanja Crnković-Pozaić attempts to estimate underground activity in Croatia by using data on employment, unemployment, the activity rate of the population and data from a pilot survey of the workforce. She finds that at its peak, underground activity may involve as much as 26% the total workforce. Given that the Croatian national income and product accounts are still in the early stages of construction and that some data inputs are of questionable reliability, it is encouraging that the three independent approaches arrived at estimates of unrecorded activity that are of similar orders of magnitude.

The two final papers attempt to estimate underground and informal activities in Poland and Hungary. **Małgorzata Kałaska** and **Janusz Witkowski** try to measure the widespread unregistered employment in Poland. As the phenomenon is not directly statistically observable they employ indirect methods based on labor force surveys. They also present survey-based estimates of the supply and demand sides of underground economy participation rates and income. Their study is rich in detailing the age, education and urban/rural distribution of unregistered workers, as well as the frequency of unregistered employment in different types of jobs. They find that both full-time and part-time employment in the underground economy amounts to roughly 16% of the total number of persons officially employed in Poland.

Endre Sik presents evidence on the nature, composition and spatial distribution of two types of informal marketplaces in Hungary. The first type of market is essentially a market for daily casual labor in which neither the employer or the employee pays taxes or social security contributions. Such markets typically involve the employment of construction workers or agricultural laborers. The second type of informal market is for goods, typically a flea market or a bazaar. Sik examines the extent to which these markets involve foreign workers or traders.

PART I
GENERAL ISSUES

1 Underground Economies in Transition: Noncompliance and Institutional Change

EDGAR L. FEIGE*

Institutions and Economic Performance

The historical laboratory in which transition experiments are taking place has revealed that liberalization, stabilization, and privatization may be necessary but are by no means sufficient conditions for creating 'market economies'. We have belatedly recognized that the successful implementation of each of these programs requires a complex set of supporting institutions, whose absence in transition economies often results in undesirable outcomes. The New Institutional Economics (NIE) is now acknowledged to be an indispensable intellectual framework for understanding economic development and economies in transition. North (1990) has persuasively argued that institutions matter insofar as they affect economic outcomes, but we still lack an explicit formulation of the critical relationship between institutional arrangements and economic performance. We suspect that a stable, credible, transparent and effective set of institutions reduces transaction costs, which in turn improves performance, but again, a precise mechanism is lacking. One hypothesis is that lower transaction costs shift economic activity and resources away from protection and predation toward production.

From the long term NIE perspective of economic history, the institutional change that shapes the evolution of societies is seen as 'overwhelmingly incremental' and highly 'path dependent'. How then, are we to recon-

---

* Emeritus Professor of Economics, University of Wisconsin-Madison. I am grateful to the members of the National Academy of Science - National Research Council Task Force on Economies in Transition for helpful comments and discussions. Questions and comments can be e-mailed to elfeige@facstaff.wisc.edu. Reprinted with permission from Transforming Post-Communist Political Economies. Copyright ©1997 by the National Academy of Science. Courtesy of the National Academy Press, Washington, D.C.

cile this 'glacial' view of institutional change with the radical transformations now under way in Central and Eastern Europe and in the New Independent States (NIS)? Are these revolutions less revolutionary and less discontinuous than they appear? What will ultimately determine their outcomes?

North (1990:91) suggests that the outcomes of revolutionary changes will depend on 'the ongoing tension between informal constraints and the new formal rules'. Formal institutions have indeed changed radically in the former communist countries, but informal institutions much less so. What, then, can we learn from a closer examination of the informal conventions, particularly when these include norms of noncompliance with the formal rules?

The NIE has taught us that every market presupposes the existence of property rights to be traded. When these rights are established, supported, and enforced in a transparent, even-handed manner under the rule of law, uncertainty and the transaction costs of exchange are significantly reduced, and economic outcomes are likely to be improved. Many of the transition economies have yet to establish the rule of law, and suffer instead from the legacy of regimes of arbitrary discretion that encouraged noncompliant behavior as the informal norm. Noncompliant behavior breeds underground economies whose persistence and consequences are now coming under increasing scrutiny in transitional economies.

If we are to understand why some transitions have been relatively rapid and successful while others have languished and suffered from huge adjustment costs, we must examine how each society has structured the relative incentives for productive, protective, and predatory behavior. These incentive structures are unlikely to be transparent, particularly when there is a lack of coherence between formal and informal institutions. When formal and informal institutions clash, noncompliant behavior proliferates, forming various underground economies. Tax evasion, corruption, bribery, organized criminality, and theft of government property become commonplace.

Many of the centrally planned economies suffered from fundamental inconsistencies between formal and informal institutions. Formal laws and contracts were often violated while informal norms, reflecting the real world calculus of effective rewards and punishments, sanctioned illegal activities. Consequentially, the transition process had to deal with a legacy of noncompliant behavior involving protective and predatory practices. One of the great challenges for a successful transformation is determining how to restructure institutions and incentives so that resources are redirected toward productive wealth-creating outcomes.

Production, Protection, and Predation

Nations have traditionally allocated scarce resources to acquire, protect, and produce wealth. A nation's growth - its ability to produce new wealth- will be determined by its technology, the quality and quantity of its total resource endowment, and the amounts of resources employed in the protection and redistribution of existing wealth. Those resources not devoted to protective and acquisitive activities can be allocated to the production of new wealth. Predatory rent-seeking practices are characterized as negative sum games because the winner's gains are overshadowed by the loser's losses as aggregate wealth declines.

As the administrative mechanisms of central planning give way to market allocations, and state ownership is replaced by private property rights, economic behavior is guided by a radically altered system of incentives, sanctions, and opportunities. Given these new institutional rules, individuals and organizations must make strategic decisions about the allocation of their scarce resources among productive, protective, and predatory activities. We might conjecture that the most constructive form of institutional change is that which provides incentives to direct resources away from protective and acquisitive activities and toward productive ones.

Production costs reflect the transformation of inputs into outputs. Transaction costs are associated with the acquisition, protection, and transfer of property rights. The linkage between institutions and economic performance depends critically on the incentive structures that flow from property rights. Efficient institutions provide incentives to minimize the sum of production and transaction costs. When property rights are uncertain and insecure, difficult to measure and monitor, costly to enforce, and inconvenient to trade, transaction costs are high, and considerable resources must be employed for the protection and redistribution of wealth. Conversely, when institutions are successful at reducing these transaction costs, resources are freed to enhance economic performance.

Institutions generate and enforce rules of behavior and rules of procedure. Rules of behavior structure incentives and constraints on permissible activities; rules of procedure specify acceptable means for amending and modifying the existing rules. Institutional change can occur in either a prescribed or a proscribed manner. Prescribed institutional change is in accordance with a society's rules of procedure, whereas proscribed institutional change comes about when behavioral and procedural rules are broadly violated. Prescribed change is typically smooth and gradual, whereas proscribed change, resulting from noncompliance with existing rules, typically appears to be traumatic and radical.

Underground economies are characterized by noncompliant economic behavior involving evasion, avoidance, circumvention, abuse, and/or corruption of the rules, as well as accompanying efforts to conceal these illicit behaviors from the view of public authorities. Noncompliance is responsible for many of the unintended consequences that often result from policy reforms. The effort to conceal underground activity systematically distorts conventional information systems and thereby complicates efforts to observe and monitor the consequences of policy reforms. These consequences and the way they are perceived thus depend in large measure on the extent to which individuals and organizations comply with the new rules. The choice to comply or not depends on the relevant incentives and sanctions and is often conditioned by the institutional structure that prevailed in the pretransition period. Therefore, institutional change is likely to be path-dependent.

When rules are circumvented by widespread noncompliance, economic performance is likely to be powerfully affected. Since institutional change is the defining feature of transition economies, any inquiry into the causes and ultimate consequences of the transition must include an analysis of the incentives and sanctions governing various types of underground economic activities. Indeed, the perception, nature, and consequences of noncompliant behavior depend on the particular rules being violated. Any analysis of institutional change in the context of transitional economies must address the consequences of noncompliant behavior as manifest in different underground economies. These include the widely observed occurrences of bribery, corruption, organized crime, financial scams, tax evasion, property theft, smuggling, money-laundering, and extortion.

Formal and Informal Institutions

Institutions represent the rules that constrain human behavior by affecting the expected payoffs for economic actors. But there are many types of institution, spanning formal legal systems and informal customs and norms. Particularly in times of social transformation, the rules of different institutions may be discordant. Macaulay (1986) observed that 'theories about the state or society tend to overlook the remarkable ability of individuals to cope with attempted regulation by evasion, manipulation, conscious ignorance of the law, and bargaining'. Eggertsson (1997) points out that 'the primary weakness of the economics of institutions is its limited understanding of the amalgam of formal and informal rules and their attendant enforcement mechanisms'.

When the institutional amalgam is hierarchical, consistent, and complementary, we most easily discern effective rules by studying their codification in formal institutions. Coherence between formal and informal norms simplifies the task of defining and enforcing acceptable behavior. Compliance with the existing institutional rules is the dominant behavior.

When formal and informal rules are inconsistent or in conflict, the effective rules germane to economic performance will depend on the extent to which individuals and organizations comply with the formal rules. Observation of widespread noncompliant behavior signals a formal system in distress. The study of noncompliant behavior (underground activities) and the incentive structures that induce this behavior provides a powerful diagnostic tool for identifying which informal institutions effectively motivate relevant economic outcomes.

Noncompliant Behaviors

Changing incentive structures affect the relative costs and benefits of complying with a newly evolving system of rules. Noncompliant behavior-evasion, avoidance, circumvention, abuse, and/or corruption of institutional rules-comprise what can be termed underground economies. A variety of underground economies can be differentiated according to the types of rule violated by the noncompliant behavior.

Noncompliant behavior is often the source of the unintended consequences observed in the aftermath of policy reforms. Moreover, since such behavior i subject to penalties, rule violators will attempt to conceal it from public view. Successful concealment distorts information and hinders our ability to perceive and interpret correctly the outcomes of policy reforms.

Radical institutional reform often creates a climate rife with noncompliant behavior. The extent, nature, and consequences of underground economic activity will affect the impact of institutional change on economic outcomes. The study of noncompliance in transition economies is likely to yield the most revealing view of the effective prevailing incentive structure, of the critical strategic behavior induced by that structure, and thus of the outcomes of policy changes.

Institutional Economics and Underground Economics

The focus of the new institutional economics is on the consequences of institutions - the rules that structure and constrain economic activity - for economic outcomes. Underground economics is concerned with instances in which the rules are evaded, circumvented, and violated. It seeks to determine the conditions likely to foster rule-violations, and to understand the various consequences of noncompliance with institutional rules. The greater the expected net benefit from noncompliance, the higher its expected incidence. Since rules differ, both the nature and consequences of rule violations will depend on the particular rules violated. Institutional economics and underground economics are therefore highly complementary. The former examines the rules of the game, the latter the strategic responses of individuals and organizations to those rules. Economic performance depends on both the nature of the rules and the extent of compliance with them.

There are, of course, as many noncompliant activities as there are rules to be violated. Feige (1990a) has shown that underground economies comprise similar types of noncompliant behavior. For example, when fiscal rules are violated, tax evasion and benefit fraud behavior is said to comprise the *unreported economy*. As suggested earlier, rule violators, mindful of penalties, will typically seek to conceal their behavior from public authorities. When income-producing activities are concealed and thus cannot be appropriately included in national income accounts, accounting conventions are violated, creating an *unrecorded economy*. Corruption, extortion, financial fraud, smuggling, organized crime, and theft of state property are examples of *illegal economy* activities.

Consequences of Noncompliance

There is a growing literature expressing concern about the prevalence of illegal activities and their corrosive effects. However, Leitzel (1997) reminds us that the consequences of noncompliant behavior depend critically on the nature of the rules being violated. The violation of 'bad' rules - 'those that prohibit voluntary exchanges - in the absence of negative third party effects' - may actually have positive economic consequences.[1] De Soto (1989) argues that noncompliant behavior that circumvents onerous regulations in developing countries effectively reduces transaction costs and therefore should be encouraged and legitimated. Corruption can also be viewed as a means of circumventing bureaucratic obstacles with 'speed money', and even organized crime has been cited as a means of providing enforcement of property rights when the state is weak and ineffectual.

The evasion, circumvention, and violation of 'good' rules - those that prohibit and regulate coercive behaviors - are likely to make society worse off. In the parlance of institutional analysis, whenever noncompliance increases uncertainty and the costs of measuring and monitoring behavior, it raises transaction costs and is likely to have damaging social consequences. Indeed, the weight of the evidence appears to be shifting in the direction of uncovering the long-term damage that results from pervasive noncompliance, particularly in the form of corruption and organized crime.[2] Bribery and corruption often encourage the bureaucracy simply to create additional artificial administrative hurdles in order to receive side payments for their removal. At the same time, organized crime and corruption are seen as a growing menace to new business establishments and as a major barrier discouraging foreign capital investments.

The extent of noncompliance is also an important factor when threshold effects dominate the dynamics of institutional change. Low levels of noncompliance with bad rules might provide a useful buffer against the negative effects of the bad rules, but widespread noncompliance can undermine the social fabric and erode political legitimacy, thereby jeopardizing policy credibility, and the fundamental principle of the rule of law.

There is now an ongoing debate concerning the consequences of various types of noncompliant behavior (see Grossman, 1989; De Soto, 1989; Klitgaard, 1991; Leitzel et al., 1995; Trang, 1994; Alexeev, 1997; Lotspeich, 1995; Shelley, 1995; Tanzi, 1994; Anderson, 1995; and Mauro, 1995). Analysis of noncompliance under the Soviet regime suggests that the circumvention of price and production controls contributed to a more efficient system and served to buffer some of the most costly consequences of allocation by administrative control. The buffer function may have extended the lifetime of the Soviet regime by ameliorating some of the costs of misallocation. But, as discussed below, the pervasiveness of noncompliance under the Soviet regime has had a pernicious effect on subsequent economic reforms.

The Legacy of Noncompliance

If we are to understand the severe adjustment costs sustained during the transition process, particularly in the NIS, we must examine the institutional structure of the earlier Soviet regime and the legacy of noncompliant 'second-economy' behaviors induced by its perverse incentive systems (Grossman, 1977). The Soviet Union's criminal code prohibited most of the private economic activities regarded as normal in Western market economies. Despite heavy penalties, however, noncompliance with the formal laws was the rule rather than the exception. Handleman (1995) describes the Soviet Union as the 'world's most heavily policed state'. Yet paradoxically, it functioned as an essentially lawless society.

Grossman (1992) has pointed out that if one were to attempt to characterize the conditions likely to 'maximize the scope and size of a country's underground economy,' one would effectively describe Soviet-type socialism. A shortage economy with state-controlled prices well below black market prices created significant incentives for internal arbitrage and speculation. Similar gaps between world prices of tradables and controlled domestic prices encouraged international smuggling. The prevalence of amorphous property rights and lax controls over state assets made the theft of state-owned property a pervasive predatory activity. Low administrative salaries combined with powerful governmental authority created rent-generating opportunities for bribery and corruption to flourish. In short, the economic incentives to engage in economic crimes were substantial, but so were the penalties.

Feldbrugge (1989) describes how the formal legal system treated economic crimes. Economic activities regarded as normal in market economies were not only prohibited under Soviet law, but also carried heavy penalties. Private enterprise and commercial middleman activities carried a maximum penalty of 5 years in prison, while speculation drew a 7-year term. Bribery and theft of state property were punishable by 15 years' imprisonment and death. Despite this stiff menu of punishments, these activities were commonplace, and indeed virtually necessary to maintain minimum living standards.

In fact, economic crimes were broadly tolerated by the Soviet regime. They served to buffer the economy from the misallocation failures of the administrative system, and acted as a means of enforcing strict political control. Tacit permission to engage in economic crimes served as a means to reward the *nomenklatura* and its clients, while the arbitrary threat of enforcing the law provided a means of maintaining strict control over political dissent.

Noncompliance with the rules was so pervasive that illegal activities comprised a vast underground economy known as the second economy. Virtually every citizen was a de facto criminal by the mere fact of being engaged in one or more of the common economic crimes. Citizens were reinforced in the expectation that no punishment would be exacted if one complied with the strict codes for appropriate political behavior. These included informal conventions signaling the extent to which different levels of the political hierarchy could dip into the pot of forbidden economic riches. Permitting a pervasive underground economy served as a means of controlling political dissention, rewarding elites, and buffering the hardships imposed by the inefficiencies of central planning. The resulting regime of arbitrary discretion was the antithesis of the rule of law.

The Rule of Law and the Regime of Arbitrary Discretion

Under the rule of law, formal statutes and judicial agencies that offer and deliver access and equal protection to all citizens govern conduct. Institutional control is exercised by the even-handed application of formal rules. The norm for behavior is compliance with the rules. When the rules are violated, a credible system of effective punishment of violators comes into play. Thus control is based on 'the application of the law'.[3]

Under the Soviet regime of arbitrary discretion, most common conduct was prohibited by formal law, which was enforced capriciously at the discretion of those in authority. Access to the system's institutional rewards and protections was reserved for the privileged few, but even then remained uncertain and uncontrolled by law. The norm of behavior was noncompliance with the rules. Penalties were assessed only rarely, and then only at the discretion or whim of the privileged elite that held effective power. Control was based on infringement of the rules, and involved both the carrot and the stick. The carrot consisted of granting the *nomenklatura* use-rights over scare resources, whereas the stick consisted of the threat to impose punishment for the commission of economic crimes.

Implications of the Legacy of Noncompliance

The regime of arbitrary discretion was the legacy and operative institution that survived the collapse of communism. Polishchuk (1997) ascribes some of the lack of progress in Russian reforms to the 'institutional void' characterized by 'missing markets'. But astride the 'institutional vacuum' were the dominant informal rules that defined de facto property rights and guided resource allocation in the second economy. Rent-seeking, rent-creating and rent-exploiting activities were pervasive.

In the transition period, policymakers hoped that 'organic growth' would produce the political and economic institutions needed to support market activities, essentially leaving the market to create the market. But this policy of benign neglect failed to produce the desired rule of law. This was due not only to the lack of a broad constituency for building market-supporting institutions, but also to the inertia of the informal norms of noncompliance.

When reforms did occur, they often legitimated the system of noncompliance that was already in place. World Bank (1996) estimates of unofficial activities suggest that in a sample of Central and Eastern European countries, the underground economy increased from 18 to 22 percent between 1989 and 1994. For a sample of NIS countries, the underground economy appeared to grow from 12 to 37 percent during the same period.[4] Increased noncompliance was associated with weakened political controls, higher tax rates, and incomplete liberalization.

Liberalization served to legitimate the pervasive black markets by legalizing behavior associated with speculation and arbitrage. The freeing up of prices conferred marketable value on many of the inventories accumulated as illegitimate wealth stocks under the Soviet regime. The creation of internal and external ruble convertibility and liberalization permitting the accumulation of co-circulating foreign currencies legitimated illegal stores of monetary wealth. Thus the reforms simply lent legitimacy to much of the behavior that had already existed in the pretransition period. In this sphere, the revolution was less than revolutionary and proved to be highly path-dependent.

Privatization legitimated the personal appropriation of state property by placing previously amorphous property rights to state assets directly in the hands of private actors. Privatization created the opportunity for privileged elites with information and network advantages to convert limited de facto use and income rights into more valuable de jure alienable rights. Not only did privatization legitimize de facto property rights, but also it offered a huge incentive to allocate resources to protective and acquisitive activities. The preference for predation over production was tied to the opportunity to capitalize long-term income streams by obtaining de jure alienation rights.

The uncertainty associated with tentative property rights also encourages appropriation of state property and discourages the type of productive investment that would normally be associated with longer economic horizons. The expected rewards from rent-seeking activities simply dwarf the expected returns from productive activities. Rent-seeking will continue to dominate as long as there are valuable unassigned property rights in the public domain, still available for privatization.

The legacy of noncompliance inherited from the pretransition period was accompanied by a pervasive distrust of government. A history of policy reversals and arbitrary confiscation had destroyed the credibility of government pronouncements and policies. Thus, the informal norm of distrusting government policy militates against every effort to establish the formal rule of law. In the absence of effective state institutions that can protect and enforce newly created property rights, these rights will remain uncertain and their exercise will involve high transaction costs.

In this effectively stateless environment, organized crime can provide a locus of authority for contract enforcement and the adjudication of contested property rights. Thus, organized crime performs a substitute enforcement service that reduces uncertainty, albeit at a high social cost. Unfortunately, the economies of scale that normally accrue to legitimate governmental institutions now accrue to the Mafia. Those public officials that retain the bureaucratic power to assign remaining public-domain property rights will continue to exploit their authority, reinforcing the legacy of corruption.

Although tax evasion existed in the pretransition period, most taxes were collected implicitly - by paying labor less than the value of its marginal product and by limiting the consumption of goods and services. In market-oriented economies, resources are paid the value of their marginal product, and taxes are subsequently collected explicitly on resource earnings. When liberalization eliminated price controls for goods and factors, the implicit tax revenue collection mechanisms collapsed, and the state suffered a significant loss of revenue, which in turn bloated budget deficits. These deficits could be financed either by creating money or by borrowing from the public. Printing money to finance the deficit simply fueled inflation and compounded the disruptive effects of the transition. It eroded the fixed incomes of the working poor and pensioners, and disguised the relative price signals of the fledgling market economy with shocks to the general price level.

The legacy of distrust of government also prevented the government from financing its deficit with the sale of public debt. In desperation, the government embraced the same informal convention of nonpayment that had been adopted by large firms. Nonpayment by firms created interindustry arrears. When the government refused to make payments for wages and pensions, it effectively forced an unwilling public to accept government debt in the form of government expenditure arrears.

The final legacy of the prereform system was a highly skewed distribution of wealth and information. Although incomes were distributed quite equitably, differential access to state resources and selective opportunities for illegal wealth accumulation created a highly unequal distribution of de facto property rights. The opportunity to convert and capitalize these de facto rights into de jure rights created a small but powerful constituency for selective privatization, but not necessarily one that would support generalized property rights.

Corruption is perhaps the most troubling legacy of the pretransition period, and it threatens the dynamic stability of the transition process. Corruption occurs at the juncture where public and private sectors meet. When public officials are granted authority to license, prohibit, tax, or subsidize economic activities, allocate favorable exchange rates, enforce trade restrictions or price controls, and distribute valuable property rights and natural resource endowments, monopoly powers are created in the public domain. Thus corruption, which involves noncompliance with the rules governing appropriate conduct in public office, is a form of government failure that occurs when public officials, acting as the agents of the state, exploit the state's monopoly powers for their personal advantage.

The extent of noncompliance will depend upon the size of the expected gains and penalties. According to Klitgaard (1988), these will be determined by the monopoly power to be exploited, the extent of discretion granted the agent(s) of the government, and the degree to which the agent is held accountable. However, the economic cost of corruption depends not only on its extent, but also on its nature. Shleifer and Vishny (1993) present an industrial organization model of corruption that shows that corruption is less costly when it is controlled by an effective cartel, like that of the Communist party during the Soviet period. In this case, the payment of a bribe is sufficient to assure the predictable transfer of scarce property right(s) and the bribe price is kept in check. The most costly form of corruption occurs when independent monopolists vie for bribes. This model best describes the current situation in the NIS, were corruption is omnipresent, yet property right transfers remain uncertain and unpredictable even after the bribes are paid. With vast, highly prized property rights remaining in the public domain, controlled by independent monopolists whose actions are unconstrained by accountability and the rule of law, predation dominates over production with devastating economic consequences.

Building a Constituency for the Rule of Law

The legacy of noncompliance with formal rules and the concomitant distrust of all public policy have resulted in great resistance to the necessary establishment of the rule of law to support and complement the still fragile property rights and market institutions of the transforming economies. The earliest privatization schemes proposed to transition governments attempted to build a powerful constituency for reform institutions by creating a massive class of private shareholders (Feige, 1990b, 1990c). It was hoped that the creation of a new egalitarian base of holders of residual property rights would produce a political lobby to establish and protect property rights and create political pressures to improve corporate governance structures. These structures, in turn, would maximize the value of the residual property rights themselves. In addition to these incentive effects, it was hoped that the equitable distribution of valued assets would serve as a safety net to cushion the inevitable decline in other government support programs.

Polishchuk (1997) argues that this program failed in its first goal, 'to prevent the rapid growth of inequality and to compensate for the loss of private savings to inflation', while it is still unclear whether the program has helped to build a constituency to protect property rights. In Russia, the scale of the privatization program was massive, creating a class of 50 million shareholders.[5] Nevertheless, the failure to include 'anticarpetbagger' provisions (Feige 1990b) to protect the residual property rights of the poorly informed public permitted wealth holdings to become even more highly skewed. Russian enterprise insiders obtained, on average, two-thirds of the mass privatization shares. By 1996, 'all employees owned an average of 58 percent of the stock'. (Blasi, et. al (1997:54) Although a key objective of the privatization program was to break the dependency linkage between enterprise managers and politicians, 'the tie proved more durable than many observers had believed or hoped'. Blasi et. al. (1997:38)

Summary

The stubborn legacy of informal pretransition norms and behavior dominates the transition economies. Those pretransition economies whose formal and informal institutions were relatively coherent had less of a legacy of noncompliance to confound the transition adjustment. But those economies in which the formal rules were largely observed in their breach inherited a profound legacy of noncompliance and distrust of government. They are also characterized by acceptance of a wide range of protective and predatory behavior that imposes severe adjustment costs on the transformation process. In this important sense, institutions matter, institutional change is highly path dependent, and it is less revolutionary than may appear at first blush.

Institutions do affect economic performance, but it is not always obvious which institutional rules dominate. Where formal and informal institutions are coherent and consistent, the incentives produced by the formal rules will affect economic outcomes. Under these circumstances, the rule of law typically secures property rights, reduces uncertainty, and lowers transaction costs. In regimes of discretionary authority where formal institutions conflict with informal norms, noncompliance with the formal rules becomes pervasive, and underground economic activity is consequential for economic outcomes.

Much of the behavior that violated the formal rules of pretransition societies has now become legitimated in the transition period. Legitimization has been accomplished by efforts to liberalize, privatize, and legalize. Incomplete liberalization - the maintenance of arbitrary gaps between buy and sell prices - produces incentives for rent-seeking, acquisitive behaviors. Incomplete privatization - the maintenance of valuable assets in the public domain with amorphous property rights – produces incentives for predation. Incomplete legalization - the maintenance of arbitrary discretion in place of the rule of law - sustains high levels of uncertainty and high transaction costs, and discourages the reallocation of resources to productive activities.

The formal rules in most of the former Soviet republics are still very far from being incentive compatible and many aspects of the old system persist unchanged. Regulatory burdens and the number of regulatory agencies have ballooned, yet the legacy of noncompliance prevails and independent monopolists willfully exploit property rights that remain in the public domain. The government's tax regime is confiscatory, organized crime extorts private taxes, and the wealth still open to rent-seeking is immense. In short, the incentive structure is such that protective and predatory behaviorcontinues to dominate productive behavior, resulting in lost output and a growing disparity in wealth that threatens the fragile transition with extinction.

Notes

1   Similar arguments can be found in Leff (1966) and Huntington (1968).
2   See Benham and Benham's (1997) account of the role of the Sicilian mafia as described by Gambetta (1993).
3   In describing the prereform Hungarian system Gabor (1989:347) distinguishes between 'control based on the application of rules' and 'control based on the infringement of rules'.
4   These estimates are based on the electricity consumption method that has been strongly critized by Lacko (this volume).

5   Nellis (1996) reports that by the end of 1994, the 15 transition countries of Central and Eastern Europe and the NIS privatized more than 30,000 large and medium-sized firms. In Russia, 16,000 large and medium-sized firms and 75,000 small business were privatized. However, an estimated 10,000 large and medium-sized firms are as yet not privatized. Blasi,et.al. (1997:26) report that by the beginning of 1996, '77.2 percent of mid-sized and large enterprises were privatized'. Moreover, some 900,000 new small business were established representing 82 percent of shops and retail stores employing 9 million people. Yet of 67 million employed Russians, 'no more than 27 million are in the private sector'.

References

Alexeev, M. (1997) 'The Russian Underground Economy in Transition' in Lippert O. and Walker, M. (ed), *Measuring the Underground Economy* Vancouver, BC, Fraser Institute, pp. 255-273.

Anderson, A. (1995) 'The Red Mafia:A Legacy of Communism' in Lazear, E. (ed), *Economic Transition in Eastern Europe and Russia: Realities of Reform*, Stanford California: The Hoover Institution Press, pp. 340-366.

Benham, L. and Benham, A. (1977) 'Property Rights in Transition Economies: A Commentary on What Economists Know:' in Nelson, J.; Tilly, C.; Walker, L. (eds), *Transforming Post-Communist Political Economies*, National Research Council, National Academy of Science. Washington, D.C. , pp. 35-60.

Blasi, J., Kroumova, M., Kruse, D. (1997) *Kremlin Capitalism: Privatizing the Russian Economy*. Ithaca, Cornell University Press.

De Soto, H. (1989) *The Other Path: Invisible Revolution in the Third World*. New York: Harper & Row.

Eggertsson, T. (1997) 'Rethinking the Theory of Economic Policy: Some Implications of the New Institutionalism' in Nelson, J.; Tilly, C.; Walker, L. (eds), *Transforming Post-Communist Political Economies*, National Research Council, National Academy of Science. Washington, D.C., pp. 61-79.

Feige, E. L. (1990a) 'Defining and Estimating Underground and Informal Economies:The New Institutional Economics Approach', *World Development* 18, 7, July, pp. 989-1002.

Feige, E. L. (1990b) 'Perestroika and Socialist Privatization: What Is To Be Done? And How?', *Comparative Economic Studies*, vol. XXXII, no.3, Fall, pp. 1-54.

Feige, E. L. (1990c) 'Socialist Privatization: Response', *Comparative Economic Studies*, vol. XXXII, no .3, Fall, pp. 71-81.

Feldbrugge, F.J.M. (1989) 'The Soviet Second Economy in a Political and Legal Perspective' in Feige, E. L. (ed), *The Underground Economies: Tax Evasion and Information Distortion*. Cambridge University Press, pp. 297-338.

Gabor, I. R. (1989) 'Second Economy and Socialism:the Hungarian Experience', in Feige, E. L. (ed), *The Underground Economies: Tax Evasion and Information Distortion*. Cambridge University Press, pp. 339-360.

Grossman, G. (1977) 'The Second Economy of the USSR', *Problems of Communism*, 26 no. 5, pp. 25-40.

Grossman, G. (1992) 'Sub-Rosa Privatization and Marketization in the USSR' reprinted in Kennett, D. and Lieberman, M. (eds), *The Road to Capitalism: Economic Transformation in Eastern Europe and the Former Soviet Union*. The Dryden Press Harcouurt Brace Javanovich, Inc, pp. 220-228.

Handleman, S. (1995) *Comrade Criminal: Russia's New Mafia*. New Haven, Yale University Press.

Huntington, S. (1968) *Political Order in Changing Societies*. New Haven: Yale University Press.

Kaufmann, D. and Siegelbaum, P. 'Privatization and Corruption in Transition Economies', *Journal of International Affairs*, Winter, 50, no.2, pp. 419-459.

Klitgaard, R. (1988) *Controlling Corruption*. Berkeley, California: University of California Press.

Kuznetsov, Y. (1977) 'Learning in Networks: Enterprise Behavior in the Former Soviet Union and Contemporary Russia' in Nelson, J.; Tilly, C.; Walker, L. (eds), *Transforming Post-Communist Political Economies*, National Research Council, National Academy of Science. Washington, D.C: 156-176.

Lacko, M. (1999) 'Electricity Intensity and the Unrecorded Economy in Post-Socialist Countries' In Feige, E. and Ott, K. (eds), *Underground Economies In Transition*, Ashgate Publishing Limited, pp. 141.

Leff, N. H. (1964) 'Economic Development through Bureaucratic Corruption', *American Behavioral Scientist* .VIII, pp. 8-14.

Leitzel, J., Alexeev, M., and Gaddy C. (1995) 'Mafiosi and Matrioshki:Organized Crime and Russian Reform', *The Brookings Review*, Winter, pp. 26-29.

Leitzel, J. (1977) 'Rule Evasion in Transitional Russia' in Nelson, J.; Tilly,C.; Walker,L. (eds), *Transforming Post-Communist Political Economies*, National Research Council, National Academy of Science. Washington, D.C, pp. 118-130.

Lotspeich, R. (1995) 'Crime in the Transition Economies' *Europe-Asia Studies*, vol 47, no. 4 , pp. 555-589.

Macaulay, S. (1986) 'Private Government', in Lipson & Wheeler (eds), *Law and Social Science*, Russell Sage Foundation, pp. 445-518.

Mauro, P. (1995) 'Corruption and Growth', *Quarterly Journal of Economics* 110, pp. 681-712.

Nellis, J. (1996) 'Privatization in Transition Economies: An Update,' Mimeograph Washington, D.C.:World Bank.

North, D. C. (1990) *Institutions, Institutional Change and Economic Performance*. Cambridge, England: Cambridge University Press.

Polishchuk, L. (1977) 'Missed Markets:Implications for Economic Behavior and Institutional Change' in Nelson, J.; Tilly, C.; Walker, L. (eds), *Transforming Post-Communist Political Economies*, National Research Council, National Academy of Science. Washington, D.C., pp. 80-101.

Shelley, L. (1995) 'Transnational Organized Crime:An Imminent Threat to the Nation-State?', *Journal of International Affairs*, 48, no. 2, Winter, pp. 463-489.

Shleifer, A. and Vishny, R. (1993) 'Corruption', *The Quarterly Journal of Economics,* August, pp. 599-617.
Tanzi, V. (1994) 'Corruption, Governmental Activities and Markets' IMF Working paper 94/99.
Trang Duc, V. (1994) *Political Institutions, Processes and Corruption in Transition States in East-Central Europe and in the Former Soviet Union.* Institute for Constitutional & Legislative Policy.
World Bank (1996) *World Development Report: From Plan to Market.* New York, N.Y.:Oxford University Press.

2 Economic Policy and the Underground Economy in Transition

KATARINA OTT[*]

Introduction

Underground (unofficial) economic activity exists to varying degrees in all economies. In most developed established market economies, the underground economy is largely a sideshow, although it can have annoying consequences. Tax revenues are reduced by tax evasion, distortions in economic information systems may at times mislead economic policy makers, and the society must deal with the consequences of socially offensive illegal behavior.

However, the more pervasive and intrusive the underground economy, the greater its influence on economic policy. Research has shown that the underground economy in Croatia has reached significant proportions - amounting to approximately 25 per cent of GDP. This paper examines the relationship between the underground economy and economic policy. We find that in transitional countries, which have a weak institutional structure for supporting market economic activity, underground economies pose a grave danger, that of undermining the establishment of the rule of law that is increasingly seen as a necessary component of successful transition.

Economic Policy

The main goals of economic policy are economic development and growth and an equitable distribution of income. In many countries, economic policy is guided by Samuel Johnson's maxim that 'decent provision for the poor is a true test of civilization'. People desire to improve their standard of living and the State is responsible for creating an institutional framework

---

[*] Director of the Institute of Public Finance, Zagreb, Croatia, e-mail: kott@ijf.hr

that serves not only to promote that growth and development, but also provides all citizens with an equal opportunity to share in the nation's progress. The goals of efficient development, high growth and income equality are not necessarily consistent. Many policy situations involve tradeoffs between efficiency and equity. Strong redistribution policies can damage the incentive structure required for efficiency and growth, whereas insensitivity to glaring inequalities can lead to political instability that can in turn weaken economic growth.

Economic policy must be based on economic analysis, but it can not ignore the ethical and political attitudes prevailing in each particular society. The poorer the country, the greater is the imperative to take care of its economic policy. Rich countries can afford to lose resources, but poor countries cannot (Dornbusch, 1993). A good economic policy is essential for the development of a country and its successful economic growth. Economic policy measures which typically benefit growth and efficiency include: state protection of ownership rights and the enforcement of contracts; maintenance of a free market; minimizing non-productive expenditures; maintaining the quality of human capital through education and health care; stimulating public and private investment in transportation and communication infra-structure, and preventing corruption and organized criminal activities.

The state must not manage the economy, but it can provide certain incentives. However, even these incentives are not completely innocent because they can lead to corruption, and tax and regulation evasion. In this situation, it is essential to have public control mechanisms of state policy that will prevent the misuse of state power.

The Nexus Between the Underground Economy and Economic Policy

Underground economic activities are of concern to economists since they affect economic outcomes in a variety of ways. To the extent that these activities are concealed and therefore go largely unmeasured, they tend to distort our view of what is taking place in the entire economy. Unreported income might not only distort the size and growth rate of observed economic activity, it will also effect the real distribution of income. Economic planners must take account of unrecorded activity if they hope to have a correct understanding of total economic activity.

The underground economy is influenced by various factors such as taxation, regulations, restrictions, and the extent of bribery of public servants. If the state dislikes the existence of the unofficial economy and it wishes to reduce it, economic policy must be directed against the factors mentioned. According to Tanzi (1983), who does not seem to be bothered by issues of democracy, civil society, and transparency, this implies that the government should reduce regulation, diminish the public sector, and lower taxation. However, each of these policies has secondary consequences that must also be addressed.

Lowering taxes will reduce the government's budget and is therefore also likely to reduce both the quantity and quality of public expenditures. If public expenditures are inefficient this policy can be justified. However, if public expenditures contribute positively to the production of needed public goods and services and redistribute income in socially desired ways, reducing them can diminish welfare and have the unintended consequence of increasing tax evasion activity. Participation in the unreported economy will depend upon the rate of taxation, the perceived benefits that accrue from public expenditures and the expected penalties from evasion. In transitional countries that require high levels of public expenditures, it may be wiser to focus policy efforts on reforming the tax system and improving tax administration and enforcement.

Recommendations for deregulation must also be approached with circumspection. Certain types of regulations that prohibit coercive monopoly behavior in labor and product markets or limit negative externalities such as anti-pollution controls are desirable rules in modern societies. Policy recommendations for deregulation must therefore specify those regulations that can clearly be identified as 'bad rules'.

In some areas, curtailing restrictions may be difficult and/or undesirable. Political bodies must decide on the relative wisdom of eliminating restrictions on trade in drugs, prostitution, or gambling. Illegal activities can either be legalized, or penalties can be increased along with enforcement efforts.

Corruption and bribery of public officials is a particularly important issue in many transition countries. When the wages of public servants are low, and many valuable property rights remain in the public domain, rooting out corruption is an especially onerous task. Privatizing these property rights, and establishing public institutions that efficiently adjudicate property right disputes is a necessary albeit not a sufficient condition for the elimination of bribery and the corruption of public officials.

Many transitional countries have high tax rates, poor tax administration, wasteful government expenditure, and transaction cost-raising regulatory systems, with valuable property rights in the public domain. These are precisely the conditions under which underground activities are most likely to flourish. In these circumstances, an economic policy that exclusively focuses on the official economy can control neither the positive nor the negative effects of the underground economy. Economic policy should therefore be interested in defining the share of the unofficial economy in the economy as a whole, as well as in individual activities. Estimates of unrecorded income are required in order to monitor overall economic activity and estimates of unreported income are necessary for determining the extent and nature of tax evasion. Until these tasks are accomplished, official statistics will remain an unreliable guide for economic analysis and economic policy management (Mikulić and Madžarević, 1997).

In order to decide which economic policy is best suited to dealing with the underground economy, we must determine its size, nature and the consequences it has on official economic activity. Kesner-Škreb (1997) emphasizes that a state wanting to reduce its underground economy can do the following:

1. In the short run, the government can increase supervision, control and punishments, thereby raising the risks and costs associated with underground activity. This would stimulate a movement from the unofficial to the official sector.

2. In the intermediate term, the government can undertake to reduce the incentives to underground activities by reducing tax rates and eliminating costly regulations.

3. In the long run the government can seek to stimulate economic growth and market transparency, reduce restrictions connected with market entry, and stimulate the growth of firms in the private sector.

4. The state must also encourage moral conduct and create a climate of public opinion against stealing from the state. The most certain way to increase tax morale is rational behavior in the spending of the state budget. Citizens who perceive that taxes are wisely and efficiently spent on quality public services have greater incentives to comply with tax laws.

The particular measures chosen by the State will depend on the size of the unofficial economy that is socially acceptable. Some countries are willing to tolerate a large underground economy as a safety value in order to preserve social peace. However, such a policy also risks the unraveling of the entire social fabric as underground and illegal activities begin to dominate the official economy.

The Influence of the Unrecorded Economy on Economic Policy

The idea of estimating the part of underground economic activity that escapes inclusion in the National Accounts is an attractive prospect in principle, but is very difficult in practice. Not only is unrecorded income difficult to identify and define, it is particularly difficult to measure. The influence that the unrecorded economy has on the economy as a whole is manifold. It influences the measurement of macroeconomic variables, decision-making in economic policy, and the efficiency with which the whole economy operates.

Not knowing the size of the unrecorded economy makes successful implementation of any economic policy very difficult. The larger the unrecorded economy, the greater will be its influence, since it distorts macroeconomic indicators in the following ways:

1. If the growth of the unrecorded economy is faster than the official economy, true growth rates are understated. If policy makers are mistakenly led to believe that the economy is in the midst of recession, then they may unnecessarily set an expansionist policy.

2. Underestimation of the GDP calls into question the correctness of all relative indicators that are derived from it. The per capita GDP appears lower than it really is, while the share of taxes, government expenditures, imports and exports in the GDP seems higher. This may lead economic policymakers to deceive themselves and/or the public.

3. The official unemployment rate will be overestimated to the extent that workers in the unrecorded economy are treated as unemployed, again leading the state mistakenly to implement an unnecessary expansionist policy.

4. Lower prices in the unrecorded sector market cause the true rate of inflation to be lower than the official figures show.

The Role of the Government in the Unofficial Economy

Criticism of the government's role in economic activity has lent force to the suggestion that in a free society the government's role should be limited. This is, of course, hard to accomplish, particularly in societies where pressures on the state budget increase as demands for public services grow. In the most developed countries, a demographic shift toward an aging population causes this. With more citizens of advanced age, pension and health insurance costs tend to rise. In transitional countries, these expenses are added to the burden of transition costs. In Croatia, there is also the added need for the reconstruction and repair of assets damaged during the recent war.

Theoretically, it seems plausible that citizens will support a taxation system that amasses the financial resources required to satisfy the citizen's demand for public services. People are willing to make a fair deal. They will assume tax obligations in exchange for the benefit of receiving public services. The unknown element arises from the ever-present free-rider problem, which is exacerbated when some citizens feel that they do not receive fair value for the taxes they pay. This is most likely to occur when the government is responsible for poor legislation, cumbersome administration, incompetence, and inefficiency of public workers, is insensitive to social circumstances, or engages in corrupt practices.

Owens and Whitehouse (1996) point out that one of the main problems of modern taxation systems is their complexity. Taxpayers have a hard time trying to understand the taxation system and tax administrators have a hard time in implementing it. All this results in increasingly complex and sophisticated tax evasion, more expensive collection of tax revenue for the state and more expensive tax compliance for the tax payers. On the other hand, the increasingly sophisticated tax evasion backfires by causing taxation systems to become even more complex because more detailed legislation is needed to fill the loopholes in existing laws. In Great Britain, for example, the total administrative and compliance cost of taxation is estimated to be 1.5 per cent of the GDP (Sandford, 1995). Two thirds of this amount refers to tax compliance costs.

In Canada, the volume of tax law tripled between 1970 and 1990. In the Netherlands it doubled. France is the only OECD country where tax legislation in the 1990s is the same as it was in the 1960s. Australia, New Zealand and Ireland have already started implementing programs to improve tax laws with the purpose of reducing tax compliance costs. There are other important changes in taxes evident in the OECD countries. Tax burdens have increased from 25 percent in 1965 to almost 40 percent in 1994. The tax base has been broadened and social insurance contributions have increased.

According to the 1995 Cato Institute report, of the about 40 million Americans who were involved in 'direct conflict' with the tax administration, most were simply confused by the complexity of the tax returns (*** 1996). Some taxpayers object to tax-paying as a matter of principle, wishing to reduce the role of the government. People sharing this attitude even organized themselves into a political party of taxpayers in the USA. In their view, the state is oppressive and tyrannical and they especially resent alcohol and tobacco taxes. These events suggest that as laws and regulations in modern societies expand, citizens are often repelled from the state and turn increasingly toward non-compliant behavior.

Some of the findings obtained from studies of the unofficial economy in Croatia indicate that the state itself can influence the trends and changes the unofficial economy undergoes. Franičević (1977) points out that the state can influence the unofficial economy directly when government officials are shown to be involved in illegal activities, or indirectly when the state shows potential participants the desirability and/or feasibility of such unofficial activities. Some more recent trends seem to indicate the wish of the Croatian State to be big, expensive and paternalistic. A growing number of people depend on the state for infrastructure investments, expensive rescues of failing firms and banks and investments in status symbols of the state. If such trends are allowed to continue, efforts to control the tax burden and the public debt will likely fail. Tax evasion is unlikely to decrease, even if evaders are faced with stricter controls and more repressive penalties.

If state investments and/or subsidies stimulate economic growth, it may present new possibilities for corruption and illegal pursuits. Heavy state participation in large projects intended as a substitute for unrealized private investments will alert tax payers to the possibility that a fiscal crisis is at hand, especially if the expected economic growth is not realized. A 'big state' means an increase in tax burdens and provides strong motivation for tax evasion to continue. A wasteful and corrupt state that exercises nepotism will only cause the unofficial economy to grow.

Causes of the Unofficial Economy

In badly organized transitional countries, with ineffective infrastructure, inadequately trained personnel and insufficient control techniques, government officials often take advantage of the possibilities offered by the unofficial economy. The activities of state officials are much more often a factor influencing the unofficial economy than is usually thought (Clark, 1988). All of these elements can be found in Croatia, especially in the first years after it gained independence.

Štulhofer (1997) explains the process taking place in countries in transition. After the initial exhilaration caused by the fall of communism (and, in the case of Croatia, also by its break with Yugoslavia), a discrepancy develops between optimistic subjective expectations and objective reality.

The reality includes impoverishment, with the unofficial economy representing one of the only means of survival. Increased inequality is another reality, caused by a widening gap between the new entrepreneurial elite and the rest of the population. Unemployment and reduced levels of public health services and pension payments stimulate tax and contribution evasion.

Transition means institutional changes that also contribute to the development of the unofficial economy. In Croatia, privatization was not transparent and had the appearance of favoring political friends and networks of acquaintances. As a result, confidence in state institutions was destroyed and noncompliance with state rules and norms became more readily justified.

Štulhofer (1997) finds a high level of opportunism in Croatia. More than two thirds of examinees were convinced that the majority of public officials were involved in corruption. The attitude that law avoidance is considered smart and not a criminal activity, and that tax evasion elevates the social status of the perpetrator is highly disturbing. This seems to indicate that exposure of tax evaders is unlikely to cause many stigmas. Perhaps some results might be achieved by appropriate exposure of the really biggest offenders from the very top political circles. This might be the only means of restoring confidence in institutions.

In spite of political rhetoric, which attributes transitional difficulties to inherited social-cultural habits, the collectivist inheritance of the socialist planning system is not the most important cause of today's relatively widespread opportunism and distrust in Croatia. Opportunism and distrust in Croatia are reflections of increased uncertainty resulting from the introduction of market competition and the deep disappointment arising from unfulfilled expectations after the breakdown of the planning system.

Awareness of a just legal system, satisfaction with the way high government officials perform their job, and perception of the extent of corruption in state institutions have proved to be very significant factors. The data show that opportunism and distrust are more frequent in larger urban surroundings with easier access to information and a higher average level of information. The fact that opportunism and institutional distrust is more pronounced in young than older respondents is another cause for alarm since it suggests the unofficial economy is likely to be a long term phenomenon.

The results of a survey of Croatian judicial statistics are alarming. The costs of breaking rules that regulate economic activities are extremely low. The total number of persons prosecuted is negligibly small and the number of those actually convicted is even smaller. The perpetrators are exposed to very low risk, since the courts of law are overloaded, employees are too busy and court decisions take years to become effective. The direct result of this situation is the generally low number of charges actually pursued (Skorupan, 1997).

Research on the unofficial economy of Croatia reveals a number of possible causes. The growth of the unofficial economy in industry, agriculture and trade appeared to be the result of inadequate financial control as well as the drop in production and real income brought on by the transition process. The unfair nature of the privatization process appears to have stimulated unofficial activities. Lack of transparency, privileged sales and corruption helped the underground economy to grow.

Some Suggestions for Economic Policy Measures Regarding the Unofficial Economy in Croatia

The state will be dealing with the problems of the unofficial economy for a long time yet to come. The first order of business is to determine the size, nature and extent of informal activities. The Ministry of Finance must address the issue of tax evasion in order to find means of improving the taxation system and its administration. The Ministry of Labor and Welfare must determine the extent to which its employment data are distorted by the unrecorded economy so as to determine the appropriate level of unemployment benefits. The establishment of a reliable system of National Income and Product Accounts must also make allowances for unreported income on tax source data.

But even when the scope of the underground economy is realized, more fundamental institutional changes must be undertaken if its detrimental influences are to be minimized. The state must provide a high professional level of state services. This requires the complete independence of the judicial system to adjudicate property right disputes in an equitable and transparent manner. All rules, regulations and procedures must be transparent and public services must be of high quality and equitably distributed.

Measures must be undertaken to restore confidence in the privatization process. Laws must be clearer and more precise and transparent in order to prevent the state administration from making arbitrary decisions and exercising unfair discretionary interpretations of the laws. Open bidding must replace bribes, corruption and other forms of rent seeking and rent creating activities.

Suggestions for Further Research into the Unofficial Economy in Croatia

Further sociological research should concentrate on measuring the perception of transition changes. How do citizens view the transparency and complexity of political, economic and legal processes? How do they judge the efficiency and equity of the judicial system?

Economic research is required to establish a system of National Income and Product Accounts that complies with the standard conventions of the UN system of national accounts (SNA). It would be useful to prepare a new input-output table in order to account for the enormous structural changes that have taken place since the last IO table was constructed in 1987.

In order to influence future trends and the success of privatization, there should be a thorough study of the effects of the unofficial economy on the privatization process so far and their proportions. New research should be based on field research in a sample of companies in which primary information would be collected to give more reliable indicators of the proportion of the unofficial economy in the process of ownership transformation and privatization in Croatia. Special attention should be paid to the acquisition of privatized companies and the development and regulation of investment funds as mediators in mass privatization.

Bearing in mind the special significance of small enterprises in the unofficial economy, their status in the Croatian taxation system should be given special attention. Is it true that the taxation system in Croatia works against small businesses because it penalizes owners for employing more workers? Does value-added tax put a relatively greater burden on small enterprises?

Conclusion

Research on the unofficial economy both abroad and in Croatia indicates that we should be skeptical about the prevailing opinion that high economic growth, economic liberalization and reduction of state involvement in the economy will automatically reduce the unofficial economy. Our concern is that the underground economy may well become a permanent feature of the Croatian economy and society. It is not simply a legacy from the past but rather an unwelcome feature of the still incomplete transformation to the market economy.

If the real source of the unofficial economy is the state itself and the way it intervenes in the economy, the unofficial economy will certainly survive. But, as Franičević (1997) points out, the legitimacy of capitalism can be established only by reliable and firm sanctions when the rules of the game are broken, and by increasing the reputation of law-makers and legal authority in general. A privatized market economy requires institutionalization and penalties when the rules are broken.

In Croatia the war created a large number of unemployed, impoverished and displaced persons, who were forced into informal activities as a survival mechanism. At the other end of the scale were the new entrepreneurs who employed people without registering them with the appropriate authorities, avoided paying taxes and contributions and regular registration in general. Croatia is now at a crossroads. Establishing a new state with new institutions after forcibly breaking with the former system of values, Croatia has two choices. It can follow those countries for which the unofficial economy is a small adjunct to the official economy. In these countries, the state monitors underground activities, is conscious of their consequences and takes measures to control those aspects that are deemed to be detrimental. There is another group of countries in which unofficial activities are the norm rather than the exception. In these countries, the rule of law does not exist as a viable institution. Organized crime has usurped many of the state's enforcement functions and the Mafia extorts tribute even as the state fails to collect taxes. Corruption, lawlessness, and anarchy have replaced the rule of law. It is up to the state, to the measures it will take within the bounds of its economic policy and within its constitutional, judicial and political norms and regulations, to decide which road it is going to take.

Summary

The unofficial economy distorts macroeconomic indicators and economic policymakers can deceive both themselves and/or the public by presenting the kind of information which best suits their goals at a given moment. In other words, they can manipulate the public by resorting to half-truths. The role of the state may also influence the unofficial economy. Our research suggests that the unofficial economy in Croatia has been embraced by some individuals and firms as a survival mechanism to deal with poverty, increased inequality, unemployment and a declining level of public services. Others have been drawn to underground activity by the incentives created by tax laws and privatization opportunities. The lack of transparency in privatization programs, the asymmetry of available information and the perception of corruption and favoritism have produced public apathy and cynicism about the legal functioning of the state. This will make efforts to control the unofficial economy more difficult.

Any economic policy directed towards prevention of the unofficial economy must reduce the incentives to participate in underground activity and increase sanctions. Standard measures include reducing tax rates and the costs of complying with regulations. More important are the huge rewards to be gotten from rent-seeking and rent-creating activities. These opportunities can only be reduced when property rights now still in the public domain are privatized in a transparent, efficient and equitable manner. The great danger in the Croatian economy is that corruption and noncompliance with the existing legal framework will become so widespread that the entire social fabric will become unraveled. The establishment of the rule of law takes generations, whereas the destruction of the rule of law can be swift and lasting.

References

Barro, R. J. (1994) 'Recent Research on Economic Growth', *NBER Reporter*, Summer, pp. 6-10.
Bawly, D. (1982) 'The subterranean economy', Mac-Graw Hill, New York.
Clark, G. (1988) 'Traders versus the state: anthropological approach to unofficial economies', Weistview Press, Boulder.
Čučković, N. (1997) 'Neslužbeno gospodarstvo i proces privatizacije', *Financijska praksa*, vol. 21, no. 1-2, pp. 259-276.
Dornbusch, R. (1993) 'Policymaking in the Open Economy: Concepts and Case Studies in Economic Performance', Oxford University Press, Oxford.
Feige, Edgar L. (1979) 'How Big is the Irregular Economy?' *Challenge*, vol. 22, November, pp. 5-13.
Feige, Edgar L. (1989) 'The Underground Economies: Tax Evasion and Information Distortion', Cambridge University Press, Cambrigde.
Franičević, V. (1997) 'Politička ekonomija neslužbenog gospodarstva - Država i regulacija', *Financijska praksa*, vol. 21, no. 1-2, pp. 295-314.
Giovannini, A. (ed.) (1993) 'Finance and development: issues and experience', Cambridge University Press, Cambridge.
Jankov, Lj. (1997) 'Monetaristički oblik neslužbenog gospodarstva', *Financijska praksa*, vol. 21, no. 1-2, pp. 157-168.
Kesner-Škreb, M. (1997) 'Neslužbeno gospodarstvo i razvoj', *Financijska praksa*, vol. 21, no. 1-2, pp. 315-328.
Madžarević, S. (1997) 'Porezna evazija', *Financijska praksa*, vol. 21, no. 1-2, pp. 241-259.

Madžarević, S. and Mikulić, D. (1997) 'Mjerenje neslužbenog gospodarstva sustavom nacionalnih računa', *Financijska praksa*, vol. 21, no. 1-2, pp. 141-156.

Mikulić, D. and Madžarević, S. (1997) 'Procjena neslužbenog gospodarstva u poljoprivredi, industriji i trgovini', *Financijska praksa*, vol. 21, no. 1-2, pp. 217-230.

Owens, J. and Whitehouse, E. (1996) 'Tax reform for the 21st century', *Bulletin for International Fiscal Documentation*, vol. 50, no. 11-12, pp. 538-548.

Peattieau, L. (1987) 'An idea in good currency and how it grew: the informal sector', *World Development*, vol. 15, no.7, pp. 851-860.

Reljac, B. (1997) 'Neslužbeno gospodarstvo u međunarodnoj trgovini', *Financijska praksa*, vol. 21, no. 1-2, pp. 195-216.

Rosen, H. S. (1996) 'Public Finance', 4th ed., Irwin, Chicago.

Skorupan, V. (1997) 'Pravni aspekti neslužbenog gospodarstva', *Financijska praksa*, vol. 21, no. 1-2, pp. 329-346.

Stiglitz, J. E. (1993) 'Overview', in Giovannini, A. *Finance and Development: Issues and Experience*, Cambridge University Press, Cambridge, pp. 343-354.

Štulhofer, A. (1997) 'Politička ekonomija neslužbenog gospodarstva - Sociokulturna dimenzija i porezna evazija', *Financijska praksa*, vol. 21, no. 1-2, pp. 277-294.

Tanzi, V. (1980) 'Undergorund Economy Built on Illicit Pursuits is Growing Concern of Economic Policymakers', IMF Survey, Feb. 4, pp. 34-37.

Tanzi, V. (1983) 'The Underground Economy', *Finance & Development*, vol. 20, no. 4, pp. 10-13.

*** (1996) The land of the free, *The Economist*, 21.12.96. pp. 69-72.

3 Between Opportunism and Distrust: Socio-Cultural Aspects of the Underground Economy in Croatia

ALEKSANDAR ŠTULHOFER*

Introduction

On a theoretical level, the *underground economy* - economic activities that are unrecorded in the official statistics and/or are unreported to the tax administration - is paradoxical. *First,* the underground economy is difficult to define neatly, which is most probably caused by the fact that the term itself 'connotes more than denotes' (Feige, 1990, p.990). The number and relative divergence of definitions (and even terminology) is a consequence of the complexity of the reality (Wiles, 1987). *Second,* most of the authors agree that the underground economy is a universal problem - since it can be found both in developing and in developed countries, in former centrally planned and in market systems, but is at the same time culturally specific. For example, the causes and forms of the underground economy in Italy are fundamentally different from the causes and forms of the underground economy in Great Britain or in the USA, just as the latter two cases are different from each other. Neither of the three cases mentioned is comparable (at least not structurally) with the African experience, which is in turn essentially different from the case of Latin-America (Portes, 1994; Portes & Sassen-Koob, 1987).[1]

The *third paradox* of the underground economy is that there is no consensus about the dynamic connection between socio-economic modernisation on one hand and the underground economy on the other. The optimistic characterisation of the *developmental paradigm*, which postulates an in-

---

* Faculty of Philosophy, University of Zagreb, Croatia, e-mail: astulhof@mudrac.ffzg.hr
The author wishes to thank Katarina Ott, Dinka Čorkalo, Ivo Bićanić, Vojmir Franičević and Krešimir Kufrin for their comments and criticism.

verse correlation between the level of economic development and the size of the underground economy, has been seriously challenged by recent findings about global growth in the underground economy (Bejaković, 1994; Castells & Portes 1989). The findings suggest that the underground economy is persistent and grows in spite of the positive dynamics of general economic development (Portes & Sassen-Koob 1987). It even seems that in some developed countries, such as Italy or Spain, economic development is directly stimulated by the underground economy.

The discrediting of this developmental paradigm brought about a change in understanding the relationship between development and the underground economy leading to the discovery of *the fourth*, and most probably the biggest, paradox. It has become unclear, as many authors point out (Feige, 1990; Portes, Castells & Benton, 1989) whether the underground economy has a positive or negative influence on economic growth and development. One thesis suggests that the underground economy has a positive influence in the short term (survival, transition towards the market economy, mobilisation of entrepreneurial energy and vitality) and a negative influence in the long term (non-transparent markets, taxation burden increases, incorrect parameters for macroeconomic analysis). This idea, however, gives no direct answer to the question of how the dynamics of the underground economy effects development in the long term. In other words, does a stable, limited-size underground economy have a positive effect, much like that of a social 'band-aid' or as an extension of social policy? Alternatively, is it the flourishing underground economy that represents a problem for economic efficiency creating a closed circle of heavy tax burden, macroeconomic short-sightedness, and the expansion of an atmosphere of immorality? Empirical arguments for or against this view are at present inadequate. The *last* paradox of the underground economy, which is especially frustrating for economists, is the imprecision of the measurement instruments. If there is any consensus among economists at all, then it is that not one of the underground economy measurement methods provides reliable data, which is confirmed by the wide range of estimates (Bejaković 1994; 1995; Portes, 1994).

All these paradoxes concerning the underground economy open the door for sociology to enter an area which is extremely important for the economic life of any community. Sociologists are inclined to empirical research and not modelling. The cultural particularity of the underground economy directly indicates benefits which empirical analysis might find in the sociological research of collective identities, values and historical dynamics of economic and other institutions (Wiles, 1987; Portes, 1994). This paper is based on an empirical analysis that is a combination of approaches called 'sociological' and 'anthropological' by Wiles (1987). He regards the former as quantitative research into the unofficial economic sphere and the latter as a qualitative approach focused on lifestyles and values. The approach proposed in this paper is a quantitative analysis of socio-cultural dimensions (social values) which stimulate - or, for that matter, discourage - the *informalization of economic activities*.

New Economic Sociology and the Underground Economy

During the last ten years, the so-called New Economic Sociology has been the dominant theoretical framework of sociological interest in economic life (Granovetter, 1990; Swedberg, 1991). Its basic postulate of the *social embeddedness* of social actions, which came about in opposition to Polany's use of the same term, is almost a truism according to which economic activities are not socially or culturally neutral.[2] This statement ceases to be trivial when analytical focus is directed onto the structure and dynamics of the embeddedness, as was done by Granovetter (1985) in his analysis of the role of networks in the effectiveness of economic transactions. Regardless of the fact that such a micro-analytical accent can be very useful in the context of the underground economy (discovering and explaining, for example, the significance of local and/or ethnic connections, functionality of traditional economic institutions), the concept of embeddedness also has a broader scope. New Economic Sociology, as I shall try briefly to explain, makes possible microanalysis as well, which is of primary importance in the creation of social and economic developmental strategies.

The significance that socio-cultural rules have for economic activities is well known (North, 1991). Labour productivity in former Yugoslavia was positively correlated with the level of modernisation (tradition of industrialism; see Obradović, 1982). One and the same institutional design proves to be effective in North Italy and ineffective in South Italy (Putman, 1993). The loyalty of older generation Chinese immigrants in the USA gathered together in rotating credit associations is inseparable from their traditional, patriarchal culture (Lyman, 1986). There are many more similar examples. Speaking in sociological terms, the socio-cultural capital of a certain community, meaning *the totality of the dominant norms and values the instrumentality of which is confirmed in the everyday life of the members* (Štulhofer, 1996), represents either a stepping-stone or a barrier to economic development.[3]

Of course, the view of the socio-cultural influence on economic variables just described is not sufficiently defined. It lacks a convincing micro-to-macro-mechanism, i.e. the operation of socio-cultural capital at the individual level. Let us therefore go back to the basic definition of the underground economy. On the micro-level, it implies that the actors (or the greatest majority of them anyway) are not only *aware* of the questionable legitimacy of their economic activities, but also that their activity in the underground economy is *not* unacceptable to their immediate surrounding. This process of *local legitimacy* of involvement in the underground economy on the part of people working in it, regardless of the fact of whether it is based on the impossibility of finding another way out of poverty or on the wish to improve a standard of living, is essential for the maintenance of their positive reputation. If that were not the case, the benefits of involvement in the underground economy would be greatly reduced by social isolation. Rationality is, simply speaking, *socially bounded* (Dietz & Stern, 1995; Portes, Castells & Benton, 1989).

Of course, the more widespread a positive attitude towards the underground economy is, the greater the expansion of respective economic activities that can be expected, although this need not always be the case. If we suppose that public discourse is equally enthusiastic about 'legitimising' tax evasion in communities A and B, the size of the underground economy will depend on the efficiency of state monitoring and sanctions in the two communities. If we go on and equalise them in that respect, the difference may perhaps be caused by different immigration contingents. The *mechanism of maintaining reputation*, the significance of which is just as instrumental (initialisation of trust in transactions) as it is affective (the role in personal identity), seems to suggest that research into dominant values will reveal the direction of current and/or potential behaviour of members in a community. In the absence of survey methods for measuring involvement in the underground economy (Bejaković, 1995; Bićanić, 1990; Portes & Sassen-Koob, 1987), research intovalues helps in outlining the rough boundaries of the underground economy.

Research Design

We shall start the analysis by identifying relevant values, or variables that enable their measurement. Bearing in mind the reasons for (Wiles, 1987)[4] and conditions in which the underground economy develops,[5] our conceptualisation includes the following dimensions: a) economic traditionalism; b) poverty; c) opportunism; d) distrust of institutions. All four dimensions are negatively correlated with the perception of the non-legitimacy of the underground economy and therefore have a positive effect on its persistence or expansion.

A) Economic Traditionalism

This category does not include the usual meaning of the concept of traditionalism in sociology, but denotes *the specific socio-cultural legacy of the former economic system*. It is plausible to suggest that a half century of socialisation within the social & economic context of the planning system - which was later partially decentralised (Sekulić, 1990) - left traces in the collective perception of the rules of the economic game, both in the official and in the 'second' economy. Numerous authors have stressed the importance of the underground economy in the formerly centrally planned economies (Feldbrugge, 1989; Gabor 1989; Bićanić, 1990; Shelley, 1990). In doing so, they have indirectly warned about the possibility that the presence of the underground economy in transitional, post-communist societies might be a consequence of conditioned 'business strategies' and widespread scepticism about state institutions. The latter coincides with the *cleptocracy thesis* (Feldbrugge, 1989), or with the 'informalization of privileges' (Portes, Castells & Benton, 1989), which explains the unavoidable role of the party-governed state in the 'second economy' as a strategy of maintaining internal stability. Of course, this strategy has resulted in a widespread perception of corruption among public servants.

B) Poverty

As ethnographic research by Pardo (1995) suggests, survival always 'legitimises' law avoidance. In extreme situations, morality and rationality become inextricable: actors justify ('rationalise') their actions by lack of choice. Bearing this in mind, the significant drop in the standard of living and increase of unemployment in all post-communist societies have strongly affected perceptions of the mandatory power of economic regulations, making the underground economy a part of the transition process.[6]

C) Opportunism

By definition, opportunism is an attitude, and conduct governed by it, which views respect for regulations exclusively as a question of cost-benefitcalculus. The public good, co-operative ethics and commitment do not exist in an opportunist's vocabulary. Opportunistic attitudes in the population indicate the inclination of actors to break all rules that do not involve high risk of punishment.

D) Distrust for Specific Institutions

Distrust for legal institutions and government is negatively connected with respect for regulations, including economic rules. From an analytic point of view, this distrust can be viewed from two sides. On one hand, people may believe that those employed in high government institutions do not have moral credibility and that because of that, they, too, need not obey rules. A widespread perception that 'those on the top' use the rules of the game to their own advantage will lead to the acceptance of behaviour in which actors attempt to avoid the situation when only they remain honest but impoverished. On the other hand, distrust for the legal system can also be a reflection of the conviction that legal protection is ineffective (or unjust), or of perception that the costs of breaking the rules are low. In both cases, but for different reasons, such distrust stimulates involvement in the underground economy.

To *operationalize* the dimensions described, we include the following variables:

a Variables that attempt to detect *economic traditionalism*: 1) to increase or to decrease differences in salaries (*egalitarianism*); 2) the state has to take care of its citizens vs. citizens must take care of themselves (*state paternalism*); 3) wealth acquisition is always at somebody else's expense vs. wealth acquisition is beneficial for all (*perception of the 'zero-sum or non-zero-sum game'*);[7]

b The extent of poverty is not measurable by our questionnaire; comp. Note 9. Some empirical outline is provided by another piece of research (Burić, 1996), according to which as many as 80 per cent of population live in households with monthly earnings between 500 (10 per cent) and 1250 (75 per cent) kunas per member. The percentage of officially unemployed persons (almost 19 per cent) completes this picture.

The indirect influence of poverty can be analysed through the analysis of the *perception of the seriousness of the problem and chances for escaping from the poverty circle*. For this reason we have included the following variables in our analysis: 1) are there more impoverished people today than before; 2) what are the chances of poor people ceasing to be poor?

c   Variables for detecting opportunism: 1) can tax evasion and tax avoidance be justified? 2) can taking bribes be justified?

d   Variables for detecting trust or lack of trust in specific institutions: 1) trust in the legal system and 2) trust in government.

The choice of variables was limited by the contents of the *World Values Survey – Croatia 1995* questionnaire. The main advantage of this questionnaire is its cross-cultural comparability; the WVS data base includes more than 80 countries around the world. (Unfortunately, partial changes of the questionnaire in 1995 as against the questionnaire of 1993 do not allow comparison of *all* the variables.) Thus, it is possible to place Croatian values in a cross-cultural context which includes: a) countries of post-communist transition (Romania, Bulgaria, Hungary and Slovenia); b) developed countries culturally close to Croatia (Italy, Spain, Austria) and c) two peripheral West European societies (Portugal and Ireland).

The analysis is divided into two parts. The first gives the results of cross-cultural comparison and attempts to test a hypothesis according to which — due to cultural inertia — countries in transition show more pronounced socio-cultural 'support' for the underground economy than the countries of West Europe. Bearing in mind the somewhat more liberal economy and greater participatory experience in former Yugoslavia than in other countries of the so-called 'East Block', the differences between Croatia and Slovenia on one side and West European countries on the other should be smaller than the differences between West European countries and the rest of the countries in transition.

The second part of the analysis will attempt to show the *dynamics* of socio-cultural factors influencing the size of the underground economy in Croatia. In the absence of longitudinal data, dynamics will be simulated by the *analysis of age groups*, based on the assumption that *cultural inertia* (inherited socio-cultural set) is more pronounced with older than with younger respondents.[8] The second hypothesis will thus be: *socio-cultural barriers to the underground economy are negatively correlated with age.*

Socio-cultural Factors and Transition

Table 3.1 shows the results of cross-cultural comparison.[9] Columns a1, a2 and a3 represent economic traditionalism, columns b1 and b2 opportunism and c1 trust in legal institutions. For easy reference, the table also shows average results (adjusted percentages) fortransitional (*average A, without*

Croatia) and West European countries (*average B*). (All the percentages are rounded.)

Table 3.1   Results of cross-cultural comparisons

(per cent)	Difference in wages should be increased (a1)	State should take more care of its citizens (a2)	Wealth acquisition is beneficial to all (a3)	Tax evasion cannot be justified (b1)	Taking bribes cannot be justified (b2)	Great trust in legal system (c1)
Romania	55	37	48	69	68	48
Bulgaria	61	35	54	60	81	46
Hungary	49	50	60	62	70	60
Slovenia	48	44	39	70	81	51
average A	*53*	*41*	*50*	*65*	*75*	*51*
Croatia	30	75	43	37	63	59
average B	*44*	*29*	*49*	*57*	*75*	*46*
Italy	47	39	64	57	77	32
Austria	42	14	64	63	72	58
Spain	46	30	41	60	74	49
Portugal	25	28	34	45	74	41
Republic of Ireland	58	30	50	50	85	47

Economic Traditionalism

Croatia shows the expected deviation from Group B in all the three indicators. The most obvious difference - which can also be interpreted as the most pronounced segment of the cultural legacy of the planned economy - is shown in the perception of state paternalism. Croatian respondents are distinct champions of the welfare state and, for the same reasons, also of state controlled income distribution.[10] Bearing in mind the fact that surveys in other countries were conducted between 1991 and 1993, the lower (or average) egalitarianism of Group A compared to Group B might be a consequence of an early enthusiasm caused by the toppling of the previous system and the resulting expectations of a fast increase of the standard of living. Another explanation, which does not exclude the first, stresses the fact that respondents from developed countries are used to established levels of income inequality, and their resulting unwillingness to support further increase of differences which would, logically, lead to extremes. (I am grateful to V. Franičević for this insight).

Opportunism

Croatia has the lowest result in both the variables (b1 and b2)[11] measuring opportunism, i.e. it displays the highest level of opportunism. In particular, the difference in attitudes to tax evasion is interesting with regard to both groups of countries, which is an unexpected finding. Calculation of the simple opportunism index (comp. Table 3.2) stresses these relations even more strongly.

Table 3.2   Opportunism index

	Opportunism Index $X = (b1+ b2)/2$ /higher result, lower opportunism/
Group A	70
Croatia	50
Group B	66

It should be pointed out that the difference between Group A and Group B is based exclusively on the lower tolerance towards tax evasion in transitional societies. Bearing in mind the complete tax inexperience of the great majority of people in the first group, this finding should be considered provisional. (The absence of differences in tolerating corruption between groups A and B[12] is contrary to the hypothesis of cultural inertia in post-communist societies.)

Distrust for Legal Institutions

Contrary to expectations, Croatian respondents take second place, after those in Hungary, in showing the greatest confidence in the legal system and are followed by the Austrians. It should be noted that contrary to the respondents from other transitional countries (where the 'excess' of trust with regard to the Group B can be explained situationally), Croatian respondents had full five years to test the efficiency of legal institutions in practice. Regardless of the fact that the confidence shown might refer to the justness of laws and the moral integrity of judges and not to the efficiency of legal protection itself, this finding seems to be systematic[13] and therefore important.

Dynamics of Socio-cultural Capital

In order to simulate the dynamics of values and attitudes associated with unofficial economic activities, the Croatian sample has been divided into three groups:

a   18-28 years of age (Group 1; N=218);
b   29-50 years of age (Group 2; N=468);
c   over 50 years of age (Group 3; N=503).

Economic Traditionalism

Analysis of economic traditionalism indicators largely confirms the hypothesis of cultural inertia. The only exception is the somewhat more positive attitude of the oldest age group towards wealth acquisition. However, a widespread tendency towards egalitarian distribution and state paternalism indicates an active presence of the collectivist legacy in all three age groups.

Egalitarianism The older the respondent, the stronger he/she prefers egalitarian distribution. On the 1 to 10 scale, with 1 meaning the extreme reduction of differences in wages and 10 an extreme increase of them, the average results obtained are as follows: Group 1 = 5.12; Group 2 = 4.48; Group 3 = 4.12. It is interesting to note that the oldest respondents' group significantly differs from other two groups ($p < .001$, F=12.21, DF=2). It should also be noted that all the age groups prefer differences to be reduced (the point of indifference is 5.5).

State paternalism All the age groups show an inclination towards extensive social services. Respondents of the oldest age group show the strongest preference for greater state care ($p < .001$, F = 9.88, DF = 2). On the scale of 1 ('the state has to take better care of its citizens') to 10 ('the citizens should take more care of themselves'), distribution results are the following: Group 1 = 3.16, Group 2 = 3.44, Group 3 = 2.8.

Perception of wealth acquisition All age groups perceived activities leading to wealth acquisition as positive, with the oldest respondents having the most positive perception. On the scale of 1 (wealth acquisition is always at somebody else's expense) to 10 ('wealth can be increased until it becomes sufficient for all'), average results by groups are: Group 1 = 5.92, Group 2 =

5.84, Group 3 = 6.24 (The Tukey test points out the difference between groups 2 and 3; p < 0.05, F = 3.02, DF = 2).

Perception of Poverty

Indicators of the perception of the dynamics and 'gravitational force' of poverty indicate a widespread pessimism in all age groups. Such an atmosphere, as has been mentioned before, makes a fertile ground for various rationalisation and side-stepping around social norms and regulations.

Poverty problem All respondents, regardless of their age, think that poverty today is a bigger problem than before. On a scale of -1 ('there used to be more poor people before') to 1 ('there are more poor people today than before'), the results are as follows: Group 1 = .68, Group 2 = .73, Group 3 = .66. The differences are not statistically significant.

Chances of escape from poverty Most of the respondents believe that the chances of ceasing to be poor are 'very slight'. Approximately 66 per cent of respondents from Group 1 were of that opinion as were 64 per cent in Group 2 and 58 per cent in Group 3. The difference among the groups is on the verge of statistical significance ($p< .058$, $hi^2=5.67$, $DF=2$), which is caused by a lower level of pessimism in the oldest age group.

Opportunism

Previous analysis has shown the surprising level of opportunism in the Croatian sample. Figure 3.1[14] shows average results of age groups in the 'tax evasion' and 'taking bribe' variables. The most interesting finding - *reverse dynamics of distribution of opportunism* (the youngest respondents show the highest level of opportunism, and not the older ones) - indicates an element of socio-cultural capital in Croatia that could stimulate expansion of the underground economy and that can not be explained by the cultural inertia hypothesis.

Tax evasion In contrast to the hypothesis, intolerance towards 'tax fraud' increases with the age of respondents. In other words, younger are bigger opportunists than older respondents. (All three age groups show statistically significant differences in 'fiscal morality'; $p< .001$, $F=17.98$, $DF=2$.)

Taking bribes As in the case of tax evasion, opportunism is stronger in the younger respondents' group. More precisely, respondents of the youngest age group are less inclined to condemn corruption than others (p< .001, F=29.46, DF=2).

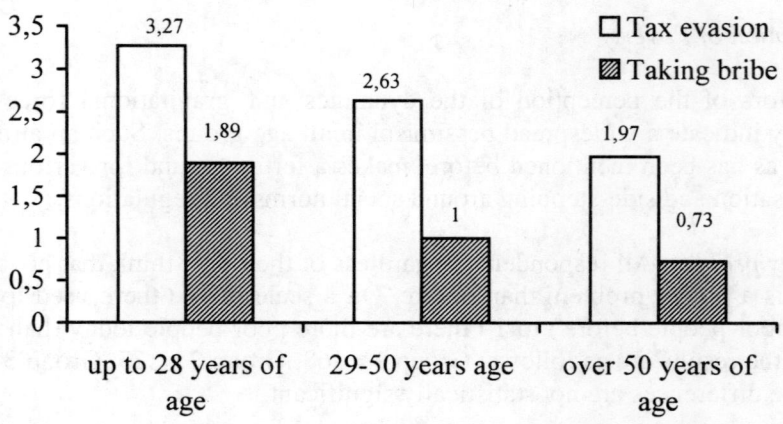

Figure 3.1 Average results of age groups on the 'tax evasion' and 'taking bribes' variables

Distrust for Institutions

The age group analysis reveals a problem which remained hidden in the cross-cultural analysis. Contrary to the cultural inertia hypothesis, it is younger respondents who mostly express distrust, and not the older ones. Distrust is very strong in working age groups, especially among respondents up to 28 years of age (*comp.* Figure 3.2; the data represent percentage of respondents who have 'little confidence' or 'no confidence' in the institutions mentioned.) If we add this finding to that concerning the highest opportunism level in younger respondents, it seems that the new generations might have a very 'underground attitude' towards the legal framework of economic activities.

Distrust for the legal system Distrust for institutions of legal protection decreases with the respondent's age. Respondents of the oldest age group differ significantly from respondents of the remaining two groups (p< .001, F=25.12, DF=2).

Distrust in government Distrust in government also decreases with the age of respondents. All the three age groups differed significantly (p< .001, F=5.8, DF=2). As in the previous variable, the greatest distrust was found among the respondents in the youngest age group.

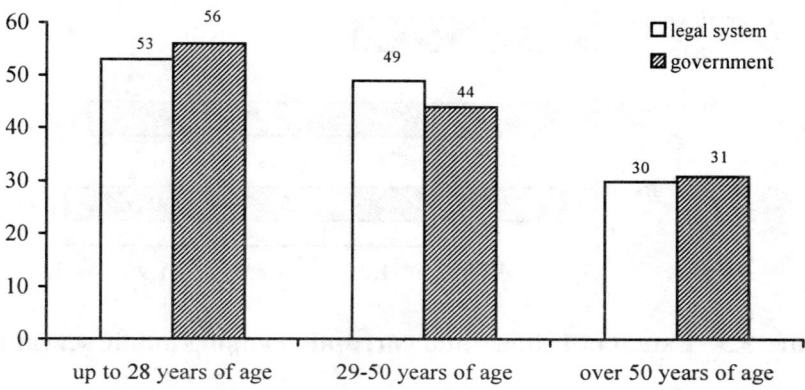

Figure 3.2 Distrust for government and the legal system

As the cross-cultural comparison shows, a relatively high level of distrust for the legal system and government[15] is not characteristic of Croatia alone. The fact, however, that younger respondents display more distrust than older ones calls for additional analysis. Bearing in mind that distrust in the institutions is a consequence of doubt either in their effectiveness or in the moral integrity of officials (the question of justness of laws will not be discussed for the time being), any explanation of the above problem requires the testing of both the possibilities. Unfortunately, the questionnaire enables only checking of the thesis according to which the lack of trust in institutions, especially formal ones, is the consequence of the belief that there is widespread corruption among public servants. Figure 3.3 shows average age group results on the scale of the 'extent of bribery and corruption' among public servants. Putting aside the fact that all the three age groups show an alarming perception of the extent of corruption (average results suggest that every second public servant *would* take bribes),[16] respondents in the first and second age group perceive corruption as more widespread than respondents of the oldest age group ($p < .02$, $F=4.08$, $DF=2$). Although the above explanation is necessarily incomplete,[17] the result according to which *75.1 per cent of the respondents in a representative national sample consider that 'most' or 'almost all' public servants are corrupt* stresses the need for further, and more focused, research into this phenomenon.

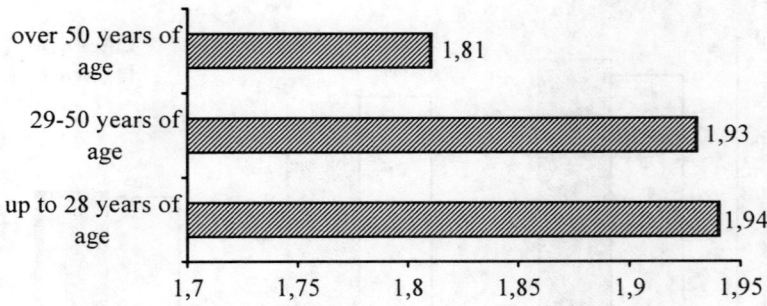

Figure 3.3 Extent of bribery and corruption among public servants

To summarise, the second part of the empirical analysis showed a pronounced presence of socio-cultural dimensions that support persistence and/or expansion of the underground economy. Especially important are findings pointing out both higher levels of opportunism and stronger distrust for the legal system in younger generations. This empirical insight could be of great importance for the assessment of the further dynamics of the underground economy in Croatia.

Socio-cultural Profile of Opportunism and Distrust

Considering non-economic influences on the underground economy, the theoretical model described at the beginning of this paper identifies four socio-cultural dimensions supporting unofficial economic activities. If such conceptualisation is valid, empirical analysis should show interconnection among these dimensions. In other words, if respondent X scores high in one dimension (let us say, on opportunism), the model assumes that he/she will have high results in other dimensions, too. Table 3.3 shows the relations among these dimensions. A plus (+) denotes a link (see Note 18) between dimensions in line with the proposed theoretical model.

Table 3.3 Linkage between socio-cultural dimensions supporting expansion of unofficial economy

	Economic traditionalism (ET)	Perception of poverty (PP)	Index of opportunism (OI)	Index of distrust (ID)
ET	***			
PP	+	***		
OI	-	+	***	
ID	-/+	+	+	***

Deviation from the logic of the model is limited to a *negative* link between economic traditionalism (ET) and opportunism index (OI), and to an ambivalent relation between ET and distrust for institutions (DI).[18] A closer look, however, reveals that the ET/OI ambivalence is a consequence of the higher opportunism expressed by non-egalitarian respondents. The 'non-egalitarians' - and not the 'egalitarians' as assumed by the model - also show a higher level of distrust for institutions (DI). On the other hand, respondents who perceive wealth acquisition as a form of theft are more inclined to distrust - a finding, which was expected by the model.

How can the above deviation be explained? *It seems that the collectivist legacy of the planned economy is not among the causes of relatively widespread opportunism and distrust in Croatia.* This thesis, which should be tested in more detail, is in direct contradiction with political rhetoric, which tends to associate transitional difficulties with inherited socio-cultural capital. It would probably be more correct to regard opportunism and distrust a reflection of an increased uncertainty (introduction of market competition), a consequence of disappointment caused by unrealistic expectations which followed after the break-down of the planning system and a perception of the political misuses of privatisation.[19]

The last step in the analysis aims to provide a rough *socio-demographic profile* of respondents who show an inclination to opportunism and distrust in institutions. Contrary to distrust, which displays no gender differences and is an impartial category, opportunism is more frequent among men ($p< .01$, $t=3.16$, $DF=1144$).[20] Table 3.4 represents the *spatial distribution* of opportunism and distrust for institutions. It shows that both dimensions grow with urban size, with the exception of Zagreb, where the level of opportunism and distrust in institutions is equal to the level of 50,000 inhabitant settlements.

Table 3.4 Spatial distribution of opportunism and distrust

Settlement size	% Opportunists (Opportunism >5.5)	% Distrusting respondents (Distrust <1.5)
up to 10.000 inhabitants	22	22
10 - 50 thousand inhabitants	29	35
50 - 500 thousand inhabitants	40	42
Over 500 thousand inhabitants (Zagreb)	31	33

Regarding other social and demographic, as well as socio-cultural characteristics, regression analysis indicates a complex background for opportunism,[21] which presents a problem in developing remedial social strategies. Of the predictors used, opportunism is significantly correlated with: *perception of just laws* (Beta/*standardised regression coefficient*/= -.22; the more just the laws are perceived to be, the lower level of opportunism), *satisfaction with people who are in power* (Beta=.15; higher satisfaction, lower level of opportunism), *household income* (Beta=.12; higher income, higher level of opportunism), and *perception of the extent of corruption* (Beta=.08; more widespread corruption, higher level of opportunism). Variables accounting for 48 per cent of variance of the distrust index are: *satisfaction with people who are in power* (Beta= -.38), *just laws* (Beta= -.25), *equality in the eyes of law* (Beta= -.14; higher perception of inequality, higher level of distrust), *father's education* (Beta=.15; higher level of father's education, higher respondent distrust) and *perception of the extent of corruption* (Beta= -.11).

Conclusion

The aim of the paper was to describe non-economic influences on the underground economy. The first, theoretical, section takes into consideration four socio-cultural dimensions (economic traditionalism, perception of 'social costs' of poverty, opportunism and distrust for institutions) which can be plausibly related either to persistence or growth of the underground economy. A basic hypothesis was also suggested according to which these dimensions were part of *cultural inertia* — a collectivist legacy of the past — and therefore more frequent in older generations.

The second, empirical part outlines two kinds of analysis — cross-cultural comparison and age group analysis — based on the results of the

World Values Survey. The first of the two analyses compared three out of the four socio-cultural dimensions in relation to a sample of transitional, developed and 'peripheral' European countries. Its results were indicative of significant cultural inertia in Croatia, but also of an unexpectedly high level of opportunism in the Croatian sample, especially in regard to tax evasion. The second analysis, with the respondents grouped into three age groups, was carried out with two purposes in mind: to discuss the distribution of socio-cultural dimensions in more detail and to indicate their dynamic component.

Two findings are especially important. First, opportunism and distrust of institutions are more frequent among younger respondents, which opens up the possibility of a 'natural' reproduction of the underground economy. Second, it seems that neither opportunism nor distrust is a consequence of a collectivist legacy, but rather a *reaction to the new economic and social conditions*. This insight, of course, implies that specific non-economic measures should also be included in strategies aimed at reducing the 'unofficial' sector.

Summary

The introduction discusses the paradoxes of the unofficial economy and the contribution of the so-called new economic sociology to the understanding of the unofficial economy as a complex socio-economic phenomenon. The central part of the paper focuses on the empirical analysis of the social and cultural factors affecting the underground economy in Croatia, based on the results of the World Values Survey - Croatia 1995 carried out on a representative national sample. The basic aim of this analysis was to distinguish the possible influence of the social and cultural heritage from the influence of the situational (transitional) variables. The first part of the empirical analysis deals with a cross-cultural questioning of the heritage hypothesis: the economic values shown by the Croatian respondents are compared with the values obtained in nine transitional and non-transitional European countries. The second part of the empirical analysis focuses on economic traditionalism, opportunism and distrust of institutions as socio-cultural factors of the unofficial economy in Croatia. Although the cross-cultural comparison indicates the effects of cultural inertia, a detailed analysis stresses the importance of the *situational dimension*. The results show a high level of opportunism in Croatia, which is primarily a reaction to the costs of transition and its political impact.

Notes

1. The denial of the possibility of the 'general theory of the underground economy' should therefore not be surprising, either (Bagnasco, 1990:306; Portes, Castells & Benton, 1989).
2. For a critical presentation of New Economic Sociology see Ingham, 1996.
3. Putnam (1993), for example, demonstrates that socio-cultural variables are better predictors of the economic development of the Italian North and South in the 20th century than the variables describing the level of their economic development in the 19th century.
4. Such as a wish to earn more (tax evasion), fight to survive or leave hopeless poverty ('black' labour) and institutional inefficiency (overbureaucracy, low costs of the involvement in the underground economy, etc.).
5. Analysing the case of Central Italy, Bagnasco (1990:168) points out the importance of traditionalism - 'deep embeddedness in family and local relationships' - for innovations in the underground economy.
6. In other words, entry into the underground economy represents an adaptive strategy.
7. The zero sum game describes strategic interaction in which the gain of one actor is equal to the loss of another actor.
8. The basic methodological problem with simulating longitudinal research via age group analysis is revealed by the fact that some of the differences in values between older and younger respondents can be lost or diminished as the latter become older (as in the famous saying: 'Revolutionary in youth, reactionary in old age'), when its members start finding jobs and getting married (In our sample, 54 per cent of respondents in the youngest age group were not employed).
9. Data according to Basanez, M., Inglehart, R. & A. Moreno (1996) Human Values and Beliefs: A Cross-cultural Sourcebook. Ann Arbor, Michigan: Institute for Social Research, University of Michigan. The data were collected in the period between 1990 and 1993 on representative national samples; Romania - N=1103, Bulgaria - N=1034, Hungary - N=999, Slovenia - N=1035, Italy - N=2018, Austria - N=1460, Spain - N=4147, Portugal - N=1185, Republic of Ireland - N=1000.

    The data for Croatia were obtained through the World Values Survey - Croatia 1995 organised by the Erasmus Gilde research team (of which the author of this study was a member), the Croatian partner of the World Values Survey Consortium (Institute for Social Research, University of Michigan, Ann Arbor). The survey was carried out in December of 1995 on a representative sample (N=1189) (The fact that the data for other countries were collected somewhat earlier reduces the reliability of comparisons).
10. Although it is impossible to measure its share within the limitations of present research, the post-war situation (a great number of refugees and displaced persons, organisational and financial aspects of reconstruction) must have had an influence on the expansion of state paternalism or maintaining its stability (I am grateful to I. Bićanić for having reminded me of this situational variable).
11. Table 3.2 shows the percentage of the respondents who consider that tax evasion and taking bribes 'can never be justified'.
12. Of course, situational explanations are applicable here as well.

13 Speaking of the perception of corruption in public services, respondents who show 'quite a lot' or 'a great deal' of trust in legal institutions (Table 3.2) significantly differ (p<.001) from respondents who show 'low' or 'no' confidence; the latter perceive more corruption.
14 On the opportunism scale (1-10; lower value means lower level of opportunism), which represents average results of respondents on 'can cheating on tax scale be justified/accepting bribe' variables, results obtained were as follows: group up to 28 years of age = 5.71; 29-50 year age group = 4.63, over 50 years of age = 3.84. (The differences between all the groups are statistically significant; p<.001, F=25.69, DF=2).
15 41.5 per cent of all respondents have 'little trust' or 'no trust at all' in the legal system and 40.5 percent when government is concerned.
16 ...and, based on this, may plan their future activities. To paraphrase a famous sociological maxim: the real extent of corruption in Croatian society is of secondary importance - what actors consider real is what matters and what becomes their reality.
17 Correlation between distrust in the legal system and perception of corruption is statistically significant (p<.001), but weak (r=.28).
18 The linkage between dimensions were measured mainly by tests of statistical difference (chi-square, F-test). For example, the link between opportunism and perception of poverty means that those who perceive an increase of poverty significantly differ in expressing opportunism from those who perceive either no changes in or a reduction of poverty. The link is positive if the difference points to the theoretically expected direction; it is both positive and negative if the difference in one indicator follows the expected and in the other the unexpected direction. The link between the opportunism and distrust indicators is expressed by the coefficient of correlation (r=.30, p<.001). Distrust index is an average result in 'distrust of the legal system' and 'distrust of government' variables, with the scale ranging from 0 ('no confidence') to 3 ('very strong confidence') (The results of age groups on the index of distrust were following: Group 1 = 1,41; Group 2 = 1,58; Group 3 = 1,87).
19 The finding that 63.3 per cent of the respondents in Croatia believe that the laws do not give equal treatment to those who are in power and the rest is very indicative. Only 10.6 per cent believe that all people are always equal in the eyes of law.
20 The same result was obtained in Norwegian research (Bejaković, 1994:97).
21 Variables the regression equation account for only 14 per cent of variance of the opportunism index. In both analyses, the variables entered into the regression analysis were: household income per month, the number of the respondent's children, educational level of the respondent, educational level of the respondent's father and mother, intensity of religious feelings, satisfaction with one's life, satisfaction with one's financial situation, the locus of control (to what extent the respondent is 'in control' of his life), perception of the justness of laws, perception of equality in the eyes of law ('laws are equal for people who have power and for those who do not') and satisfaction with people who are in power ('How happy are you with the way the people who now have power perform their job?').

References

Bagnasco, A. (1990) 'The Underground Economy', in A. Martinelli & Smelser, N. (eds.), *Economy and Society,* Sage, London.

Bejaković, P. (1994) 'Siva ekonomija u svijetu i osnovica za njeno analiziranje u Hrvatskoj'. *Financijska praksa,* vol. 18, no. 2, pp. 79-107.

Bejaković, P. (1995) 'Metode mjerenja i fenomen sive ekonomije u Hrvatskoj'. *Financijska praksa,* vol. 19, no. 4, pp. 317-346.

Bićanić, I. (1990) 'Unofficial Economic Activities in Yugoslavia' in M. Los (ed.), *The Second Economy in Marxist States,* MacMillan, London.

Burić, I. (1996) 'Prema košnici, ili prema socijalnoj bombi?' *Privredni vjesnik,* 5. February, pp. 6-7.

Castells, M. and A. Portes (1989) 'World Underneath: The Origins, Dynamics, and Effects of the Underground Economy', in A. Portes, M. Castells & Benton, L. (eds.), *The Infomal Economy: Studies in Advanced and Less Developed Countries,* John Hopkins University Press, Baltimore.

Dietz, T. and P. Stern (1995) 'Toward a Theory of Choice: Socially Embedded Preference Construction' *Journal of Socio-Economics,* vol. 24, no. 2, pp. 261-279.

Feige, E. L. (1990) 'Defining and Estimating Underground and Underground Economies: The New Institutional Economics Approach', *World Development,* vol. 18, no. 7, pp. 989-1002.

Feldbrugge, F. (1989) 'The Soviet Second Economy in a Political and Legal Perspective', in E. Feige (ed.), *The Underground Economies,* Cambridge University Press, Cambridge.

Gabor, I. (1989) 'Second Economy and Socialism: The Hungarian Experience', in E. Feige (ed.) *The Underground Economies.* Cambridge University Press, Cambridge.

Granovetter, M. (1985) 'Economic Action and Social Structure: The Problem of Embeddedness', *American Journal of Sociology,* vol. 91, no. 3, pp. 481-510.

Granovetter, M. (1990) 'The Old and the New Economic Sociology: A History and an Agenda', in R. Friedland & Robertson, A. (eds.), *Beyond the Marketplace,* Aldine, New York.

Ingham, G. (1996) 'Some Recent Changes in the Relationship Between Economics and Sociology', *Cambridge Journal of Economics,* no. 20, pp. 243-75.

Lyman, S. (1986) *Chinatown and Little Tokyo.* Associated Faculty Press, Millwood, NY.

North, D. (1991) 'Institutions', *Journal of Economic Perspectives,* vol. 5, no.1, pp. 97-112.

Obradović, J. (ed.) (1982) *Psihologija i sociologija organizacije,* Školska knjiga, Zagreb.

Pardo, I. (1995) 'Morals of Legitimacy in Naples: Streetwise about Legality, Semilegality and Crime' *European Journal of Sociology,* vol. 36, no. 1, pp. 44-71.

Portes, A. (1994) 'The Underground Economy and Its Paradoxes', in N. Smelser & Swedberg, R. (eds.), *The Handbook of Economic Sociology,* Princeton University Press, Princeton.

Portes, A., Castells, M. and L. Benton (1989) 'Conclusion: The Policy Implications of Undergroundity' in A. Portes, M. Castells & Benton, L. (eds.), *The Infomal Economy: Studies in Advanced and Less Developed Countries.* John Hopkins University Press, Baltimore.

Portes, A. & S. Sassen-Koob (1987) 'Making It Underground: Comparative Material on the Underground Sector in Western Market Economies', *American Journal of Sociology*, vol. 93, no. 1, pp. 30-61.
Putnam, R. (1993) *Making Democracy Work*, Princeton University Press, Princeton.
Sekulić, Duško (1990) 'Samoupravni i 'etatistički' model razvoja', in R. Kalanj (ed.), *Modernost i modernizacija*, Hrvatsko sociološko društvo, Zagreb.
Shelley, L. (1990) 'The Second Economy in the Soviet Union', in M. Los (ed.), *The Second Economy in Marxist States*, MacMillan, London.
Štulhofer, A. (1996) 'O racionalnosti, normama i institucijama: evolucija sociokulturnog kapitala kao model institucionalne promjene', *Društvena istraživanja*, vol. 4, no. 6, pp. 953-81.
Swedberg, R. (1991) 'Major Traditions of Economic Sociology', *Annual Review of Sociology*, no. 17, pp. 251-76.
Wiles, P. (1987) 'The Second Economy, Its Definitional Problems', in S. Alessandrini and Dellago, B. (eds.), *The Unofficial Economy*, Gower, Aldershot.

PART II
POLICY ISSUES

4 Tax Policy, Tax Evasion and Corruption in Economies in Transition

ROGER A. BOWLES[*]

Introduction

Economies in transition seem to be at least as vulnerable to corruption of their tax administration as any other economies. The economic, social and political reengineering which comprises the process of transition creates many uncertainties and many opportunities for exploitation by the unscrupulous. The institutions intended to generate the financial flows from taxation on which the state depends are usually given strong powers and the temptation for bureaucrats and politicians to abuse these powers for personal gain may be very great. This is potentially a very destabilizing force because abuse on the part of those inside the system may well lead citizens to become disenchanted with the activities of the state and weaken their own will to support the state and pay the taxes on which it depends.

But, of course, economies in transition are by no means unique in wanting to maintain the credibility of their tax administration. All states rely on tax revenue to finance the collective provision of goods and services and all tax administrations run the risk of leakage in the process of collecting revenue. Our prime purpose in this paper is to develop a rather simple model of corruption of tax administration. It is a model which has corruption on the part of the *tax official* as its focus, but we take pains to emphasize that this kind of corruption is only one part, possibly only a rather small part, of the corruption story. We argue that political corruption may play at least as great a role as what we term 'administrative corruption'. But it is a form of corruption that lends itself less readily to the tax evasion type of economic model that we employ. One of the important consequences of our model is that it demonstrates the degree to which there may

---

[*] Institute for Fiscal Studies, University of Bath, UK, e-mail: hssrab@bath.ac.uk

be a strong link between administrative corruption, the choice of tax policy and the citizen's decisions about tax evasion. The model also illustrates the point that a policy that appears to be tough on corruption, imposing heavy penalties on officials discovered to be taking bribes, for example, may not be particularly effective and can even be counterproductive.

Fiscal Administration in Economies in Transition

It is not hard to find melodramatic accounts of the problems involved in collecting tax revenue in transitional economies. OMRI (1997b) for example reports the Russian Tax Service saying that 26 of its inspectors were killed, 74 injured, 6 kidnapped and 164 threatened with physical violence in 1996. Eighteen tax offices experienced bomb blasts and shooting incidents. As if that were not enough, the tax service suffered financial hardship because of delays in payment of wages. At this time the service was under great pressure from the government to increase tax collection because the IMF had suspended payments of loans on the grounds of inadequate tax collection.

Measures taken to try to improve tax collection, according to Meier (1996) included the launch of a 'Temporary Extraordinary Commission', called the Vcheka, with armed tax police empowered to 'storm illegal enterprises' and shut them down. The tax police are reported to operate on a bounty system, which enables them to keep 50% of what they collect. The worry appears to be however that this may simply encourage the police to choose 'soft targets' such as Western businesses operating in Russia and, in effect, to hold them to ransom. This could obviously be very damaging in the longer term both to the pace of economic development and the amount of tax revenue that can be collected because it might well frighten off both foreign investors and Russian entrepreneurs. Bounty schemes, particularly if they are not expected to continue indefinitely, can have the effect of encouraging what one might term the exploitation or 'looting' of taxpayer goodwill.

More ominously in some respects, the Time report by Meier goes on to note that many of the huge industrial groups have massive arrears of unpaid tax. It is suggested that under pressure from the tax police some of the debts had been paid, but that many firms with good political connections have not settled their tax liabilities. In a rather similar vein, OMRI (1997a) reports that Presidential Chief of Staff Anatolii Chubais has apparently not paid income tax on very high earnings even though he was placed in August 1996 by Yeltsin in charge of the new tax commission, Vcheka.

These problems are by no means restricted to the Russian Federation, however, although they may be more spectacular and better documented there. Speaking broadly, there is plenty of evidence that the transition process in many countries has been accompanied by a fall in the tax revenue to GDP ratio. There are many factors contributing to this decline and the picture is complex. We have no grounds for supposing that the Russian situation is in any way representative of economies in transition, or that corruption (or more precisely, an increase in corruption) is to blame.

The process of transition from a system of physical allocation through plans under communism to a more decentralized system of monetary incentives and private profits prompts important changes in the nature of the economy and in the relationship between the taxpayer and the tax administration. This change is partly a consequence of the fiscal reform that accompanies transition and partly of the changes in fiscal administration resulting from the changing relationship between the taxpayer and the state.

These changes are perhaps most evident at the level of the enterprise. Enterprise taxation under physical planning plays a quite different role from the one it plays under a market system. The objectives are different and the pattern of taxation is quite different also. Individual negotiations over the scale of transfers between the enterprise and the state are replaced, at least in principle, by a more rule-based system, and the application of a set of standard tax rates entails a different mode of thought for both the enterprise manager and the tax official. The information needed to manage an enterprise's activities, to compute its tax liabilities and so on are quite different under a market or a physical planning system.

The experience of many economies in transition has been one of acute fiscal crisis. Pressure on the expenditure side of the public finances has come particularly from growing poverty problems associated with decontrol of prices and the loss of employment security. On the revenue side, receipts as a percentage of GDP have fallen overall, and there have been quite marked changes in the pattern of revenue collection (Table 4.1). In many cases tax rate structures remain complex and many 'special provisions' are made to encourage particular sorts of activity or enterprise. Complexity and one-off arrangements are of course very conducive to corruption, and more generally to wasteful rent-seeking behavior on the part of tax officials.

Table 4.1   Transition and the structure of tax revenue

	Tax Revenue		Income Tax				Domestic Tax		Social Security	
			Corporate		Personal					
	Pre	Post	Pre	Post	Pre	Post	Pre	Post	Pre	Post
Albania	44.2	20.0	11.5	3.5	0.0	0.6	22.6	8.2	4.9	2.5
Bulgaria	49.4	18.8	23.3	4.6	4.1	-	11.1	6.2	9.6	8.0
Croatia	33.0	31.2	4.0	0.5	4.8	4.7	8.4	14.6	17.6	11.4
Czech Republic	53.1	43.9	10.9	7.7	6.9	3.2	17.8	11.6	12.6	15.4
Hungary	48.5	47.5	7.7	1.8	0.0	6.3	17.3	14.3	18.7	17.6
Poland	26.5	23.9	11.4	5.9	3.4	6.3	8.9	9.0	6.7	3.0
Russia	38.5	28.5	12.2	10.4	4.4	2.7	11.8	7.9	3.5	5.3
Slovakia	53.1	27.2	10.9	6.5	6.9	4.3	17.8	14.0	12.6	12.7

Source: Adapted from Table 6.5 in EBRD (1994)

It seems natural to ask whether it is tax administration or tax policy that is to blame for the crisis, or whether it is simply inevitable that public finances have to go through a trough as part of the process of transition. There seems to be a consensus amongst commentators that there is an element of truth in each of these explanations. The World Bank (1996), for example, concedes that '...improving tax administration require(s) long-term institution building and tend(s) to lag behind market liberalization'. The EBRD (1994) puts emphasis on tax policy reform, arguing that 'To generate adequate revenue, the tax system needs to be extended to cover emergent bases and, in particular, different types of enterprises'. As we will show in a more formal way below, it is important to consider tax policy and tax administration in conjunction with each other. Tax evasion and corruption are two of the real threats to successful tax collection and they have to be tackled in tandem.

Before we go on to develop a more formal model of bureaucratic corruption it will be useful to put this type of corruption in context. It will be illustrated by an examination of the relationship between various kinds of corruption and by the provision of an example of the relationship between tax policy, tax administration and corruption.

Types of Corruption

In a companion paper to this one, Bowles (1997), I have set out a taxonomy of some of the principal types of corruption to which a tax administration might be subject. That paper identifies four 'pathways' through which corruption may occur, and I take this opportunity to review each of them briefly.

Bureaucratic corruption, the type we model below, is a comparatively straightforward matter compared with some of the other types. It usually involves a 'front-line' official who deals directly with members of the public. There are many possible variants: the corruption may be of a 'one-shot' type, where there is basically a chance encounter, or it may be part of a continuing relationship between an official and a prospective taxpayer. In a one-shot case, the tax official may actually uncover a consignment of untaxed goods or may simply threaten to run a check on a taxpayer's declaration of personal income. In either event the taxpayer may try to bribe the official not to pursue the matter any further. In the context of a continuing relationship, the taxpayer may pay a regular premium to the official in the expectation of protection from a regularly recurring liability. A smuggler bringing consignments of goods into the country repeatedly through the same airport or road customs post might reach an arrangement with the local tax chief to ensure that nothing more than a 'cosmetic' search is conducted of couriers.

Political-administrative corruption refers to instances where the taxpayer makes use of political influence to secure special treatment by officials. Like bureaucratic corruption this can take many forms, ranging from a one-off payment by a taxpayer to a regular payment, either to the politician's political campaign fund or to the politician's own private funds. The capacity of politicians to 'deliver' protection regularly will depend on the degree to which the legislature and the administration are independent of each other. The greater the degree of independence the more difficult it becomes for the politician to 'intervene' in the process of tax administration on behalf of a 'constituent'.

Political-legislative corruption refers to cases where the taxpayer seeks to make what might be termed 'more legitimate' use of the political process in the search for more generous treatment by the tax authorities. Most legislatures take some account of special pleading by taxpayer groups of various kinds in formulating their tax policy, and making decisions about its implementation. Lobbying by producer groups might, for example, result in more generous treatment of manufacturing investment for tax purposes. Where lobbying by itself seems not to be working too well, the temptation to bribe politicians to put special treatment for a group onto the agenda may be strong. The profits (and employment or export orders or whatever) may be substantial and the politician may find it easy to prepare compelling social reasons for supporting such moves. Indeed, if you watch too many

English TV programs like 'Yes, Minister' you could be excused for believing that in some countries taxpayers collectively support the payment of civil servants whose main function is precisely to prepare unlikely answers to criticisms of any policy which appears to favor one particular group over another.

Judicial corruption is an unpalatable prospect but is said to exist in many countries. In many democracies elaborate measures are taken to ensure that the judiciary enjoys full independence from the government of the day and that, financially, it is provided for sufficiently well for there to be no reason for taking bribes. Nevertheless it is often alleged that judicial corruption continues. In the field of tax administration the judiciary has an important role to play as a third party arbitrator in ensuring that both taxpayers and tax administrations abide by the laws to which they are subject.

Tax Policy, the Underground Economy and Corruption: An Example

Taxation of alcoholic drinks has been a popular source of tax revenue in many countries for a long time. The smuggling of these products has likewise been a popular activity for a long time, as has the clandestine production of alcohol. The reasons are obvious enough: the tax rates (whether excise duty, sales tax, profits tax or whatever) have often been set rather high or have been higher in one country than another and the rewards to evasion have thus been considerable.

Sometimes, of course, there are legal devices for avoiding some of the taxes; at present, for example, British consumers are allowed, under European Law, to buy alcohol in countries such as France, where it is taxed more lightly, for consumption on return to the UK. Wine and beer are now imported into Britain by individuals for private consumption (as the law allows) on quite a large scale. But the same goods are also imported through the same channels by restaurateurs and by individuals who intend to resell the product through informal markets. This is not legal, but it is an attractive activity because effective enforcement is difficult.. The potential damage to the domestic drinks industry, however, is sufficient to ensure that legitimate, taxpaying firms affected press for firm action against illegal importers.

In the case of Russia, it is estimated that illegal sales of alcohol are enormous: a recent estimate puts the share of the illegal sector at 70%. This is the principal reason why the share of federal budget revenue raised from these products (which had been as high as 50% under the czar's government at the beginning of the century) has fallen from around one third in the Soviet period to 3.5% in 1996: OMRI (1997c). The illegal sales are the result of various kinds of underground activity. Shipments into Russia of vodka and pure alcohol from other CIS states with lower tax rates allow smugglers to make profits if the after tax price in, say, Belarus, is lower than the legal market price for the product in Russia plus the shipping cost. Despite threats to increase the number of customs posts on the country's borders, it seems that the illegal imports remain a significant source of supply to the market. Whether this implies that Customs officials are corrupt is difficult to say, but it is quite easy to imagine that the smugglers would at least try to bribe officials if they wanted to avoid capture.

Illegal domestic production, another part of the underground economy, will likewise represent a revenue loss and also create incentives for clandestine producers to attempt to bribe tax officials in the event of detection. This is, then, another example where the corruption and evasion levels depend directly on the size of the tax rate imposed on domestically produced and/or imported goods. At lower tax rates it would not be worthwhile smuggling or producing the good illegally, and if these activities disappeared then obviously the incentive to corrupt officials would disappear as well.

A Model of Corruption

Strategy

The model of corruption we develop here is not entirely original in its approach. Like many of the other models of corruption which have been developed in recent years by economists it owes its foundations to the Allingham and Sandmo (1972) approach to tax evasion. That model was itself an extension of the Becker (1968) model of criminal behavior. The model developed in this paper exploits an analytical device suggested by Cadot (1986) and applied in a similar way by Bowles and Garoupa (1997) in their model of police corruption. We allow both the size of bribes and the proportion of tax officials who are corrupt to be endogenous within the model. In many other models either or both of these variables is made exogenous.

The model, which is most readily interpreted in the familiar light of models of tax evasion as a model of income tax, can be readily adapted to a variety of tax settings such as smugglers evading excise duties. It can be summarized in the following way:

- Legislation already in place fixes a tax rate plus penalties for evasion by taxpayers and also for officials who take bribes.

- The government fixes the volume of anti-evasion investigation work the tax administration is to do, and the amount of counter-corruption work it is to do.

- The taxpayer decides whether to make a truthful declaration of his or her tax liability, knowing the probability with which the return will be scrutinized and the penalty which applies to dishonest declarations.

- When making a tax declaration decision, the taxpayer is assumed to infer both the likelihood that he/she will be investigated by a corrupt rather than an honest official and also the likely size of bribe to be paid in the event of a corruptible official being encountered.

We assume that taxpayers differ in their attitude towards evasion, but are all neutral as regards taking risks. The honesty decision for the taxpayer is treated as dichotomous: there is a choice between complete honesty and complete dishonesty. This is comparable with the economic model of crime where the individual decides whether or not to commit an offence. But it is clearly more restrictive than the approach taken in more sophisticated models of tax evasion where the taxpayer can vary the degree of 'underdeclaration' continuously over the unit interval. The officials are all assumed to be risk neutral, but they differ in their attitudes to taking bribes. The taxpayer knows the parameters of the distribution of these attitudes but is unable to identify the exact position of any individual official in the distribution: he or she will only learn whether an official is corrupt after having been discovered to have underdeclared.

Our rationale for making these rather strong, simplifying assumptions is that we wish to make the underlying structure of the model as simple as possible. Many models of corruption aim for a higher degree of generality than we do. Our purpose is to construct as transparent a model as possible of the interaction between the various elements in order to throw light on the interactions between tax policy, tax evasion and corruption. To make the analysis accessible it is essential to impose tight restrictions. The corollary, of course, is that our model is far too crude to use for policy design purposes. It is intended as a basic framework that can be extended in various directions.

Notation and assumptions

We begin with a description of the taxpayer. The taxpayer's situation is summarized as follows:

- Y = income
- t = (proportional) income tax rate
- z = penalty rate, payable on undeclared income revealed by investigation
- p = probability of the taxpayer's return being investigated
- c_i = psychic (or 'stigma') costs of evasion for the i-th taxpayer
- the probability that investigation will reveal the taxpayer's true income is set to unity
- the distribution of stigma costs is assumed to be uniform on the interval $[c^l, c^u]$

The tax official's position is summarized similarly as:

- q = probability of a taxpayer investigation being audited by the tax administration's own anti-corruption division
- S_j = punishment cost to j-th official if investigation reveals collusion with taxpayer
- b = bribe charged by a corrupt tax official
- the punishment cost is, at least in part, subjective and is non-observable by the taxpayer
- punishment costs are distributed uniformly on the interval $[S^l, S^u]$

Analysis

Our initial objective is to derive an expression for the amount of evasion to be expected. Since we are assuming that taxpayers discount for the bribery possibility when making their income declaration, we begin by looking at corruption since this will have to be anticipated by the taxpayer from the outset.

If the parties find themselves in the position where an official has conducted an investigation that reveals an underdeclaration by the taxpayer, then the nature of their bargaining is likely to go as follows. The marginal official, indifferent between taking and refusing a bribe, has punishment cost we will denote S^-. This official does not know whether investigation of the taxpayer will, in the event, be double-checked, or audited, but, like others, assigns to audit a probability q. Given our assumption of risk neutrality we may infer that for this marginal official the expected cost of taking a bribe b is such that $b = qS\tilde{}$. This expression, which is illustrated in Figure 4.1, simply provides a correspondence between the size of the bribe and proportion of officials who will find it attractive. Any bribe, such as b_1 in the diagram, translates into a proportion of officials, who will take it. We will write this proportion, as r, where:

$$r = (S\tilde{} - Sl)/(Su - Sl) \tag{1}$$

We can also, however, use this critical value $S\tilde{}$ as providing a *threat point* (of $qS\tilde{}$) in the (implicit) bargaining which takes place between taxpayers and officials as to the level of the bribe. Since we derived this value for the marginally corrupt official, we know that any bribe below this level will be turned down by the marginal official, giving a contradiction.

The maximum the taxpayer will be prepared to pay as a bribe will be zY because it would be cheaper for the taxpayer to become honest and pay the penalty rate z on undeclared income at any bribe in excess of that level. This therefore defines a *threat point* for the taxpayer in bargaining with the official.

By assuming that the parties reach a Nash bargaining point, we have now determined the size of the bribe. It will have to be midway between the threat points and thus satisfy:

$$b = .5(zY - qS\tilde{}) = qS\tilde{} \Rightarrow S\tilde{} = zY/3q \tag{2}$$

Or, equivalently, $b = zY/3$.

The proportion of tax officials for whom corruption is worthwhile can thus be inferred immediately by solving (2) from the parameter values of z, Y and q and substituting this value into (1) to get the proportion, which we label r. This proportion is interpreted by the taxpayer as the probability that they will be able to bribe an official, conditional on their underdeclaration having been detected.

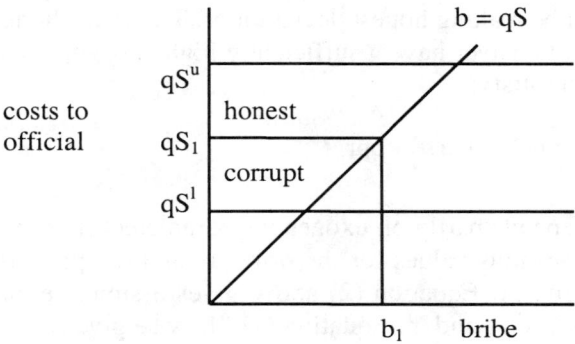

Figure 4.1 The official's bribe decision

The Evasion Decision

For a risk neutral taxpayer (with psychic costs c_i) the decision to make an honest initial declaration of income will require that the honest strategy has at least as high a payoff as the dishonest one. This is equivalent to the condition:

$$Y(1-t) > [Y(1-z) - b]prq + [Y-b]pr(1-q) + [Y(1-z)]p(1-r) + Y(1-p) - ci \quad (3)$$

The right hand side of this expression has four terms which summarize the 'lottery' represented by underdeclaring and a fifth term which gives the psychic cost when evading. The lottery terms refer in turn to (a) the possibility of investigation by a corrupt tax official who is subsequently investigated by the anti-corruption squad, (b) investigation by a corrupt official who is not checked (c) investigation by an honest official (whether or not he or she is audited), and (d) no investigation.

In the case of (a) we assume that when the tax official is subsequently discovered by the anti-corruption squad to have taken a bribe, the taxpayer will subsequently be required to pay tax at the penalty rate z: but no punishment is imposed on the taxpayer in this case, perhaps because they agree to collaborate with the tax department in standing witness against the official alleged to have taken a bribe. The bribe cannot be recovered in this case, so the cost to the taxpayer is the bribe plus the penalty rate. It would not, in any event, be difficult to incorporate heavier punishment for the taxpayer into the model.

By rearranging (3) we can derive an expression giving the proportion of taxpayers who will be making honest declarations. To induce honesty we require that an honest taxpayer have a sufficiently high subjective aversion to being discovered to satisfy:

$$c_i \geq Y[t - zp(1-r(1-q))] - bpr \qquad (4)$$

This condition depends partly on exogenous parameters (t, z, p, Y and q) and partly on endogenous values for the bribe, b, and the proportion of officials who are corrupt, r. Equation (2) above gives a simple expression for the bribe, b in terms of z and Y. Equation (1) likewise gives a value for r which can be written in terms of the support (S^u, S^l) of the distribution of tax official punishment costs in relation to the bribe. Expression (4) thus has the capacity to characterize the amount of tax evasion in relation to a wide range of variables, a number of which are controllable. It would be possible to write down a rather messy expression by making the relevant substitutions into (4) for b and r. It is tidier to write down an expression where b is expanded but where r is written in the form $r(z,Y,q,S^l,S^u)$ to indicate that its value depends on z, Y and q and on the support of S:

$$c_i \geq Y\{t - zp - zp[2 - 3q]r(z,Y,q,S^l,S^u)/2\} \qquad (5)$$

For many purposes the most interesting question is how this condition, which is derived in the Appendix to the paper, will respond to changes in the system's parameters, particularly those over which the government might have control. In order to derive the relevant partial derivatives, let us denote by X the value of c_i which just meets the weak inequality (5). The results are as follows.

Change in the tax rate

$$X_t > 0$$

This implies that an increase in the tax rate t will raise the critical value of psychic costs at which consumers will find it optimal to declare honestly. Since we have assumed the distribution of psychic costs to be fixed exogenously, the increase in the critical value X is equivalent to saying that a smaller proportion of taxpayers, other things remaining equal, will now submit an honest tax return. Intuitively this makes sense: the cost of honesty has increased relative to dishonesty, and this inclines a higher proportion of taxpayers to cheat.

The impact of the tax rate change on the extent of corruption can also be derived. On our assumption that the penalty tax rate, z, is set independently of the tax rate itself, nothing about the increased evasion has any effect on the level of the bribe or the proportion of officials who are corrupt. But there are more evaders now, and so we would expect there to be an increase in the incidence of corruption. We have assumed, implicitly, that there are no additional psychic barriers for the taxpayer when it comes to corruption: once the dishonesty barrier is broken at the filing stage, the taxpayer thereafter aims simply to minimize costs.

Change in the investigation probability

$$X_p < 0$$

A rise in the probability of a taxpayer's return being investigated will reduce the amount of evasion. The increase in this probability deters evasion because it adds greater weight to the downside payoffs associated with dishonest declarations. Evasion now appeals to fewer taxpayers, and more of them find that the psychic cost of evasion exceeds the net monetary gain it offers. The increase in the investigation probability has no impact beyond this initial effect. This is because it does not in any way influence the bribe level since it has no effect on the threat points for either side.

Change in the penalty tax rate

$$X_z < 0$$

A rise in the penalty rate of tax, other things equal, will be likely to reduce evasion. This may seem obvious although, at least in our model, the reasoning is a little more complex than in the case of the previous two findings and the sign of the derivative is no longer completely free of ambiguity. The reason for the complication is that because a higher penalty rate makes detection more costly for the consumer this will influence the size of the bribe, via the consumer's threat point (zY). By raising this level, the increase in the penalty rate raises the bribe. Taxpayers, that is to say, have to concede that it is now worth paying more as a bribe if they have made a false declaration than it was previously. The higher bribe itself deters some evasion, but this is offset at least to some degree by the fact that a higher proportion of officials will now find it expedient to take bribes. An increase in the number of officials taking bribes will raise the probability of being able to bribe an official in the event of the taxpayer being caught evading and this (other things equal) will tend to encourage more evasion.

The overall impact on the amount of evasion however, as we demonstrate in the Appendix, is likely to be negative. Fewer taxpayers find evasion worthwhile because the extra cost of getting caught and having to pay a higher level of bribe exceeds the advantage of a higher likelihood of finding a corrupt official.

Change in the audit probability

$$X_q > 0 \text{ or } < 0$$

An increase in the audit probability, q, has an ambiguous effect on X. This may seem odd at first glance: surely if the authorities get tougher on officials, that is bad news for potentially corrupt taxpayers? It is true that the immediate effect of the increase is to reduce the proportion of officials taking bribes, since they are now more likely to get caught. From the taxpayer's perspective this will mean fewer corruptible officials: it will also mean that a bribe is more likely to be detected. Both these factors will encourage greater honesty in reporting income initially. But alongside these 'initial' effects are further adjustments some of which work in the other direction. The increase in the expected costs to officials of taking bribes and the resulting rise in the threat point of officials will find expression in an increase in the level of bribes. Although this too will tend to depress the amount of evasion, it will also have the effect of raising the proportion of officials prepared to take bribes. The net effect on evasion will depend on the relative strength of the various effects.

Implications and Concluding Remarks

Whilst the derivation of some comparative static properties of the model represents a useful start it is by no means the full story. We have focused only on the evasion decision, without tracking through the implications for the extent of corruption itself. The amount of corruption is determined within our model as the product of the probabilities that: (a) evasion occurs, (b) an investigation is done and (c) a dishonest official is involved.

A substantially more serious challenge is the derivation of a full-scale 'optimal solution' for the model. In incentive contracting terms the problem could be characterized as follows: Laffont and Tirole (1993). The legislature can manipulate the tax rate and the tax administration's budget (say, B) to maximize a welfare function containing the gross amount of revenue collected and the cost of resources used in collection, both valued at some appropriate set of shadow prices. This problem is soluble, in principle, provided that the tax administration is assumed to behave in a perfectly passive way and chooses a pair of values of p and q consistent with both its budget B and with the maximization of social welfare. But if it were to be assumed that either the legislature or the administration were itself vulnerable to political corruption of some sort then agendas might change. This would necessitate more of a public choice kind of analysis than the public interest approach implicit in the incentive contracting approach.

Without pursuing these more ambitious targets is it possible to draw any worthwhile lessons from the analysis of section 5? Our main objective here was to set out as simple as possible a model of the interaction between tax policy, tax evasion and corruption, and to do this we have made many assumptions which other authors have been keen to relax in their analysis of evasion. From this literature it is well established that apparently quite innocuous relaxations of the restrictions imposed can substantially damage the 'commonsense' findings of basic evasion models: for a recent review of the evasion literature, Pyle (1989). It is quite clear that the model developed here will be very sensitive to many of the same criticisms.

Whilst an integration of evasion and corruption models seems a desirable objective to pursue, it may not be easy to achieve. From a policy point of view, however, there may be considerable urgency in the search for configurations of tax policy and administrative parameters that will yield maximum revenue. Raising tax rates is unlikely ever to be enough by itself to raise revenue collection performance, even if the efficiency impact of such change is small. The incentives that higher tax rates create for evasion, for the corruption of tax officials (and possibly legislators and judges as well) and for other related rent-seeking activities are such that high taxes may simply prove uncollectable.

We have not pursued here the implications of our findings for the design of tax administration in any detail. It seems clear, at least in our model, that raising penalty rates and investigation probabilities shows more promise than increasing audit probabilities as a means of tackling evasion. Raising tax rates seems to prompt both more evasion and more corruption. Whether economies in transition can avoid the twin evils of evasion of taxes and the corruption of tax administration seems unlikely at present. But whether they could avoid further problems by reducing tax rates in an effort to prevent abuse must remain an open question for the present.

Summary

Effective collection of taxes has been a problem in many economies in transition, as is evidenced by a decline in the tax revenue to GDP ratio. This paper develops a model designed to explore various influences on two of the most widely blamed causes of this decline, namely the taxpayer's propensity to evade tax and the tax official's propensity to behave corruptly. Using a solution concept proposed by Cadot (1987), and developed in the context of police corruption by Bowles and Garoupa (1997), we investigate some of the possible interactions between factors such as tax rates, the penalty structure, social attitudes and efforts by the tax administration to control corruption. We show that there are subtle interactions, and that efforts to reduce evasion may only increase the incidence of corruption. We look also at the relationship between the corruption of tax officials and other 'pathways' to corruption that the reluctant payer of tax may exploit.

References

Allingham, M. G. and Sandmo, A. (1972) 'Income Tax Evasion: a theoretical analysis', *Journal of Public Economics,* no. 1, pp. 323-38.
Becker, G.S.(1968) 'Crime and Punishment: an economic approach', *Journal of Political Economy*, vol. 76, no. 2, pp. 169-217.
Bowles, R. (1997) 'Anti-corruption Policy' in C.T. Sandford (ed.), *More Key Issues in Tax Reform*, Fiscal Publications, Bath.
Bowles, R. and Garoupa, N. (1997) 'Casual Police Corruption and the Economics of Crime', *International Review of Law and Economics*, vol. 17, no. 1, pp. 75-88.
Cadot, O. (1987) 'Corruption as a Gamble', *Journal of Public Economics,* vol. 33, pp. 223-44.
EBRD (1994) *Transition Report*, October, EBRD, London.
Laffont, J. J. and Tirole, J. (1993) *A Theory of Incentive Procurement and Regulation*, MIT Press, Cambridge.
Meier, A. (1996) 'Russia's New War on Taxes', *Time*, Dec 16.
OMRI Daily Digest (1997a) 'Chubais Behind on His Taxes', *OMRI Daily Digest* 16, Pt. 1, 11 January 1997.
OMRI Daily Digest (1997b) 'Hazards of Tax Collection', *OMRI Daily Digest* 19, Pt. 1, 20 January 1997.
OMRI Daily Digest (1997c) 'State Reintroduces Monopoly of Alcohol', *OMRI Daily Digest* 246, Pt. 1, 30 January 1997.
Pyle, D. (1991) 'The Economics of Taxpayers Compliance', *Journal of Economic Surveys,* vol. 5, no. 2, pp. 163-198
World Bank (1996) *'From Plan to Market: World Development Report 1996'*, New York, The World Bank/OUP.

Appendix - Derivation of Principal Results

Taxpayer's Evasion Decision

We can summarize the taxpayer's evasion decision by considering the pay-offs in the various states of the world in conjunction with the probability of each of them occurring. We are using r here to represent the probability of encountering a corrupt official.

Outcome	Payoff to taxpayer	Probability
evade: investigation: corrupt: audit	$Y(1-z) - b - c_i$	prq
as above, but no audit	$Y - b - c_i$	$pr(1-q)$
evade: investigation: honest official	$Y(1-z) - c_i$	$p(1-r)q$
as previous but no audit	$Y(1-z) - c_i$	$p(1-r)(1-q)$
evade: no investigation	$Y - c_i$	$(1-p)$
honest declaration	$Y(1-t)$	1

To be persuaded to file an honest declaration (given only a choice between declaring all or nothing) the taxpayer will require that the following condition be met:

$$Y(1-t) > [Y(1-z) - b]prq + [Y-b]pr(1-q) + [Y(1-z)]p(1-r) + Y(1-p) - c_i \quad (A1)$$

Expanding this condition we can write:

$$Y(1-t) > Yprq - Yzprq - bprq + Ypr - Yprq - bpr + bprq$$
$$+ Yp - Yzp - Ypr + Ypzr + Y - Yp - c_i$$

So that:
$$Y(1-t) > Yzp[r(1-q)-1] + Y - bpr - c_i$$
$$c_i > Y - Y(1-t) - Yzp[1-r(1-q)] - bpr,$$

giving:
$$c_i > Yt - zpY + zpY(1-q)r - bpr \quad (A2)$$

The problem of course is that the values b and r are both endogenous in the model. In order to be able to explore the impact of policy change, we have to eliminate these variables as well. This is inconvenient, because it makes the model substantially more complicated. The level of the bribe, b, can be replaced by the expression (zY/3). The proportion of tax officials who are corrupt, r, could be written in rather general form as $r(z,Y,q,S^l,S^u)$, giving:

$$c_i > Yt - zpY + zpY[1-q]r - zYpr/3$$
$$c_i > Yt - zpY + zpY[2-3q]r(z,Y, S^l,S^u)/3 \qquad (A3)$$

For many purposes the most interesting question is how this condition (A3) will respond to changes in the system's parameters. In order to derive the relevant partial derivatives, however, we need first to be more explicit about the form of the relationship r(.), thus we write it as:

$$c_i > Yt - zpY + zpY[2 - 3q][(zY/3q) - S^l]/3[S^u - S^l]\} \qquad (A4)$$

Denote by X the value of c_i which just meets the weak inequality (A4). This X can be interpreted as the net financial gain from non-declaration i.e., from evasion. If the value of X increases, then a higher proportion of taxpayers will find evasion gives a positive net payoff. Denote by k the difference $[S^u - S^l]$, giving:

$$X = Yt - zpY + \{zpY[2 - 3q]/3\}[(zY/3q) - S^l]/k \qquad (A5)$$

or, equivalently [we use both below]:

$$X = Yt - zpY + \{zpY[2 - 3q]\}[(zY - 3qS^l]/3qk \qquad (A5a)$$

The partial derivatives of X with respect to the parameters at the government's disposal can then be written as:

(1) $\qquad X_t = Y > 0$ (unambiguous) $\qquad (A6)$
(2) $\qquad X_p = -zY + zY[2 - 3q][(zY/3q) - S^l]/3k \qquad (A7)$

The ratio $\{[(zY/3q) - S^l]/k\}$ already defined as the ratio r must lie between zero and unity. We can rewrite (A7) as:

$$X_p = -zY + zY[2 - 3q]r/3 \qquad (A8)$$

Since q, too, lies in the unit interval, the term (2-3q)/3 is restricted to values between [-1/3, +2/3]. This is sufficient to ensure that:

$$X_p < 0 \tag{A9}$$

(3) Recalling that:

$$X = Yt - zpY + \{zpY[2 - 3q]/3\}[(zY - 3qS^1)/3qk] \tag{A5}$$

This formulation makes it clear that the volume of evasion will respond to a rise in the penalty rate z in a rather complex way. This is because the rise in z causes a rise in the bribe and in the proportion of officials choosing to be corrupt. The taxpayer now faces higher punishment if caught, but has a higher probability of finding an official to corrupt. There are clearly countervailing pressures here and the net effect depends on their relative strengths.

$$X_z = -pY + pY[2-3q][(zY - 3qS^1)/9qk + (Y^2zp[2-3q]/9qk) \tag{A10}$$

$$X_z = -pY + \{pY[2-3q]/9qk\}\{zY - 3qS^1 + zY\} \tag{A11}$$

$$= -pY + \{pY[2-3q]/9qk\}\{2zY - 3qS^1\} \tag{A12}$$

If we impose the restriction $\{2zY-3qS^1\}[2-3q]/9qk < 1$, then:

$$X_z < 0 \tag{A13}$$

It is not easy, however, to think of compelling reasons either why this condition should be met or why it should not be met.

(4) Recalling (A10):

$$X = Yt - Yzp + (zpY[2-3q]/3k)\{(zY/3q)-S^1\} \tag{A10}$$

$$X_q = [-Ypz/k][(zY/3q)-S^1] + [-3zY/9q^2][Ypz(2-3q)/3k] \tag{A14}$$

$$= [zpY/k][(-3Yz/9q) + S^1 - 3Yz(2-3q)/27q^2] \tag{A15}$$

$$= Ypz\{[-3Yz/9q]\{1 + (2-3q)/3q\} + S^1\} \tag{A16}$$

$$= Ypz\{[-2z + 9q^2S^1]/ 9q^2\}/k \tag{A17}$$

$$\text{sign }\{X_q\} = \text{sign }\{-2z + 9q^2S^1\} \tag{A18}$$

We cannot sign X_q unambiguously, although there are grounds for supposing it might be positive. The first term, $-2z$, is likely to be small but negative. The lower bound on the costs faced by officials if they are caught taking bribes, S^1, is likely to be relatively large with the result that the derivative is likely to be positive, which would imply that a rise in the audit probability gives rise to an increase in evasion. This may be somewhat counterintuitive, but it occurs because the higher bribe it provokes causes more officials to take bribes.

5 Policies Dealing with Tax Evasion
CEDRIC SANDFORD[*]

A major problem of developing countries and economies in transition is low tax effectiveness - the so-called 'tax gap', by which a substantial proportion of the maximum potential revenue from a given tax structure remains uncollected.

This statement is only another way of saying that such countries face a major problem of tax evasion. Tax evasion is the failure, by an individual or organization, to pay tax legally due, or alternatively the claim of a refund to which they are not legally entitled.

Tax evasion takes one or both of two main forms:

1. An understating of taxable income, profits or sales and excise tax receipts (of which the extreme form is a failure to declare any such income or receipts by not making a tax return or not registering for a particular tax when legally required to do so).

2. An overstating of tax exemptions, allowances, reliefs, credits (of which the extreme form is to claim credits in excess of tax liability).

These are the main but not the only forms of tax evasion. For example, delaying payment, especially in times of inflation, is a form of evasion. Tax evasion embraces both deliberate acts and unintentional evasion arising from ignorance of the law or forgetfulness. Tax evasion ranges from minor omissions to major fraud.

We can illustrate tax effectiveness and tax evasion by reference to a simple diagram (Figure 5.1).

---

[*] Institute for Fiscal Studies, University of Bath, UK.

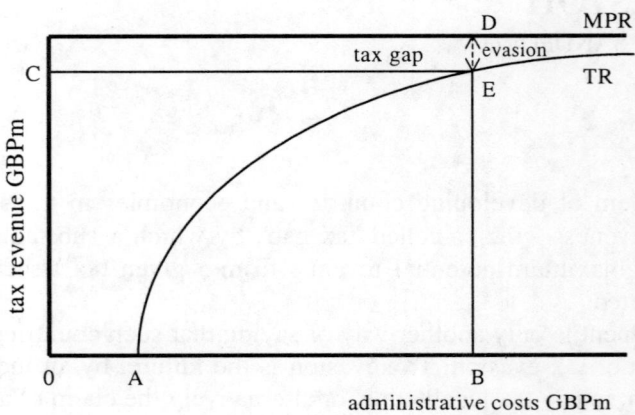

Figure 5.1 Relationship between costs and revenue[**]

On the horizontal axis we show administrative costs, i.e., the costs to the revenue authority; on the vertical axis, tax revenue. Note that the scales are different, one unit on the horizontal axis relating to 100 units on the vertical axis. The line MPR represents maximum potential revenue i.e. tax rate(s) times tax base at a particular time. The MPR is difficult to calculate with any degree of precision; it will obviously rise or fall as a result of changes in tax rates or tax base, but is also affected by decisions of the courts about the legitimacy of tax avoidance schemes,

The total revenue curve (TR) begins at a point (A) to the right of the origin because some administrative costs have to be incurred before any revenue can be collected. The curve rises very steeply at first; additional units of administrative costs will generate very substantial revenue. But as total revenue begins to approach the MPR line, the curve flattens out. Additional increments of administrative cost generate decreasing additions of revenue and the curve becomes flatter and flatter the closer it gets to the MPR. Once the tax is in the operational area (to the right of point A) the vertical distance between the total revenue curve and the MPR line is the tax gap or tax effectiveness gap i.e. the measure of evasion. Thus, if OB is the administrative cost, the revenue collected is OC and the tax gap (the extent of evasion) is DE. This formulation can be applied to a single tax or the tax system as a whole.

**   I am indebted to Dr Peter Dean for the idea of this diagram.

Some assumptions underlying the diagram need to be mentioned. It assumes constant prices and incomes and a given administrative 'technology' — i.e. a given administrative structure. If, for example, unit labor costs rise as more tax administrators are employed, or if the tax administrators get a salary increase, the curve would move to the right and the cost-revenue relationship would increase. If, on the other hand, there were an increase in administrative efficiency, more revenue would be collected for any given administrative cost.

Policy on tax evasion can be thought of as having two broad aspects, which are to some extent interconnected but can for convenience, be analyzed separately.

1   How far should a government proceed along the horizontal axis, i.e. how many resources should be put into tax administration?

2   How can the position of the curve be raised i.e. how can we reduce the tax gap for any given level of administrative cost?

How Many Resources Should be Allocated to Tax Administration?

The natural response of economists, thinking of the theory of the firm, is to say that resources should continue to be employed in tax administration up to the point at which marginal cost (MC) equals marginal revenue (MR); i.e. more resources should be put into tax administration as long as the incremental addition to tax revenue exceeds the incremental addition to administrative cost.

This raises two issues — the conceptual and the practical. Let us start with the practical, in particular, what should count as revenue, what should count as marginal costs and how do we measure them?

What Should Count As Marginal Revenue?

Clearly the extra tax directly collected in the year of investigation as a result of additional enforcement activities should count as revenue; but should an allowance be made for the present value of the future tax revenue expected from its continuance in future years (on the assumption that convicted tax evaders will behave themselves in the future)?

Again, should we include in marginal revenue additional tax arising from the deterrent effect that the knowledge of additional enforcement activities may generate; and even include the present value of the tax revenue generated by a continuation of the deterrent effect beyond the year of investigation? Should fines collected as a result of enforcement activities count as marginal revenue?

What Should Count As Marginal Cost?

Increasing enforcement activities may not only increase administrative costs (the costs to the revenue authorities); they may also put up tax compliance costs (i.e. the tax which taxpayers have to meet, over and above tax revenue, in complying with the legal obligations laid upon them). An increase in enforcement activities may frighten honest taxpayers, who may now feel that they need to be increasingly meticulous about their accounts, or perhaps employ an accountant to make sure that they are doing everything correctly. In other words, ideally, the cost to take into account is not just the cost to the revenue authorities, but the cost to the economy, marginal social cost or marginal 'operating cost' (i.e. administrative cost to the revenue authorities plus compliance cost to the taxpayers).

How Do We Measure Them?

Clearly, some of these items are very difficult if not impossible to measure: such as the present value of revenue from the deterrent effects, determining marginal administrative cost where resources are jointly supplied, or measuring the marginal compliance costs resulting from additional enforcement activity. But the conceptual problems are even more fundamental.

Conceptual

There are reasons for querying whether the MC=MR principle is appropriate. The tax revenue, which is the outcome of the application of real resources to tax administration, represents a transfer of income. Resources applied to tax administration do not generate new goods or services. Thus the analogy of the firm is misleading. The rule of equality between MC and MR does not tell us what total resources should be applied to tax administration. The realization that tax revenue is transfer suggests that the level of resources applied to tax administration should be less than that at which MC=MR; but how much less? Moreover, there is a contrary argument: that tax administrative resources should be increased beyond that point where MC=MR. The gap between the total revenue curve and the MPR line represents the extent of tax evasion. It can be argued that tax evaders should be pursued as criminals - they steal from the rest of the community. No one argues that police expenditure on catching criminals should be related to the loot that can be recovered from them. (In that case plain murderers would not be pursued at all!) Additional expenditure on tax administration, so the argument goes, is therefore justified even when the incremental cost is greater than the increment of revenue gained - to bring criminals to justice.

Where does all this lead us in practice? A government has to take a decision about the total resources to be allocated to a revenue department; it may, indeed should, take account of the considerations we have outlined as well as other economic and political considerations. Whilst a revenue department may properly urge the case for an increase in budget because of the additional revenue that it could generate, the more practical decision for a revenue department is, given its total budget, how to allocate its resources. Here the marginal principle is helpful.

There are some expenditures of a revenue department, in the shape of H.Q. staff and overheads which, whilst essential, cannot directly be related to revenue yield. There are others, notably customer services, which add to costs in the short term but, in the long run, may reduce administrative costs (because, with the benefit of guidance, more taxpayers get their returns right in the future) and even increase revenue (because taxpayers come to view the tax office in a more favorable light and comply more willingly). But for sections concerned with enforcement, such as audit and investigation branches, the marginal principle is important.

It can be argued that resources in these activities should be so allocated that the ratio between administrative costs and revenue is the same, at the margin, for all taxes and sections of taxes. If this is not so, then additional revenue can be raised from the same total resources by transferring resources from where the cost/yield ratio is high to where the cost/yield ratio is low and continuing so to do until the ratios equalize. (It should be noted that we are talking about marginal cost and marginal revenue. The average cost of collection of Tax A may be higher than that of Tax B, but it may still pay (i.e. generate more income) to transfer resources from B to A).

Indeed the same principles apply within a tax to different income levels, socio-economic groups and types and sizes of business and other characteristics of tax filers. Thus, to over-simplify, if income tax applied only to taxi drivers and publicans and the cost/yield ratio is lower for taxi drivers than publicans, enforcement activities should be increased for taxi drivers and reduced for publicans until the ratio is the same for both.

In practice many revenue departments attempt something like this by what is sometimes referred to as 'risk analysis' - concentrating resources in areas where the risk of revenue loss is greatest. In so doing they simplify the issue by ignoring the indirect revenue increases which may come from increased enforcement and concentrating on the direct revenue gain; and without taking effects on compliance costs into the calculation save, perhaps, not pursuing enforcement in too aggressive a manner.

The most famous and thorough example of this kind of work by a revenue department is the discriminant function analysis until recently undertaken by the Internal Revenue Service of the United States, leading to the Discriminant Index Function (DIF) (Graetz, M.J., J.A. Dublin, L.L. Wilde, 1989). About every three years the Internal Revenue Service conducted the Taxpayer Compliance Measurement Program (TCMP) which was a series of special audits, which covered some 50,000 taxpayers randomly selected except for some heavier weighting of high income taxpayers. The audits were exceptionally comprehensive and the prime object was to identify the characteristics of those taxpayers who, if audited, would generate above average revenue. The details of the analysis were kept secret. Filers were given a DIF score according to their characteristics. The higher the DIF score the more likely that an audit of the return would yield additional revenue above a threshold amount. The prime purpose of the DIF score was to select returns for routine audits (which are less comprehensive that the TCMP audit). In calculating the revenue yield, the uncollected tax plus fines from would-be evaders were taken into account. No allowance was made for deterrent effects or future yield (Roth, Scholz and Witte, 1989).

It may be of interest to readers that, in his November 1996 Budget, Mr. Kenneth Clarke, the then United Kingdom Chancellor of the Exchequer, inaugurated what he described as a 'Spend to Save' initiative to which he allocated £800m. Most of this projected expenditure was to combat benefit fraud, but £187m for Inland Revenue was expected to bring in about ten times as much over three years (with 1,000 extra tax inspectors and another 1,000 transferred from other duties as processing work was computerized). Additional money for Customs and Excise was expected to yield a similar or higher ratio (Financial Times, Nov 27, 1996).

Referring back to our diagram, in so far as more resources are put into tax administration using the same methods, then evasion diminishes as we move to the right along the curve. In so far as a revenue department adopts more effective methods than hitherto within a given budget (such as better targeting in its audit program) then the effect is to raise the position of the curve. We now turn to other ways of raising the curve.

Raising the Position of the Curve

Methods of raising the curve i.e. reducing evasion from broadly the same administrative cost can be considered under 3 heads, which might be thought of respectively as the administrative, the economic and the socio-psychological approach:

- minimizing evasion opportunities;
- reducing the net advantages of tax evasion;
- reducing the willingness to evade i.e. fostering voluntary compliance.

Minimizing Evasion Opportunities

In his writings on tax evasion Wallschutzky, (1993) rightly stresses the importance of minimizing opportunities for evasion. This may be achieved in a number of ways, of which the following are among the most important:

(a) An administrative structure whereby tax is deducted at source wherever possible, whether it be PAYE for employees, dividends and interest of businesses or interest of banks and other financial institutions. If direct deduction at source is not possible the next most effective method is a system of financial reporting which can provide information to cross-check with the taxpayer's own statements. Least satisfactory is sole reliance on the statement of the taxpayer.

It was William Pitt the Younger who first introduced income tax into the United Kingdom in 1798, during the Revolutionary War with France. The tax was abolished in 1802 with the Treaty of Amiens, but re-introduced in 1803 by Addington at the Exchequer, when hostilities started in the Napoleonic War. If Pitt takes the credit for introducing the tax, Addington must receive equal plaudits for putting it on a sound administrative footing. He introduced taxation at source where possible. The effect: almost the same yield as Pitt's Act from half the rates (Sabine, 1966).

There is much to be said in favor of the UK income tax by which the vast majority of taxpayers pay the same marginal rate of tax. As a result, deduction at source is easier and more accurate and, because of this feature and a cumulative PAYE system, for most taxpayers the correct amount of tax is deducted without the need for them to complete a tax return - thus minimizing compliance costs for the ordinary taxpayer. Unfortunately deduction at source is not possible for self-employment earnings. In connection with deduction at source, it is important to have only a short time lag between the collection of tax by the third party (e.g. the employer) and its payment to the revenue authorities and to enforce payment by the due date. Delayed payment amounts to evasion and the extent of evasion may be considerable if the inflation rate is high.

(b) Opportunities for tax evasion can be reduced by a simplified tax structure which minimizes the number of exemptions, reliefs, concessions and rebates, all of which can be a source of false claims. This statement applies equally to sales taxes as to income and capital taxes. The form of tax may also be important - thus a VAT is generally considered to be less evasion prone than an RST because of its self-policing properties, the audit trail and the fact that only a proportion of the revenue is collected at the vulnerable retail stage. On the other hand if the VAT contains extensive zero rating it opens the way to false claims. Even the existence of multiple rates can encourage evasion by claims that sales relate to lower-taxed goods rather than higher-taxed.

(c) A further vital component in minimizing the opportunities for evasion is an honest tax administration. Corrupt officials invite evasion. I shall not enlarge on this matter which is the subject of another paper, but a key factor here is also a simple tax structure, which minimizes tax officer discretion.

(d) Some countries, such as Australia, have found it useful to give all taxpayers a unique tax identification number, which has to be used, for example, in the opening of a bank account. If no number is forthcoming, tax is deducted from the interest on the account at the top marginal rate.

Reducing the Net Advantages of Evasion

The second method is to reduce the net advantages of evasion by increasing the risk/gain ratio. This method is based on the traditional economic approach following Allingham and Sandmo, (1972). The taxpayer is viewed as an amoral (if not immoral) rational being concerned to maximize his/her expected utility. Four elements are involved - the level of income, the tax rate on the relevant band of income, the probability of being caught and the penalty if caught. The risk of being caught is increased by more audit or more effective audit activity (which we have already discussed) - making evasion less attractive; a higher penalty structure has the same effect. It is generally taken that the higher the income the more the gain from evasion and the lower the tax rate the less the gain; but there are some complicated interconnections.

It is usually maintained that the higher the income, the less people are averse to risk. If the effect of reducing the rate of tax is to increase net of tax income, this reduces aversion to risk and acts in the opposite way to the effect of the tax reduction, leaving the net outcome unclear. On the other hand if the tax rate reduction is compensated for by an increased tax take elsewhere, either by broadening the tax base or by raising other taxes, there will be no income effect and the lower tax rate can be expected to reduce the gain from successful evasion.

However, there is a further problem of interconnections. Often the tax penalty is a fixed multiple of the tax unpaid e.g. twice the unpaid tax plus the tax due. If so, then the penalty falls with the tax rate. So the tendency for evasion to fall with a lower tax rate is reduced or offset. However, it is obviously open to a government, if lowering tax rates, to raise the multiple or to impose some additional fine.

Two further comments need to be made about this approach to reducing tax evasion. First, the deterrent effects of increased audits or higher penalties only apply if would-be evaders are aware of these changes. In fact it is the perception that their chances of being caught have increased that will deter, even if the perception does not accord with reality. It is vital, therefore, that publicity be given to an anti-evasion program, that increased penalties are highlighted and convictions made public, by number if not by name, to generate the perception of increased risk and reduced gain.

A second consideration is that too much emphasis on convictions and punishments may be counter-productive. A heavy-handed policy may set up attitudes which militate against voluntary compliance. On the one hand convicted evaders (and others who have witnessed their punishment) may feel that they have been treated with excessive harshness and may develop an anti-tax department attitude of 'we'll get even'. Whilst such convicted evaders may be more careful in the future, they may then take every opportunity to evade in circumstances where they are most unlikely to be discovered. One of the limitations of the Allingham and Sandmo analysis is that it assumes that all evasion carries the same probability of detection. In practice this is not so. Some evasions are almost guaranteed to succeed; others are more risky.

The second unfortunate effect of a heavy handed policy is that, as we have mentioned above, even entirely honest taxpayers feel threatened. As a result, their compliance costs may rise, either because they become over-meticulous with their tax record keeping or/and because they decide to shelter behind an accountant and hence incur professional fees. This, in itself, is an unfortunate use of resources, but, also, as we shall argue in the next section, high compliance costs generate resentment and militate against voluntary compliance. In so far as compliance costs are tax deductible, they actually reduce tax revenue.

This economic analysis is interesting and subsequent work has increased its sophistication; it is useful in focussing on some of the instruments, which can be adjusted to combat evasion, but it is far from being the whole story.

Reducing Willingness to Evade

The third category focuses on attitudes and motivations to behavior. Reducing willingness to evade means fostering a positive attitude towards tax paying and the tax department. As some recent researchers, Coleman and Freeman, (1996) argue, it is a matter of researching into why people wish to evade taxes and then doing something about it. They particularly look at what they call 'cultural background' - influences which formed early attitudes such as family values, civics, peer groups, aspirational group attitudes and personal experiences.

In what follows some of the more important issues that emerge from research in this field are put forward. Much of the research is reviewed in Roth, Scholz and Witte and Roth and Scholz, (1989), but not all of the propositions can be regarded as having been conclusively validated by research findings. Some must be regarded as more in the nature of plausible hypotheses. Unfortunately, too, none of the proposed measures for promoting voluntary compliance is likely to have speedy results. In what follows we group the considerations under three heads, starting with the broadest and most abstract and narrowing to the personal experience of the individual.

Commitment to Obey the Law

The overall weight of evidence from various kinds of research suggests the importance of commitment to obey the law for tax compliance. 'Commitment to obey the law refers to the individual's perceived moral obligation to obey, based on internalized beliefs and attitudes' (Roth, Scholz and Witte, 1989). Clearly, then, any way of maintaining and increasing that general commitment will maintain or increase tax compliance; important in this regard are features such as demonstration of the fairness of elections; the impartiality of the law; the independence of the courts; the availability of a cheap, speedy and accessible appeal system; and a strong civic sense.

Conviction of the Integrity of Government and the Efficiency and Equity of Government Expenditure and Taxation

Unfavorable to tax compliance are a series of negative perceptions of government: that government is corrupt; that it is wasteful in its expenditure (e.g. by extravagant buildings); that in its expenditure it favors certain ethnic groups or economic classes over others; that taxation lacks horizontal and vertical equity.

There is a link between avoidance and evasion. If the poor see the rich avoiding taxes on a large scale, the poor, who lack avoidance opportunities, are more likely to engage in evasion. The relationship between tax and expenditure is sometimes referred to as the exchange relationship.

The stronger the feelings of inequity are the less inclined will taxpayers be to see their hard-earned money going to be wasted in extravagant or inefficiently run schemes, lining the pockets of corrupt politicians and civil servants, or favoring some group to which they do not belong. The remedy would seem to be to show that these perceptions are untrue; to keep government clean and ensure that any breaches of conduct are severely punished; to provide detailed information about just how the taxpayers' money is spent.

There is much circumstantial evidence that complexity in a tax system and, in particular, high tax compliance costs, have negative effects on tax compliance. Thus, the small businessman, who faces disproportionately high compliance costs for his own income tax, sales tax and the tax he has to collect from his employees, may well revolt against paying his due amount. He may feel that it is bad enough to have to pay tax in the first place, but to have to incur high compliance costs in order to do so and to have to act as the unpaid tax collector for the government in collecting sales tax from his customers and income tax from his employees is to add insult to injury. In these circumstances the small business taxpayer may decide that he will cheat on his tax return at least to the extent of recovering the compliance costs that the government imposes on him.

There is some limited evidence in the United States that complicated tax forms discourage some less educated taxpayers from filing. Further, some very detailed aspects of the tax code (for example, in the United Kingdom in the field of fringe benefits) are not adhered to by all taxpayers from ignorance or from the feeling that it is just not worth the hassle.

The answer, therefore, is to seek to minimize tax compliance costs. Governments should publicly express their intention so to minimize them (subject to other objectives), automatically take them into consideration in all tax policy discussions and, like the United Kingdom, New Zealand and

Australia, require Compliance Cost Assessments (CCAs) from the revenue departments for changes in the tax law.

There is also a case, under strictly controlled circumstances, for compensating taxpayers who have incurred exceptional compliance costs. For example, suppose a taxpayer has been the subject of an in-depth investigation as a result of which he has emerged blameless; there is a strong case in equity, for compensating him for the exceptional compliance costs which that investigation has imposed on him.

Relationship to the Tax Office

The relationship between the taxpayer and the tax office is an important element in achieving compliance. A helpful customer services unit; a special small business unit which is aware of the needs and stresses of the small business man; above all, an attitude on the part of the tax office by which taxpayers are seen as clients, to be helped; as people innocent until proved guilty. Bad personal experience of a tax office militates against compliance (generating a 'we'll get even' mentality) whilst a good experience has the reverse effect.

A particularly important aspect is an appropriate complaints system. In June 1993 the United Kingdom Government set up a Citizen's Charter Complaints Task Force, which listed seven principles which should characterize a complaints system, it should:

- be easily accessible and well publicized;
- be simple to understand and use;
- allow speedy handling with established time limits for action and keep people informed of progress;
- ensure a full and fair investigation;
- respect people's desire for confidentiality;
- address all points at issue and provide an effective response and appropriate redress;
- provide information to management so that services can be improved.

However efficient it is, there are bound to be some mistakes in a large organization, and how well complaints are dealt with is very important in generating a favorable atmosphere amongst taxpayers.

An interesting and very successful experiment in the United Kingdom has been the appointment of an Adjudicator, since 1993, initially for Inland Revenue with subsequent extension to Customs and Excise and the Contributions Agency. The Adjudicator, Elizabeth Filkin, doesn't deal with technical issues of tax and tax liability (for which there is a separate appeals system) but with complaints against the administration of the revenue departments (Elizabeth Filkin, 1997).

These three approaches, the administrative, the economic and the socio-psychological should not be seen as separate or competitive, but rather as complementary.

Summary of Most Important Policy Measures for Tackling Evasion

– Fostering a commitment to obey the law.

– Taxation at source wherever possible.

– A simple tax system with minimum tax expenditures (in other words with a tax base which is measurable, observable and verifiable).

– An efficient system of auditing to maximize revenue from given resources.

– Regular reviews of the penalty structure - particularly important in times of inflation - with appropriate publicity for increased penalties.

– Public spending which is perceived as non-wasteful and equitable.

– Taxes which are perceived as equitable.

– An honest and customer-friendly tax administration.

Summary

The paper uses a simple diagram relating the cost of tax administration (horizontal axis) and tax revenue (vertical axis) to demonstrate the 'tax gap' or level of tax evasion. In terms of the diagram, policy to minimize tax evasion revolves around two issues: (1) how many resources should be put into tax administration (movement along the curve); and (2) how can we raise the position of the curve i.e. raise the tax yield for any level of tax administration cost. The first entails a discussion of the appropriate relationship between administrative cost and revenue yield at the margin. The second looks at three complementary approaches: minimizing evasion opportunities (the administrative approach); limiting the likely advantage from evasion (the economic approach); and reducing the willingness to evade (the socio-psychological approach).

References

Allingham, M. G. and A. Sandmo (1972) 'Income Tax Evasion: A Theoretical Analysis', *Journal of Public Economics*, vol. 1, pp. 323-338.

Coleman, C. and L. Freeman (1996) 'Taxpayer Attitudes to Voluntary Compliance', paper in series *Current issues in Tax Administration*, ATAX, University of New South Wales.

Filkin, E. (1997) 'Dealing with Complaints - The Adjudicator: A United Kingdom Experiment' in. C. T. Sandford (ed.), *Further Key Issues in Tax Reform*, Fiscal Publications.

Financial Times, November 27, 1996.

Graetz, J. M., J. A. Dublin and L. L. Wilde (1989) 'United States' in IFA Cahiers de droit fiscal international, *Administrative and Compliance Costs of Taxation*, general reporter C. T. Sandford, Kluwer, The Netherlands.

Roth, J. A., J. T. Scholz and A. D. Witte (1989) 'Tax Payer Compliance', vol. 1 and vol. 2, University of Pennsylvania Press, Philadelphia.

Sabine, E. E. V. (1966) 'A History of Income Tax', George, Allen & Unwin.

Wallschutzky, I. (1993) 'Minimising Evasion and Avoidance' in (ed.), C. T. Sandford, *Key Issues in Tax Reform*, Fiscal Publications, Bath.

6 Russia's Underground Economy During the Transition
SVETLANA GLINKINA[*]

An analysis of the situation in Russia demonstrates that the underground economy is a dynamic phenomenon involving the criminalization of the state economic system. Today, we are observing the criminalization of all stages of the economic process including production, distribution, product exchange and consumption. This criminalization now includes financial activities, property relations, foreign economic activities, and consumer market. The criminalization of the Russian economy represents a national problem with vast international consequences.

Definitions of the Underground Economy

Different authors have suggested different definitions for the concept of the underground economy. In the widest sense the underground economy comprises all the economic activities that are not registered in the official statistics (Feige, 1979). This definition covers the unrecorded activities that are excluded from conventional measures of the GDP of the country and the unreported activities and incomes that escape taxation and registration.

Maria Lacko, following Carter (1984) distinguishes three main elements of the underground economy: an informal economy comprising production in households, do-it-yourself activities and barter transactions between individuals; the unrecorded economy comprising activities where income is unreported or the production of commodities and services are legally not-licensed; and the unreported economy involving tax avoidance and evasion. I identify three sectors of the underground economy and base my analysis on the following structure:

---

[*] Center for East European Studies, Institute of International Economic and Political Studies, RAS, Moscow, Russia, e-mail: sveta-cl@ropnet.ru

- *The unofficial economy,* which consists of legal forms of economic activity producing goods and services not covered by official statistics and therefore escaping taxation;
- *The criminal (or illegal) economy,* which includes all forms of economic activity specifically banned by law;
- *The fictitious economy,* which implies speculative transactions and different kinds of swindles with a view to receiving and transferring money, including contrived rent-seeking.

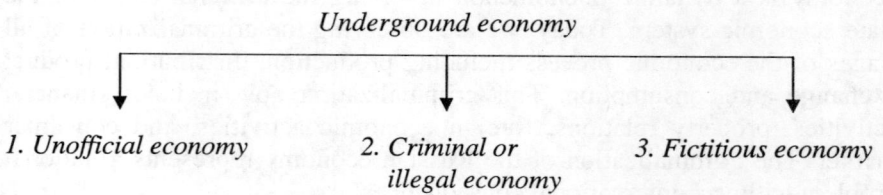

In many countries, particularly those in a difficult period of transformation, the underground economy may account for a sizable share of all economic activity. But there may be a considerable variation in the underground economy between countries with otherwise similar prospects and general socioeconomic backgrounds.

There may be a structural difference in the share of criminal activity in overall output, in the scope of the fictitious economy, and the development of the unofficial economy as a result of burdens of economic administrative regulations and high taxation rates, and different correlation between the sectors of the underground economy.

As a result of structural differences there may be different consequent problems, such as the failure fully to collect budget revenues, corruption, and the emergence of criminal economic links. There may also be variations in the effects on income distribution, in some cases increasing, in others decreasing, income disparities.

So, the role and structure of the underground economy may be one more very important indicator for comparative analysis of reform process in post-socialist countries. Analysis suggests that the role and structure of the underground economy in a country undergoing a change of system may be a yardstick for deciding whether or not reforms are succeeding. Use of this indicator requires consideration of the main trends that are taking place in the underground economy in the Former Soviet Union (FSU) and Central and Eastern Europe (CEE).

Main Trends in the Development the Underground Economy in Post-Socialist Countries

Unofficial Economy

The World Bank (1996) estimates of the unofficial economy in 14 post socialist countries, comprising 9 from the FSU and 5 in Central and Eastern Europe (CEE) from 1989-1994, reveal a large overall growth in the importance of the underground economy throughout the region.[1] The overall share for the combined unweighted sample has more than doubled, from about 15% of overall output in 1989 to a share exceeding 30% by 1994. On average, almost one-third of the economy in post-Soviet countries is thus underground. But there is high variance in the evolution and the share of the underground economy in the analyzed countries.

In the late 1980's, CEE countries appeared to have a substantially larger share of activities in the underground economy than those in the FSU (approximately 20% vs. 12%). Yet the early nineties saw a very sharp increase in underground activities in the FSU (its share tripling to 36%) while the overall share in the CEE sample rose slightly, amounting to between one-fifth and one-quarter. Within the FSU the 1994 estimates for the underground share vary from merely 12% in Uzbekistan to almost 50% in Ukraine; while within the CEE countries the estimates range from 14% in the Czech Republic to 28% in Bulgaria. The share of the underground economy appears to be related to the level of economic and political liberalization and the success of macro-economic stabilization. The relatively low underground economy shares observed in Uzbekistan, on the one hand, and the Czech Republic on the other are accounted for by different circumstances. Uzbekistan has had little economic liberalization and even less political liberalization but has maintained tough enforcement mechanisms. In sharp contrast, the Czech Republic has had a high degree of political and economic liberalization from 1990 onwards, liberalized the economy very rapidly, stabilized its macro-economy, and developed market institutions and enforcement mechanisms faster than other countries in the region.

Such countries as Russia, Ukraine, Moldova and Kazakhstan are found to have the highest underground economy share among the 14 CEE/FSU countries in the sample. These high proportions are explained by the low initial role of commerce and services in the economy of these countries, by the high degree of political liberalization, by lack of macro-stability and undeveloped market institutions.

This suggests that as reform programs encompassing macro-stabilization, liberalization and privatization are implemented and bear fruit, (as they have been in some CEE countries), a reverse cross-over of activities towards the official economy does take place. Poland and Romania are examples where the share of underground activity has decreased since 1989.

The influence of the underground economy is contradictory. The underground economy plays a positive role, mitigating the large drop in official GDP of the countries. The very deep declines in official GDP overstate the true fall in overall GDP. This is particularly the case in countries that initially had a low underground economy share and which experienced the largest declines in official GDP. Thus, this 'mitigating' effect of the underground economy was particularly marked for the FSU countries. In the FSU about one-half of the decline in official GDP was accounted for by underground activities while only one-half was a bona fide decline in national output. This mitigating role of the underground economy resulted in a lesser overall GDP decline than the official GDP figures suggest, as well as in significantly less inter-country variance in overall GDP declines than when performance was measured by official GDP.

From a national welfare standpoint the underground economy has had a positive side. It has helped keep the economies afloat as the costs of producing efficiently in the official economy have often increased. It has also debunked the myth of 'lack of entrepreneurship' or 'lack of readiness for the market' on the part of FSU citizens. Furthermore, it has provided valuable market experience to such budding entrepreneurs. The underground economy is a very important resource for additional incomes of citizens. The existence of underground incomes in such countries as Czech Republic Poland, Hungary helps to decrease incomes disparities.

At the same time, the emergence and growth of a large underground economy poses serious concerns, which on balance dominate. First, the effective management of the economy by the state is undermined. The taxation and foreign exchange base that any state needs to manage its economy is eroded by the rapid flight from the official to the underground economy. Macro-economic stability is thus harder to attain and sustain. Further, the legitimacy of the overall legal and regulatory system is challenged. This can take years to reverse.

Second, however large the underground economy may be, it is mostly a 'survival economy', where trading, services, state asset stripping and a focus on short-term turnover drive out a longer-term view. Large scale and more sophisticated investments are virtually absent, and they are crucial for the longer-term growth prospects of the country.

Criminal Economy

The criminal situation in Russia and in some states of the FSU is much worse than in the countries of CEE. There are a number of explanations for this phenomenon:

- First and foremost is the sheer volume of wealth that became available for distribution and redistribution during the transition in the states of the FSU and CEE. The estimates of the World Bank show, for example, that the value of Russian land resources totals about thirty trillion dollars. The world has not previously known such high levels of profit rates as we have in some branches of post-Soviet economies.

- Underground economic relations have developed above all because the former state system was destroyed, and the long-established links between separate industries and whole territories were disrupted. Since the destruction of the Soviet Union, the borders between new states are permeable, presenting few obstacles to smuggling or other forms of criminal entrepreneurship.

- The criminalization of post-Soviet economic life is a self-generating process, largely due to the slackening of efforts in economic crime control. Some quarters try to excuse these omissions by pointing to the need to harness the underground economy's capital to the advancement of economic reform.

- The legal system of the FSU is inadequate. The inherited Soviet legal system is insufficiently developed in commercial and in criminal law. In Russia the situation was further complicated by the 1993 power struggle between the president and the legislature. The new constitution of December 1993 has not clarified the situation. The law is often interpreted by presidential decree. Moreover, the lines of authority between Moscow and the regions are ill defined so that central and local regulations are often in conflict. The participants in the criminal economy exploit such ambiguities.

Due to these reasons post-Soviet space has become the center of criminal actions and links. The Russian Ministry of the Interior reports that there are 5,700 organized criminal gangs currently active in the country, of which 30% specialize in illegal financial and real estate transactions. Others are connected with drugs, the antique markets, the smuggling of natural resources and people. Over 47,000 crimes connected with illegal narcotics operations have been revealed in Russia for the year 1994 alone. Approximately 10,000 people have been accused. Forty-six tons of narcotics, valued at approximately 120 billion rubles, have been confiscated. According to experts, no less than 700 tons of narcotics, valued at approximately 4 trillion rubles, were in circulation last year. Specialists say that over two million people in Russia and approximately 6,500,000 people in countries of the CIS regularly use drugs. Forecasts suggest that within the next five years this figure will at least double. The law actually contributes to this; in Russia, one can freely use narcotics; it is only illegal to keep or sell them.

A basic tendency in Russia's drug market is the transfer from the natural to the synthetic narcotics trade. Last year approximately 210 underground laboratories in Moscow were destroyed. Today this problem is extending far beyond the bounds of Russia and the CIS countries. According to expert forecasts, the near future is more than likely to see the transfer of heroin technology from Afghanistan and Pakistan to Central Asian countries such as Uzbekistan, Tadzhikistan and Turkmenistan. Unemployment, corruption, the lack of natural resources and developed industry, and the complete control over law enforcement agencies established by local authoritative regimes will evidently promote this.. However, while this narcotics intervention is only being expected, the expansion of exports of narcotics from CIS countries has already begun. After the fall of Balkan narcotics channels, Russia will now be a leading factor.

Another large-scale business involves the antique market. In Europe alone - France, Germany and Italy - there exist approximately 500 stores that specialize in the trade of Russian relics. A large portion of this merchandise is contraband. According to Russian special services, at least 40 international groups with extensive infrastructures are active in this illegal business. With their help, illegally exported Russian paintings and icons eventually end up at British auctions.

A significant number of illegal migrants from Africa and South-East Asia also arrive in Europe, particularly in England, by travelling across the territory of the former Soviet Union and Russia. Today, the smuggling of people has become a very lucrative international business. It costs those wanting to emigrate to Europe approximately $7,000-$10,000 to be smuggled across borders complete with false entry visas. According to experts from Russia's Federal Migration service, in the past two and a half years alone, no less than 300,000 émigrés from Asia and Africa entered western countries through Russia.

Underground operations in the sphere of finances are also conducted on an increasing scale. An outstanding example is Russia's largest scale fraud involving forged mutual account bank documents. According to various estimates, as a result of this operation, in the course of a year, between 3-5 billion dollars were stolen from the State. In Russia this is referred to as a Chechen action, since its executors, as a rule, were members of Chechen criminal groups and many traces of this fraud led to the city of Grozny. However, specialists are sure that this action was planned in Moscow with the direct participation of important heads of the Central Bank of Russia, members of Parliament, and leading officials of the former KGB and prominent commercial banks.

It is no accident that the major organizers of this fraud have not yet been named, since everything possible is being done to conceal the traces of this large-scale crime.

Speaking of banks, according to experts from law enforcement agencies, up to 85% of these institutions in Russia are directly connected with criminal economic structures (Rossiskiye Vesti, 1994). The Mafia even has a complete series of tested methods on how to subjugate disobedient banks.

Russia's commercial bank system is extensively engaged in laundering money from illegal sources. The climate for such operations is favorable because, unlike Western countries, the depositing procedure does not require a check on the source of the money. Moreover, cash transactions are widely practiced.

Samples of criminal activities in CEE countries are very often closely connected with the underground transfer of resources from the FSU. In 1992 - 1994, at least 20% of the petroleum and one third of the metals produced in the country were smuggled across the border. Nearly 10% of the smuggled goods are transported to the Baltic countries. Thus, tiny Estonia, which produces no non-ferrous metals at all, has become one of the biggest non ferrous metal exporters.(Novaya Yezhednevnaya Gazeta, 1994). Close to 70% of the raw materials shipped by rail through Lithuania from Russia fail to reach the intended destination, that is, the Russian city of Kaliningrad. According to the Ministry of the Interior of the Russian Federation (RF), in Lithuania at least four powerful Mafia groups specialize in 'switching' the flows of Russian goods to different addressees. Thus, every single day in 1993, a trainload of 147 barrels of oil 'disappeared' in Lithuania. It was established that railway personnel, customs officials and executives of Lithuanian foreign trade bodies were involved in these operations (Global Finance, 1994).

Criminal groups in Russia control over 40,000 individual businesses, including some 2,000 enterprises, 4,000 joint-stock companies, 7,000 cooperatives, 7,000 small businesses, 407 banks, 47 exchanges and 697 agricultural markets. Corrupt officials assist one out of every seven gangs in committing crimes (Rossiskiye Vesti, 1994).

Fictitious Economy

Since the beginning of the transition, the character, mechanisms, and scope of the fictitious economy have completely changed, largely as a result of the rapidly increasing role of distribution in economic life, and the development of the privatization process.

One of the most important constituents of the reforms in post-socialist countries is the group that benefits from the privatization of the economy. Privatization occurs in these countries in different socio-economic and institutional environments that define its specific character. There are some different approaches to privatization in academic literature:

- Privatization as transfer of ownership of assets (corresponding to existing enterprises) from the public sector to private economic actors, ultimately to households.

- Privatization as increased reliance on the private institutions of society and decreased dependence on the government for the satisfaction of people's needs. Privatization is the act of increasing the role of the private sector, or decreasing the role of government, in an activity or in the ownership of assets (Savas, 1989/90);

- Privatization as the removal of the central state authorities from decision-making about the allocation and utilization of existing state-owned capital assets within the process of systemic change (Mihalyi, 1992).

These approaches do not contradict to each other. Each of them is connected with a particular level of analysis: economic, socio-economic or sociological. Using these various approaches to the privatization process gives us very different picture of the most frequent forms in which underground economy activities appear in the area of privatization. For example privatization as the transfer of state assets from the public to the private sector has been accompanied in all post-socialist countries by:

a   Allocation of favorable conditions for purchasing of parts or whole companies on the principles of political clientelism. This takes the form of setting the price lower than the real value of a company, giving specially favorable conditions and time-limits for payment and payment by installment.

b   Allocation of managerial loans without real mortgage guarantees by the state-owned banks to a selected number of managers close to the ruling strata.
c   Repayment of shares or loans from the assets of the privatized company, fictitious recapitalisation, concealment and privatization of the company's profit by majority owner managers and against the interest of remaining shareholders and similar illegal activities.
d   Criminal activities such as corruption, bribery, fraud, fraudulent bankruptcy before privatization.
e   Morally and legally dubious and non-sanctioned privatization activities such as purchasing discounted shares ;
f   Informal stock markets (Čučković, 1997).

In the framework of the third approach, economic and legal research must be supplemented by the analysis of informal, underground relations between state administration, management of enterprises, state property agencies, foreign investors, local authorities, and workers and employees. In this case, the third segment of underground economy – the fictitious economy plays a particular role in privatization.

There are many deliberate attempts to misrepresent the real picture of privatization in former socialist countries, in particular, in Russia. The following table presents a graphic idea about the real process going on in Russia.

The national economic infrastructure has been privatized briskly on 'semi-official' grounds. In 1988-1993 concerns were founded instead of ministries, commercial banks instead of state banks, and various exchanges, joint ventures, trade houses instead of state supplying and trading organizations. Economic power has been privatized without any social control and without any legal basis. Payments from the state budget were actively 'privatized'. 'To operate' with both the budget and the Central Bank of the Russian Federation is the main business direction of any 'serious' commercial structure with the slightest pretensions; this is actually the basis of the explosive growth of corruption in the country.

Table 6.1   Main objects and methods of privatization in Russia and participating parties

	Objects	Methods	New proprietor
1.	National economic infrastructure	Creation of commercial structures on the base of existing state economic entities without necessary legislation and social control	Upper management of transforming state bodies, representatives of the nomenclature.
2.	Property owned by political and public organizations	Creation of commercial structures, export of capital	Members of the nomenclature (top officials of public and political organizations and their close associates)
3.	State budget, public funds and foundations	Granting of all sorts of social credits and tax privileges	Corrupted officials and staff, and 'grateful' beneficiaries
4.	Funds owned by state enterprises	Employment of various forms of 'pre-privatization' (founding of small co-operatives, leasing etc.); widely varied forms of mass privatization with and without compensation	Work collectives (employees of industries and organizations); Management; Former operators in the underground economy; Bureaucracy;
5.	Savings of the population	Establishment of voucher and investment funds, founding of a bank system and new social security organizations	Staffs of relevant funds, foundations and organizations

The easiest and most popular method of privatization on the second guideline was the so-called 'milking the credit cow'. It works as follows. The Russian Central Bank gives a special loan to a factory at a low (for Russia) interest rate of 25% per annum to pay overdue debts to other enterprises or back wages. The money, however, goes straight to the commercial bank associated with the factory, which re-lends it at something closer to the country's real interest rate of 250% per year. The difference then gets pocketed or deposited in an overseas bank account. The volume of such loans in the last nine months of 1994 alone was 6.5 billion rubles. This may help explain why, although the Central Bank keeps pumping out more money, the country's enterprises never seem to get any healthier. Some managers and commercial bankers have made enormous profits, but Russia's factories are producing less, not more.

Illegal tax allowances for favorite commercial structures can be viewed as a peculiar form of budget fund privatization. In the period of 1993 through the first half of 1994, the amount of these allowances exceeded the expected income receipts resulting from monetary privatization (Ross, 1994). By the end of 1993 less than 30% of total circulating assets could be related to the share of state and municipal property (Kuzenkov, 1994). This fact, which has not been advertised by the official statistics, could explain many problems of non-payments that strangle the national economy.

Numerous investment and privatization funds, completely free of control at the initial stage, have privatized a substantial amount of individuals' monetary means, mostly vouchers, and there is not the faintest chance of tracing these transactions. The list of 'non-formal' means and 'non-advertised' objects of Russian privatization could be extended. There were also very many 'non-formal' actions during the official part of privatization program, as state enterprise assets were assigned to the private sector.

In many countries, participation in the redistribution of the national wealth and the government budget offered higher expected returns than normal productive activity. As a result, the economic entities invested more and more time, effort and resources in redistribution via different mechanisms, including rent-seeking. They invested in incumbents, whose exercise of discretion provides a source of income, thereby creating corrupt links to the Mafia.

The fictitious economy in transitional countries today is closely connected with rent-seeking. The picture of rents in these countries is very complicated. There are numerous classes of rents that are a natural consequence of market valuation and opportunity cost of supply.

One natural result of the transition is the existence of contrived and non-contrived but contestable rents (a rent is contestable if the beneficiaries are subject to a decision-maker's discretion). It is often difficult to distinguish between contrived and non-contrived contestable rents in economies in transition. They arise for a number of reasons:

- the concentrated market structure when the formerly planned large state enterprises are released to function in a market environment,
- the transformation in the transition of state property to private wealth via privatization and other means,
- the ambiguity surrounding property rights when privatization is delayed,

– political and bureaucratic discretion to influence wealth, assignment and income distribution.

A typical example of a contrived rent is monopoly profit. Many contrived rents are created in the framework of international trade policies. Holders of quota rights to artificially restricted quantities of imports or exports earn rents equal to the difference between world and domestic prices. Protectionism policy also provides rents for owners of domestic factors of production. Contrived rents can also be provided directly via the government budget, in the form of direct transfers or as subsidized credits to designated groups. Rent can also be associated with political and bureaucratic positions, via private returns from discretion to assign rents: a customs inspector can earn a rent, as can a government.

There are many opportunities for rent creation and rent seeking in transition:

a. Monopoly rents. The monopoly rents were sustained because competition often took the form of a contest as to who would acquire the sole supply rights of a former state enterprise. Normal competition in the supply of output was replaced by the practice of so-called representative - 'upolnomochennej', often assigned to a bank or particular exporter. For example, competition did not take the form of a competitive offer to supply a product to a retail store, but rather, in contesting the right to be the sole supplier of a product to the store. The competition was thus to establish the claimant to the rents from noncompetitive supply.

b. Rents from delayed privatization. The ambiguous property rights sustained by state ownership allow management and government officials' discretion in decision making that creates and assigns rents. The discretion can be exercised in the prices that the non-privatized enterprise pays for inputs and sets for the delivery of outputs in transactions with the private sector. High input prices and low delivery prices transfer profits to the private sector from the state enterprise. We may consider this process one of the underground ways of expanding the private sector in a transitional economy, a part of underground privatization.

c. Rents from the process of privatization can be connected with:

- asymmetric information (by reporting lower than actual profitability; managers and other insiders can hope to reduce the valuation of property to be privatized and thereby create a rent to be realized by purchasing state property at less-than-market prices);

- opportunity to control the privatization process (in many cases where the privatization process has been controlled by managers themselves, state property was sold at artificially low transfer prices, to beneficiaries who were often family and friends, or individuals with political and corrupt ties).

d. Rents attendant on a political position. Rents can accrue to an individual as a consequence of the individual's discretion to make decisions that transfer incomes to others. For example, it is valuable to have the discretion to decide who should receive an export quota, or to decide who should be able to buy state property at a preferential price. Since individuals seeking to benefit from such decisions will be prepared to pay part of the anticipated benefits to achieve a resolution in their favor, this in turn makes displacement and replacement of the individual exercising the discretion valuable.

Tough competition between economic entities for rents is the main goal of pseudo-economic activity in many countries of transition. The means whereby the competition is conducted is often outside the law closely connected with crime and corruption.

The existence of a complicated system of rents is especially unfavorable in Russia because of the specific character of the mechanism by which resources are allocated and authority is delegated. Under this new mechanism (local corporate, monopolistic regulation) certain institutions (15-20 financial-industrial groups) in the existing economic system take advantage of their position. The concentration of the production facilities, capital and corporate power gives them local control over production and consumption parameters (volume, quality and structure), market performance indicators (pricing and sales growth through marketing practices) and indicators governing social life. These groups are pseudo-state - pseudo-private. They have very close links with bureaucrats, bureaucratic structures and political forces. Their cooperation leads to the creation of corporate-bureaucratic structures (clans), whose non-economic rivalry has come to replace the mechanism of state management.

The government hierarchy is corrupt at all levels. Both bureaucrats and the police are poorly paid, and are therefore especially eager for the extra sources of income, which organized crime can provide. This allows organized crime gradually to extend its hold on whole sections of the government apparatus.

Under the influence of this mechanism, the Russian economy has split into spheres with high or low degrees of incorporation. The highly incorporated sphere contains industries with a technological monopoly (and so highly concentrated production facilities), a market monopoly (an ability to regulate prices and the operations of suppliers and customers on a local scale) and an institutional monopoly. This sphere includes the holders of most of the liquid resources and of the corporate-bureaucratic structures, including the fuel and energy complex, the finance and trade complex and the more export-oriented firms in manufacturing. It amasses vast profits at a rate quite unprecedented anywhere in the world.

The other, non-monopoly, sphere is plagued by shortages of resources and inadequate management and technology. It covers reproduction of the labor force, production of consumer goods, and a large part of the farming complex. The highly incorporated sphere enjoys enduring advantages in prices, funding and credits.

The difference in the potentials and perspectives of these two economic spheres polarizes the society. It paves the way for narrow circles to earn astronomical profits by dominating specific mechanisms of resource allocation and power delegation. It constitutes the main source of the underground economy.[2]

From many points of view the situation in Russia is unique. While such countries as the Czech Republic, Hungary, Poland, Slovenia have shown real results in the way of the creation of efficient market mechanisms, Russia exhibits contention and competition for rents. The CEE societies leave individuals with no option but to engage in productive activities while Russia offers broad opportunities to acquire wealth by influencing redistribution. All claims to property and income are now contestable. The society loses the resources used in attempts to influence the distribution of income, when the same resources could have been used in productive activity to add to national income. A rent-seeking society experiences lower growth. Rather than accumulating capital, it is dissipating resources in contesting and defending redistribution.

So there is an ever widening social stratum whose interest is aligned with maintaining illegality in the business sphere, and taking part in the growing underground economy. As a consequence, there is an unprecedented growth of business crime, a diversification of offences, and resistance to fighting them.

Summary

In many countries, particularly those in a difficult period of transformation, the underground economy now accounts for a sizable share of all economic activity. But there is considerable variation in the underground economy in countries with otherwise similar prospects and general socioeconomic backgrounds. At first there may be structural differences with different shares of criminal activity in overall output, different scope for fictitious activity, and different development of the underground economy because of tax and regulation burdens. Structural differences may create different consequent problems. There is the failure of tax collection, the emergence of criminal economic links, and the growth of corrupt practices. There may also be a variation in the effect on social distribution, increasing or decreasing income disparities. The role and structure of the underground economy may be one of the more important indicators for comparative analysis of the reform process in post-socialist countries.

For a variety of reasons, the share of underground activity in modern Russia is one of the highest among the transitional countries. A huge volume of formerly state held wealth has suddenly become available for redistribution during Russia's transition. Over the past decade Russia has experienced changes that have shaken its very identity as a nation. It has lost 40% its population and a quarter of its territory.

The destruction of the Soviet Union disrupted the long-established links between separate industries and whole territories. Borders between new states became permeable, presenting few obstacles to smuggling or other forms of criminal activity. The weakened state became unable to fulfill many traditional functions, and organized crime became a substitute for many government functions. The criminalization of Russia's economy has been a major feature of the transition, defeating the rule of law, and making the transition to a market economy all the more difficult.

Notes

1 Analysis concerns Russia, Ukraine, Moldova, Belarus, Uzbekistan, Kazakhstan, Latvia, Estonia and Lithuania in the FSU and Czech Republic, Poland, Hungary, Bulgaria and Romania in CEE. For estimation was used the macro-electric methodology.
2 Only in 1992 the new Russians received through the direct and indirect subsidies (subsidized credits, export quotas, subsidies to food import) incomes exceeding 75% of GDP). 'Izvestija', June 20, 1996.

References

Carter, M. (1984) 'Issues in the hidden economy', *Economic Record*, vol. 60, pp. 209-221.

Čučković, N. (1997) 'The underground economy and the privatization process in Croatia', paper presented at the International Workshop, *'The importance of underground economy in economic transition'*, Zagreb, 16-17 May 1997.

Feige, E. L. (1979) 'How big is the irregular economy?', *Challenge*, vol. 22, pp. 5-13

Kuzenkov, A. (1994) 'Privatization and the national wealth redistribution', *Problems of forecasting*, no. 4, p. 69.

Lacko, M. (1997) 'Do Power Consumption Data Tell the Story? (Electricity Intensity and Hidden Economy in Post-Socialist Countries)', mimeo.

Mihalyi, P. (1992) 'Privatization in Hungary'. Institute of Economics, Hungarian Academy of Sciences. Bp., p.1.

Ross, J. (1994) 'A price for shock therapy', *Independent Newspaper*, no. 10, p. 4.

Savas, E. S. (1989/90) 'Taxonomy of privatization strategies', *Policy Studies Journal*, vol. 18, Winter, pp. 343-335.

Tanzi, V. (1980) 'The underground economy in the United States: Estimations and Implications', *Banca Nazionale del Lavoro Quarterly Review*, vol. 135, p. 427.

7 Political Economy of the Unofficial Economy: the State and Regulation

VOJMIR FRANIČEVIĆ*

In my paper entitled 'The Basic Characteristics of the Unofficial Economy' (Franičević, 1996), I tried to show that institutions are the most important factor for explaining the unofficial economy. I also wanted to show that the unofficial economy is systematically and structurally characterized, susceptible to business cycles and socio-culturally adapted. I expect that this will prove true also in the case of Croatia.[1] In my approach to the political economy of the unofficial economy in Croatia, I shall deal with the established and publicly known facts and with analytically well established claims.[2]

The process of transition has a very strong influence on the unofficial economy and its relationship with the official one. This paper will concentrate on the transitional state as a generator of motivation and barriers to unofficial economic activities. The main theme will, therefore, be certain political economic aspects of the unofficial economy in Croatia. My starting point will be those approaches in which the unofficial economy is derived from the behavior of actors who take part in economic processes within the structure of limitations and motivations provided by the state itself through its intervention, regulations and sanctions (Tokman, 1992; Tokman-Klein, 1996; Franičević, 1996).

Introduction

Given the sparse empirical insight into current economic, social and political processes in Croatia, it is difficult to undertake a detailed analysis of such a complex and heterogeneous phenomenon as is the unofficial econ-

---

*   Professor at the Faculty of Economics, University of Zagreb, Croatia,
    E-mail: franicevic@oliver.efzg.hr

omy.[3] This is even truer because Croatia is presently in a period of extensive and thorough economic, social and political transformation, the characteristics of which add to the complexity of the unofficial economy. Contrary to the ('normal') unofficial economy as we find it in countries with transparently defined economic systems and institutions, with a stable 'institutional structure of accumulation',[4] the unofficial economy in Croatia is in a process of transition itself. It is in a process of change, from the unofficial economy based on the political and economic logic of a self-governing, socially-owned economy (Glas et al., 1988; Bićanić, 1990) towards the unofficial economy typical of highly developed Western economic systems (Thomas, 1992, Greenfield, 1993). Many characteristics of the unofficial economies in developing countries are being reproduced along this path (De Soto, 1989; Portes, Castells and Benton, 1989; Tokman 1992; Tokman and Klein, 1996). These characteristics are a consequence of the significant institutional and regulatory gaps that still exist in Croatia, of yet unfinished market processes and of the low credibility level of the sanctions in cases of illegal conduct. At the same time, however, they are also a consequence of the enormous significance and role the economy of sheer survival has for the majority of Croatian citizens.

The main characteristic of the transitional process is the transformation of ownership, institutions and regulations. This means a thorough and fundamental redefinition of relations that exist between the state and the economy as well as between politics and civil society. This makes possible deep changes in the economic and industrial structure, which were impossible in a socialist economy. Liberalization of the Croatian economy has filled markets with new actors, new demands and organizational solutions. The explosive dynamics and spontaneity of entrepreneurship in many instances and in many ways have preceded the ability of the state to place them within the desirable regulatory framework. Demand for regulation usually comes after the object of regulation has become established and recognized in a political process as something that should be regulated. There is no doubt that this process has been and still is too open to informality, trying to establish its own 'rules of the game'. In addition, many aspects of regulation taken over from the previous economic system have shown themselves to be inadequate, and have actually allowed, and sometimes even forced, entrepreneurs to resort to non-institutional informal behavior.

Not only have the 'rules of the game' changed in the above processes, but so have the 'playing fields' and the 'players'. This makes the period of transition remarkable in the following ways: old economic and social actors adapt or new ones emerge, social positions, social wealth and political influence are re-distributed. This leaves a lot of space for the unofficial economy, since everything is open, and also provides it with a strong and unique stimulation. Many 'games', and especially privatization of state and/or socially-owned property, are played to the final number of moves, which are just sufficient to make this property private. Since potential benefits are high and the sums and the 'game' itself final, the motivation to break the rules of the transition game (Čučković, 1996), which anyway lacks credibility, is almost irresistible. In such a setting, as the theory of games suggests, the non-co-operative outcome will prevail (Frank, 1994).

The war in Croatia also played a significant role. It encouraged certain entrepreneurial activities to take place and profits to be made. It also led to a high tolerance level and/or the low resistance of institutions to their linking up with parallel trends of the peacetime economy. The non-transparency and arbitrary decision making in the privatization process (Čučković, 1996) only made this inter-connection stronger. At the same time, the capacity of the state to penalize the many informal activities of war-entrepreneurship were completely inadequate even when it was actually trying to do so. Frequent justification of the most obvious and extreme war profiteering on the pretence that special conditions existed in the new state, accompanied by occasional ritual threats of sanctions, did nothing to suggest to entrepreneurs that the risk might be too high. Rather, it supported widespread public suspicions that even parts of state's political mechanisms were involved.

The Croatian entrepreneurial scene was formed at the crossroads of liberalization, privatization and war-entrepreneurship, which together gave rise to a wide range of actors whose success was based on rough, and often 'network'-assisted breaking of laws and moral standards. While the penalization of such activities was very insufficient indeed (Skorupan, 1996), the transfer of money derived from those activities into the official economy was relatively easy. This not only resulted in the development of 'success models', but also in cynical disbelief in the rule of law and in politicians[5] - the most dangerous element preventing any government attempt to reduce the unofficial economy. And politicians did precious little to dissuade citizens in their beliefs. On the contrary![6] Even the most flagrant suspicions of illegal or immoral conduct by politicians and/or big privatization 'magicians' usually remained unresolved and unheeded. Many 'discovered' cases never attract penalties of any kind. This is exactly the right way for the state to provide its citizens, along with all other public goods, with a mechanism of collective rationalization for joining the unofficial economy! The effect is well known: the more actors there are, the more efficient the mechanism is (Henry, 1978). The moral dimension of the Croatian economy may therefore prove to be the key restrictive factor in attaining legitimate economic growth and also one of the most significant factors in expanding the unofficial economy.

The processes of economic liberalization and privatization have imposed upon many actors enormous economic and other costs. The stressed 'transitional crisis' has only made the unfavorable economic trends preceding it worse (Franičević and Kraft, 1986). Although economic and institutional crises in former Yugoslavia had already started to become serious in the '80s, the transition itself had a very recessionary impact. Generally speaking, 'transitional crises' can be ascribed to the simultaneous shocks of supply and demand caused by dramatic institutional change and the requirements of stabilization. In Croatia, this was additionally sharpened by the dissolution of the Yugoslav market and the war in Croatia and Bosnia and Herzegovina.

This transition shock, accompanied by a substantial reduction in the real value of state transfers and other acquired rights, resulted in a variety of consequences, which stimulated or even forced actors into the unofficial economy. It suffices to mention only the enormous growth in unemployment and the dramatic decline of the real income of employed and retired persons (Crnković-Pozaić, 1996; Franičević and Kraft, 1996). Stabilization policies, deflationary in their character, have only succeeded in making the pressure stronger. As the process of restructuring, with rare exceptions, has not seriously started yet (Mateša, 1996), it may well be expected that thousands of workers forced to seek their daily bread in the unofficial economy will be appearing in the labor market for years to come. Current government attempts to establish credible sanctions against debtors in the economy, who are already heavily insolvent, will make the above development even more stressed[7] (Franičević and Kraft, 1996).

We should also add that the after-effects of the war have not yet been overcome and this drastically worsens the social situation. Together with its whole tragic course, the war resulted in hundreds of thousands of individuals struggling to survive. In spite of all the enormous efforts of government and other institutions, their struggle led to the increase of various specific 'entrepreneurial' activities starting from rummaging through garbage, beggary and prostitution all the way up to black marketeering, illegal trade and theft. These and similar activities are all referred to as the unofficial economy (Bejaković, 1995).

Finally, unofficial economy activities are characterized by a specific socio-cultural context in which individuals and organizations operate. The rationality of their actions is bounded, mediated by institutions and adapted to circumstances (Franičević, 1996c) and strongly dependent on cultural and social capital in general (Štulhofer, 1996b). Individuals involved in economic processes are not 'rational economic individuals' from orthodox textbooks of neo-classical theory. Instead, their decisions are based on their past, their routines and on social norms and values (Hodgson, 1993). Key elements of this context referring to their involvement in the unofficial economy are:

a   the influence of path dependency (North, 1990). The socialist economic system was for decades rich in unofficial economic activities that were usually politically tolerated (Bićanić 1990). It is likely that this habituation of the actors to the unofficial economy will influence their behavior in the future, too. This is especially true because privatization and transitional crises create a unique combination of opportunities, incentives and pressures that make actors become involved in the unofficial economy, either as a way of acquiring enormous profits and market advantages or, simply, to survive;
b   the influence of traditional socio-cultural values of particular local communities, especially those reflecting the dominant attitude towards the law and state authorities or those which facilitate 'networking' (Powell, 1990) of individuals and firms that are deeply 'embedded' (Granovetter, 1985) in their social context.

It can be expected that those socio-cultural environments where both the above elements are present, will largely influence both the readiness and the ability of individuals to engage in unofficial economy activities (Štulhofer, 1996b). It is quite possible that the strong expansion of entrepreneurship in some traditional communities and the areas where their members tend to live (for example, Dubrava-Sesvete area in Zagreb) has been supported by their distinct socio-cultural capital. It allows them to generate within the unofficial economy the required level of trust and a credible sanction system within the community itself (Portes et al., 1989; Portes, 1994; Franičević, 1996). Unfortunately, in this respect, as far as Croatia is concerned, apart from some anecdotal evidence, we know unforgivably little. More detailed and deeper research into economic, sociocultural and anthropological characteristics of such entrepreneurship, the role of 'networks' in it and the levels and mechanisms of informality would definitely improve not only our understanding of one of the most expansionary sources of entrepreneurship within the unofficial economy, but would also prevent us from making gross simplifications about economics, politics and values.[8]

The fact that the unofficial economy in Croatia is rich in survival activities, characterized by universality and diversity, is responsible for the belief that economic growth, accompanied by increased wealth and real incomes in the official economy, will in itself be the best long-term solution for the unofficial economy (Bejaković, 1995). Although it can really be expected that the level of the unofficial economy in Croatia will to a certain extent decrease, providing a more significant level of economic growth is achieved, a more important fact is that its structure and phenomenology will change as well. Since the unofficial economy develops primarily from the relationship of the state towards the economy, the unofficial economy in Croatia will be closely connected with the political and economic, as well as with the social and political characteristics of the state.

Is the state, then, going to be liberal, professional, competent and 'small'? Or is it going to be corporate, paternalistic, filled with corruption, nepotism and incompetence, as well as 'big' and wasteful? Or will it be something else entirely? Lasting contours of the relation between the politics and the economy as well as between the state and the market in Croatia are being established in collective, political choices made by numerous actors in the process of transition. They also establish the structure of opportunities, motives, costs and benefits from working in the unofficial economy. This makes research into the 'political economy' of the unofficial economy in Croatia so important.

The following sections discuss the effects of privatization and state regulation on the unofficial economy. We then go on to examine how the lack of professionalism and the inefficiency of the state motivate actors, particularly small firms, to engage in the unofficial economy. The last section contains concluding remarks concerning the connection between the transitional state as found in Croatia and the unofficial economy.

Privatization

Through the process of privatization, a huge amount of assets has been redistributed to individuals, families, social groups and entire local communities. This fact makes the 'privatization game' very special, an almost irresistible magnet for numerous unofficial economy activities and a high level of opportunism is therefore to be expected. Opportunism also includes relativization of social norms and rationalizations for breaking them.

Many opportunistic activities are against the law while others may be legal, but nevertheless, leave a bitter taste of unethical conduct in the mind of the public. Typical examples of this are shares obtained well below their true value, 'hostile take-overs', and trading with privileged information. Generally speaking, privatization includes illegal procedures in the process of buying and/or paying for assets and also procedures which are neither regulated nor sanctioned. But even conduct formally legal can, if it seems unethical, lead to increased cynicism on the part of the public towards formal institutions, making the rationalization of engagement in the unofficial economy easier.

The role of the state is essential since the process of privatization gives extreme power to persons responsible for its management. It makes it possible for them to influence the conditions of asset acquisition and selection of owners. The less transparent is the process and the more dependent it is on discriminatory conduct of the government and civil servants, the greater is the likelihood for the creation of an informal property market under their control. When public, democratic control is lacking, judicial independence questionable and inefficiency monumental,[9] it is only to be expected that such markets will flourish. The aforementioned elements are, to a greater or lesser extent, characteristic of all transitional economies also, but Croatia has some special characteristics:

1 The war, which made possible rapid acquisition of significant assets, but which also enabled 'laundering' of such assets through the privatization process. Many top managers of former socially-owned companies have been very successful in the processes of privatization. At least some of them cannot account for their current wealth either from the income they formally enjoyed in the system of social ownership or from relatives living abroad.

2 The legacy of the self-governing socialist management structure. Managers had both the skill and the knowledge necessary to achieve success in privatization. One of them was their 'orientation towards style and functional strategies and against ideology' as a source of flexibility and efficiency, 'especially in times of quick and sudden changes' (Pusić, 1992:118). Management structures possessed precious sociocultural capital, i.e. 'networks' of informal connections, trust and reciprocity, which they were successfully able to exploit. This was the most important element that made them successful in the privatization process, even in situations when it was against the wishes and efforts of political structures.[10]

3 The political 'design' of Croatian capitalism (Franičević-Kraft, 1996). Instead of acting as a supervisor of the formal rules of the game, the ruling party has engaged in meritocratic privatization, political selection of owners and even in open nepotism. This has simply encouraged

a symbiosis between the unofficial economy and unofficial politics - politics outside actual constitutionally based institutional control.

4   Finally, the rules of privatization in Croatia. The models of privatization through transformation of social ownership, of asset-valuation, of the sale of shares held in the state funds — all of them proved to be: (a) non-transparent; (b) extremely favorable for the creation of gray assets markets; (c) inadequately shielded from corruption.

Regulation of the Market Economy: What 'Rules of the Game' to Chose?

Numerous new laws and regulations are being adopted in the process of forming the new institutional foundations of the market economy in Croatia. The laws and regulations impose certain restrictions on firms and companies, give them rights and benefits, but also impose costs connected with gaining and retaining legality (Tokman, 1992:12). In other words, those actors in economic processes who make decisions and create interactions within a defined regulatory and institutional environment are part of the official economy.

But there are also potential gains and profits which can be achieved through activities outside the legal framework. The majority of informal activities by Croatian entrepreneurs take place within business entities belonging to the official economy. The actors in the unofficial economy are only occasionally completely outside the official economy, an insight that is important for understanding the dynamics of the unofficial economy and for the formulation of appropriate policies to deal with non-compliant behaviour.

The State

The state as an institution, can stimulate the unofficial economy either directly (when it takes part in the unofficial economy itself), or indirectly (when it signals to private actors the desirability and/or feasibility of engagement in the unofficial economy). The high costs of the Croatian post-socialist state makes working in the official economy expensive. The current trends in Croatia indicate that it is the ambition of the state to be 'big' (Kesner-Škreb, 1996), 'expensive' and 'paternalistic'.

Paternalism can be seen in the enormous number of citizens who depend on state help and in the increasing number of those to whom the state has made commitments either through direct subsidies or various concessions in imports.[11] There is also the tendency of the state to engage in big infra-structure investments and in expensive rescues of failing banks and companies, including some private ones (Ramljak, 1996). A number of activities depend almost completely on the state: education, health service and culture. The attempt on the part of the state to maintain its monopoly and the obligations that this involves are obvious in quite a number of them. Enormous investment in status symbols should also be added to the list, the symbols not only of the young state, but also of its officials, which results in huge inefficiency and wastefulness.[12]

The state sends its taxpayers multiple signals that its costs will continue to be high. Th large commitments the Croatian state has made to various groups of its citizens and foreign countries must be met. The possibility of a fiscal crisis suggests that taxes are unlikely to decline. On the contrary, they might even increase, particularly if promises of high economic growth are not realized. If such trends continue, the current efforts by the Government to decrease the tax burden and the public debt, which would also lessen motivation for tax evasion, will lose their credibility.[13] This means that incentives for tax evasion will continue to exist, in spite of the growth of financial discipline on the part of tax payers due to the establishment of a Tax Administration and Financial Police (Madžarević, 1996).

The engagement of the state in large projects is a poor substitute for private investments (Franičević & Kraft, 1996). Growth based on state investments and/or subventions encourages rent seeking and corruption. If the state is also wasteful, we can expect a high level of unofficial activity. To reduce this underground economy would require the following:

1   High professional standards for public and state administration services accompanied by increased competency and the development of a distinctive working ethics.[14] This is specially important with regard to the key personnel (Pusić, 1995);

2   Complete independence of the judiciary and exclusively parliamentary control of the inspection institutions;[15]

3   Transparent regulations;[16]

4   True democratic control by citizens and their representatives over all state institutions and the activities of officials.

5   Increased penalties for tax evasion, improved public services and a decrease in the share of public expenditure in the GNP.

Such reforms would require a decisive break with the tendencies of 'paternalistic capitalism' which are all too obvious in Croatia. Success will depend on the ability of the actors in political processes to implement such changes.[17]

Small Firms: Forced to Engage in Unofficial Activities?

The number of small firms in Croatia has been growing extremely rapidly, and there are many indications that much of the growth is in the unofficial sector.[18] Although both medium and large firms engage in many operations and work practices which actually fall within the unofficial economy,[19] there is no doubt that small firms have greater opportunities and are exposed to far less risk when they do so.

The very fact that small firms are exempt from many regulations and obligations means that they operate in a regime which is significantly less formalized in comparison with the one in which large firms operate. But this is only one side of the story. Small firms have more opportunities and greater need to operate in the unofficial economy, whether it concerns entrepreneurial exploitation of the unofficial economy or the economy of sheer survival. In a situation when former social and state sectors constantly cut employment, self-employment has become necessity for many people. This fact explains not only the sudden explosion of small firms (Biljan-August and Lovrić, 1995), but also its concentration in sectors with low entry barriers. 'Marginal entrepreneurship' is concentrated in the areas where entry is very easy such as trade, services and 'unregistered sales' (Mikulić and Madžarević, 1996) in markets, market places, pedestrian underpasses, and other 'peddling' locations. The majority of small firms in Croatia are engaged in activities of this kind. Of all small firms, 48.1 per cent are engaged in trade, 17.7 per cent in financial and other services and 7.4 per cent in construction (Popović, 1996; Kaštelan-Mrak and Vehovec, 1995). In addition there are small cafés and numerous craftsmen who also engage in trading activities.

Small firms experience both greater opportunities and needs for hiding unofficial economic activities. High taxes and contributions for employees present a significant burden on businesses already exposed to fierce market competition because of the relatively low capital labor ratios and the above average labor intensity. Their small size excludes economies of scales which are otherwise present in meeting the requirements of many regulations. Blažić (1995) describes the tendency in modern taxation systems to discriminate against small firms by favoring capital investment while penalizing employment. Croatia also has extremely high rates of payroll taxes and contributions. A value added tax, with high compliance costs and none of the economy of scales available to large firms, will also put a relatively higher burden on small firms.[20]

An important part of the story of small firms is their unfavorable position in the capital market which drives them to the gray market (Franičević, 1995b). This, like so many other aspects in the Croatian transition process, has not been sufficiently researched. Precious little is known about how small firms are actually financed. The only pieces of information we have to rely on are the regular complaints by small entrepreneurs who cite their unfavorable position in the capital market, together with high taxes, as their greatest problem.

Finally, a note about services. The liberalization of the Croatian economy has opened a lot of space for an accelerated spread of service activities. The more liberal development of the institutions of civil society did the same for an increase of alternative forms of self-help and self-provision, existing side by side with the traditional ones that are part of the existing economic structure. Many of these activities take place in the unofficial economy. This is a very important part of everyday life and should be adequately researched to provide significant information about trends and changes in socio-cultural values, which influence preferences concerning official services such as health, education and entertainment. We wish to learn the extent to which dissatisfaction with the quality of service offered by the public sector influences development of the unofficial markets.[21]

Conclusion: A View of the Political Economy of the Unofficial Economy in Croatia

Economic liberalization and privatization have opened an unexpectedly large space for business activities in Croatia. Business people and entrepreneurs have latched on to the many opportunities trying, of course, to make the best of them. At the same time, there has simply been no regulation of many forms and ways of conduct, and for many the existing regulations simply were not credible. Huge spaces opened up to informal economic activities and were used by small and large firms alike, but also by citizens, either as the input owners or as taxpayers.

The process of institutional and regulatory 'design' of the capitalist economy has taken — and is still taking — place, according to (presumably the best) models of developed market economies. A government with an adequate political mandate, but with insufficient capacity for effective monitoring and credible sanctions in cases of non-compliance is implementing this.[22] The reasons for regulation of business activities are well established in the economic literature, but so is the fact that the compulsory regulations impose costs upon the actors (Feige, 1990; Tokman, 1992; Tokman & Klein, 1996). Regulation also sets up barriers to the market competition. These costs and barriers can now, especially when it comes to dealing with marginal actors who have managed to keep their head above water in the open, non-regulated regime, become an enormous obstacle both from the standpoint of costs and the competence required for running a business 'by the book'.[23] On the other hand, their avoidance can reduce costs, increase profit and strengthen one's position in the market. Numerous opportunities provided by regulations — either by avoidance of regulations or by achieving regulatory monopoly or rents — are taken advantage of in the unofficial economy.

The unofficial economy in Croatia cannot be limited, not even primarily, to the 'survival' strategies. Many entrepreneurs take advantage of opportunities and promptly react to restrictions imposed upon them by the level, forms and costs of regulation. Various combinations of events (recession, unemployment, etc.) and cultural background (the inherited and widespread acceptance of engagement in the unofficial economy and the practical experience of doing so) strongly influence the appearance and characteristics of the unofficial economy in Croatia. Nevertheless, the primary interest of any policy seeking to reduce the role of that unofficial economy must definitely be in the institutional sphere. An understanding of the relationship between the state and the economy — and wider, of the state and society — is essential for an understanding of both the development and the characteristics and effects of Croatia's unofficial economy.

Dynamic contexts, such as transitional ones, seem to present a paradox as far as the unofficial economy is concerned: it surfaces simultaneously as both a consequence of existing regulation and of its non-existence. Sometimes the unofficial economy is simply an answer to the inadequacy of existing regulations, sometimes (probably most often) it means profitable avoidance of regulations and sometimes it indicates new practices which are not yet regulated. On one hand, the state tries to make its regulatory system as watertight as possible, at the same time increasing the costs and complexity of adhering to it and producing a basic structure of incentives for engagement in the unofficial economy. On the other, entrepreneurs who constantly find new opportunities to gain profits in the liberalized environment, signal at the same time potential areas of regulation to the state.[24] The dynamics of the unofficial economy depends in large measure on the above processes, but also on the ability of the state to increase the credibility of institutions concerned with prevention and/or sanctions against illegal economic activities as one of their primary functions.

When speaking of the generation of the unofficial economy, the motives of private actors are usually studied — of business people, entrepreneurs, employers, workers and consumers — who react to their environment according to the constraints it imposes and/or to the opportunities it offers. But, if the relationship between the official and unofficial economy is distinctly defined by economic and social institutions which are given regularity and credibility by the state, if institutional formation and regulation is a state matter and a part of the political process, then the following aspects cannot be avoided: (a) the problem and character of political choice itself and (b) the motives and conduct of the actors concerned in it. The border line between the official and unofficial economy is problematic in Croatia not only because official and unofficial economic activities are intermeshed and not only because the dynamics of privatization and market transformation influence the demand for deregulation, but also because the very producer of formality and regularity — the state itself — shows inclinations to take part in the 'grey zone' of both politics, law and economic life. Consolidation of a democratic political system and the functioning of a state showing respect for law and order seem to be the essential prerequisites for keeping the unofficial economy at bay.

Those who assume that the increase in employment and productivity in the official economy and rise in real wages and incomes will provide the main mechanism for a reduction of the unofficial economy and of the whole range of its side effects are definitely right. However, if we accept the fact that the main source of the unofficial economy is in the state itself and in the way it intervenes in the economy, then it seems logical to expect that the unofficial economy will be with us forever. This entails the following:

1. The unofficial economy in Croatia will come closer to the unofficial economy of developed mixed Western economies when the normalization of the market economy and the appropriate institutions take place;

2. Its share and importance will then to a certain extent be less. It is not realistic, however, to expect that the unofficial economy will disappear as long as regulation itself continues producing both costs and opportunities and the political system continues to make possible the creation of markets for rents.

For the above reasons, it seems probable that the unofficial economy is likely to be a permanent characteristic of Croatian economy and society, rather than a mere legacy of almost surmounted history or a consequence of the still not completely finished transformation into the capitalist market economy through comprehensive institutional, social and political engineering. Believing in the possibility, not to mention the necessity, of complete elimination of the unofficial economy might well lead to unforeseeable consequences in which, paradoxically, its transformation into a true parallel, hidden economy might be just one of the results.

Summary

The unofficial economy in Croatia is under the strong influence of transitional processes. Privatization gives extraordinary and unique opportunities to the actors and power to persons responsible for the management of the privatization process, the implementation of which is non-transparent. This situation results in a high level of inclination to illegal and/or unethical conduct. Regulatory and institutional economic structures develop through the formation of the market 'rules of the game', but so does the structure of opportunities for and benefits of working in the unofficial economy. In addition, many activities are not regulated and some are inadequate. Regulations impose costs upon the actors and their avoidance (in the framework of the unofficial economy) brings advantages and benefits, especially if sanctions are not credible, as is the case in Croatia. Incentives for rent supply and demand are numerous and are a significant contribution to the expansion of corruptive activities. The state itself, due to its size, inefficiency and inclination to paternalism, is also a significant source of the unofficial economy. The importance of institutional reforms (professionalisation of state services, judicial independence, transparency of regulations and procedures, openness to the public) should be stressed, but so should all other reforms that would increase the benefits of paying taxes and other contributions. This calls for rationalization in public revenue expenditures, diminishing their share in the GDP and an increase in the quality of public sector services. A break with the tendency towards 'paternalistic capitalism' is necessary. The role of small firms in the unofficial economy is also discussed. Small firms have more opportunities, but also greater need, to operate through the unofficial economy. This is a consequence of their greater susceptibility to the costs of adherence to the regulatory framework, but also of the big role of 'marginal entrepreneurship' within the economy of survival. Although it may be expected that economic growth will decrease the role played by the unofficial economy, it will nevertheless remain a permanent characteristic of the Croatian economy. Its dynamics will depend both on the character of the developing regulatory regime, on the character of the state itself and on its capability to increase the credibility of its sanctions. It is obvious that this is a problem not only of an economic, but also of political character.

Notes

1. Socio-cultural aspects of the unofficial economy in Croatia are analyzed in more detail in Štulhofer (1996a and b).
2. The analytically well established claims mentioned refer in a rather high measure to the analytical contributions of other collaborators in the project entitled *The Unofficial Economy in the Republic of Croatia*.
3. While the associates in the Project point out the very high level of the unofficial economy in Croatia (Crnković-Pozaić, 1996; Madžarević and Mikulić, 1996; Mikulić and Madžarević, 1996, Jankov, 1996; Radnić-Ivandić, 1996), analysis of specific forms and especially motives and conduct of actors in the unofficial economy is not possible without more detailed field research.
4. 'Institutional structure of accumulation' should be understood to cover all those basic institutions and economic and social regulations which mediate in the relations between work and capital, state and capital and state and citizens ensuring a stable relationship between capital accumulation demands and legitimacy of order. (For more detail see Franičević, 1986).
5. This is supported, though indirectly, by the data from Štulhofer 1996a (on opportunism and corruption expansion).
6. If, for example, the first session of the Croatian Parliament had adopted proposals to put public officials under obligation by the law to report their property status before taking over their public functions and after leaving it, that would have meant some 'strategic commitment' with enormous positive moral external effects. Today, this would mean ratification of the '*status quo*' situation and would, therefore, have far weaker credibility.
7. Due to the possible increase of member of over-indebted firms going bankrupt.
8. Relevant sociological and anthropological starting points already exist, for example, in the works of D. Tomašić, J. Županov, D. Rihtman-Augustin and others.

9   This is clearly visible from the hundreds of thousands of yet unsolved cases in courts that will have to wait their turn for years to appear before the overloaded judges. D. Kalogjera warns that 'the legal system in the economy is near collapse. Claims are practically inactionable, and their collection has come to be a new cost (and, we should add, also a source of specific informal activities), which is increasing and becoming increasingly more difficult to record and increasingly closer to criminality. Lawsuits are not being settled and judicial protection of trade relations has practically ceased to exist. Registrations are slow and unreliable. Offence and criminal procedures are falling behind the pace of living' (Kalogjera, 1996). This has much wider implications for the flourishing of unofficial activities than those concerning the privatization process itself.

10 Government policy regarding the so-called 'old foreign currency household savings', which were to become the main source of manager bank credit made business easier (deliberately so?) for managers (Čengić, 1995:156). It is not hard to see that the sources of managerial credits are usually the banks with which the managers used to have business as well as other kinds of connections in past years. On the other hand, it should not be surprising that managers of the state-owned banks, in operations of a questionable nature, showed most confidence in those who had already established their reputation by, among other things, the number of informal operations in the old system. There is no doubt that delay in the privatization of banking made possible the unexpected success and consolidation of the old manager structure in the privatization game. In the midst of all this, managers also succeeded in capitalizing skillfully on the loyalty of workers (formed in the self-governing system) in 'their' firms. (Čengić, 1995:156).

11 The following groups of people directly depend on state transfers: the poor, children, retired persons, war victims, displaced persons and refugees, persons who receive their salaries on non-regular bases or do not receive them at all, the unemployed -- approximately 2 million people in all (Gatarić, 1996:27). The system of transfer delivery itself is extremely expensive and non-transparent. Expenses for persons employed in the Social Welfare Funds are, for example, higher than the value of the social program for 100,000 social card holders, or for their 230,000 family members (Gatarić, 1996:28).

12 This is also supported by numerous reports on audit performed which were submitted to the Croatian Parliament by the State Audit Office during 1996. The reports, however, do not refer to those wasteful activities that were covered by completely legal decisions.

13 The obvious concern of the Governor and the Council of the Croatian National Bank regarding the 'expansionary fiscal policy and accumulation of state debt' speaks fluently of the alarming tendencies of state expansion (Knežević, 1997).

14 'State administration cannot work properly if the rules are constantly changed and their implementation is conditioned upon personal discretion, gifts and corruption' (Kregar, 1994: 60).

15 There is no doubt that the examples of 'political rationality' in selective use of the Financial Police does nothing to promote either its credibility or the professional ethic of its members. An institution crucial to curtailing the unofficial economy should not be the tool of political opportunity.

16 Regulations and procedures should be designed bearing in mind their potential to induce corruption. Priority should be given to 'simple, easy to monitor, rules... over ones that give great discretion to poorly paid officials'. Various rights (to pollution, exports, etc.), licences and the like, can be objects of open auctions (Rose-Ackerman, 1994:28).

17 Objective difficulties in achieving and implementing consensus about the changes, which impose significant costs upon actors, call for caution, but so does the experience of numerous countries where the political and economic system was based on distinct state commitment towards various interests and needs. The example closest to us is the system of socialist self-government.

18 The number of firms registered in Croatia grew as follows: 5512 (1989), 7991 (1990), 16643 (1991), 26009 (1992), 35595 (1993), 49732 (1994), 59922 (1995). Small firms accounted for the following growth dynamics: 2064 (1989), 5651 (1990), 14542 (1991), 24093 (1992), 33781 (1993), 48021 (1994), 58072 (1995). The share of small firms in this is: 37.4 (1989), 70.7 (1990), 87.4 (1991), 92.6 (1992), 94.9 (1993), 96.6 (1994), 96.9 (1995). (Biljan-August and Lovrić, 1995; Primorac, 1996). Registered number of persons employed followed the following dynamics: 136266 (1991), 158916 (1992), 155515 (1993), 185901 (1994) and 198696 (1995). (Kaštelan-Mrak and Vehovec, 1995; Popović, 1996). The number of persons employed per firm, however, shows a constant decline: 9.37 (1991), 6.59 (1992), 4.60 (1993), 3.87 (1994), 3.42 (1995).

19 Subcontracting reduces risk and increases flexibility (of, for example, employment) by avoiding regulatory barriers, which do not apply to small firms or which small firms can avoid more easily (Franičević, 1995a). Unfortunately, there are no data on subcontracting in the unofficial economy. Instead of the highly needed research and studies, there are only numerous indications (obtained from labor inspections, various 'advertising papers', articles in newspapers, etc.) indicating its importance for the explanation of the sources and mechanisms of the unofficial economy in Croatia. Work at home seems to be very widespread (from making clothes to performing the intellectual services required by the official economy), and so does sub-contracting in construction works.

20 In reaching this conclusion, she refers to the experiences of other countries, such as Great Britain. Research has shown that VAT is 'the first in the scale of burdens state regulation imposes upon small firms ' (Blažić, 1995:245).

21 This is equally as true for going to a private dentist, who largely operates in the unofficial economy (since the official dentists require long waits and offer questionable service), as it is for seeing a person who practices 'bio-energy' in a hotel and advertises in the press, operating completely in the unofficial economy and offering an 'alternative' even when the official alternative no longer exists.

22 In societies which go through rapid social changes, Kregar points out, 'social behavior', typically, 'does not conform to legal norms. Legal rules are treated as obstructions to be by-passed informally... Problems relating to the ambiguous nature of rules are compounded by the extraordinary mixing of traditional myths with rational standards.' While the institutions, regulations and laws are identical to standard foreign models, the difference in implementation 'is obvious. Precise regulations and consistent interpretation give way, in fluid situations, to exemptions. Eventually, exemptions granted to friends, compatriots, clans, sects, or due to corruption and bribery, swallow the rule.' Implementation of the law becomes 'ritual'. In fact, 'without (such) re-interpretation, the state cannot function' (Kregar, 1994). It is not difficult to recognize elements of Croatian reality in the above description.
23 This also includes another possibility: transition is also a period of learning for many completely inexperienced actors. Non-compliance can, therefore, also be a consequence of ignorance. However, we do not expect this share to be very important.
24 Let us, for example, take the services of chiropractors. Today, they are completely outside the official economy, although they are tolerated. It is probable that requests for regulation will come from both sides of the market (supply and demand). It is also possible that complete formalization will take place resulting in entry of chiropractors into the system of health insurance. Then regulation will become a motive for working in the unofficial economy (similar to other private medical practices).

References

Anušić, Z. (1996) 'Inflacija ne dolazi u obzir' (interview), *Poslovni svijet, Večernji list,* svibanj 8.
Arrow, K. J. (1963) 'Social Choice and Individual Values' rev. ed, John Wiley and Sons, New York.
Bejaković, P. (1995) 'Metode mjerenja i fenomen sive ekonomije u Hrvatskoj', *Financijska praksa*, vol. 19, no. 4, pp. 317-346.
Besley, T. (1995) 'Savings, Credit and Insurance', in Behrman J. and T. N. Srinivasan (eds) (1995) *'Handbook of Development Economics'*, vol. III, Elsevier.
Bićanić, I. (1990) 'Unofficial Economic Activities in Yugoslavia', in Los, M. (ed), (1990) *'The Second Economy in Marxist States'*, The Macmillan Press, Houndsmills, pp. 85-100.
Biljan-August, M. and Lj. Lovrić (1995) 'Strukturni značaj malih i srednjih poduzeća za gospodarstvo Republike Hrvatske i Primorsko-goranske županije', in *Zbornik radova*, Ekonomski fakultet Rijeka, vol. 13, no. 2, pp. 49-59.
Blažić, H. (1995) 'Porezna politika u funkciji razvoja malih i srednjih poduzeća' in *Zbornik radova*, Ekonomski fakultet Rijeka, vol. 13, no. 2, pp. 239-250.
Crnković-Pozaić, S. (1996) 'Neslužbeno gospodarstvo mjereno radnom snagom', *Financijska praksa*, vol. 21, no. 1-2, pp. 169-194.
De Soto, H. (1989) 'The Other Path: The Invisible Revolution in the Third World', Harper and Row, New York.

Čengić, D. (1995) 'Manageri i privatizacija: Sociološki aspekti preuzimanja poduzeća', Alinea, Zagreb.
Čučković, N. (1996) 'Neslužbeno gospodarstvo i proces privatizacije', *Financijska praksa*, vol.21, no. 1-2, pp. 259-276.
Državni ured za reviziju (1996) *'Izvješća o obavljenim revizijama'*, Državni ured za reviziju, Zagreb.
Feige, E. L. (1990) 'Defining and Estimating Underground and Informal Economies: The New Institutional Economics Approach', *World Development*, vol. 18, no. 7, pp. 989-1002.
Franičević, V. (1986) 'Radikalna politička ekonomija: Traganje za alternativom kapitalizmu SAD', Centar V. Bakarić/Globus, Zagreb.
Franičević, V. (1995a) 'Small Firms and Networks: Some Policy Consideration', *Zbornik radova*, Ekonomksi fakultet Rijeka, vol. 13, no. 2, pp. 285-300.
Franičević, V. (1995b) 'Financiranje malih poduzeća u komparativnoj perspektivi', *Računovodstvo i financije*, vol, 16, no. 5, pp. 43-54.
Franičević, V. (1995c) 'Problemi s racionalnim ekonomskim čovjekom', *Revija za sociologiju*, vol. 26, no. 3-4, pp. 151-168.
Franičević, V. (1996) 'Temeljne značajke neslužbenog gospodarstva', *Financijska praksa*, vol. 21, no. 1-2, pp. 45-70.
Franičević, V. and E. Kraft (1996) 'Economic development in Croatia: Is Croatia facing a growth impasse', paper presented at the conference *'Economic Reconstruction and Development Policies in the Yugoslav Successor States'*, School for Policy Studies, Bristol, 27-28 June 1996, pp. 1-40.
Frank, R. H. (1994) 'Microeconomics and Behavior', 2nd ed, McGraw-Hill, New York.
Gatarić, Lj. (1996) 'Socijalna pomoć za dva milijuna ljudi', *Banka*, vol. 7, no. 12, pp. 26-28.
Glas, M., S. Kukar, M. Simončič and I. Bićanić (1988) 'Siva ekonomija v svetu in v Jugoslaviji, Delavska enotnost, Ljubljana.
Granovetter, Mark (1985) 'Economic Action and Social Structure: The Problem of Embeddedness', *American Journal of Sociology*, vol. 91, no. 3, pp. 481-510.
Greenfield, H. I. (1993) 'Invisible, Outlawed, and Untaxed: America's Underground Economy', CT: Praeger, Westport.
Henry, S. (1978) 'The Hidden Economy: The Context and Control of Borderline Crime', Martin Robertson, London.
Hodgson, G.M. (1993) 'Economics and Evolution: Bringing Life Back into Economics', Polity Press, Cambridge.
Jankov, Lj. (1996) 'Monetaristički oblik neslužbenog gospodarstva', *Financijska praksa*, vol. 12, no. 1-2, pp. 157-168.
Kaštelan-Mrak, M. and M. Vehovec (1995) 'Dinamika razvoja sektora malog poduzetništva u prijelaznoj ekonomiji Hrvatske', in *Zbornik radova*, Ekonomski fakultet Rijeka, vol. 13, no. 2, pp. 61-79.
Kalogjera, D. (1997) 'Trgovački sudovi 'krivi' za visoke kamate' (interview), *Poslovni svijet, Večernji list*, 8 January, 1997.
Kesner-Škreb, M. (1996) 'Neslužbeno gospodarstvo i razvoj', *Financijska praksa*, vol. 21, no. 1-2, pp. 315-328.

Knežević, D. (1997) 'Oprez sa zaduživanjem u inozemstvu', *Večernji list*, 10 January, 1997.
Kregar, J. (1994) 'Deformation of Organizational Principles: Corruption in Post-Socialist Societies' in Trang Duc V. (ed), pp. 47-60.
LaPalombara, J. (1994) 'The Structural Aspects of Corruption', in Trang Duc V. (ed), pp. 33-36.
Madžarević, S. (1996) 'Porezna evazija', *Financijska praksa*, vol. 21, no. 1-2, pp. 241-258.
Mateša, Z. (1996) 'Za administrativnu kontrolu plaća nema više razloga' (interview), *Poslovni svijet, Večernji list*, svibanj 29-30.
Madžarević, S. and D. Mikulić (1996) 'Mjerenje neslužbenog gospodarstva sustavom nacionalnih računa', *Financijska praksa*, vol. 21, no. 1-2, pp. 141-158.
Mikulić, D. and S. Madžarević (1996) 'Procjena neformalnog gospodarstva u poljoprivredi, industriji i trgovini', *Financijska praksa*, vol. 21, no. 1-2, pp. 217-230.
Mueller, D. C. (1989) 'Public Choice II', Cambridge University Press, Cambridge.
North, D. C. (1990) 'Institutions, Institutional Change and Economic Performance', Cambridge University Press, Cambridge.
Pejovich, S. (1995) 'Economic Analysis of Institutions and Systems', Kluwer Academic Publishers, Dordrecht.
Popović, J. (1996) 'Trgovci i kafići vrte najviše novca', *Večernji list*, 28 November, 1996.
Portes, A. (1994) 'The Informal Economy and Its Paradoxes', in Smelser Neil J. and Richard Swedberg (eds) (1994) *'The Handbook of Economic Sociology'*, Princeton University Press, Princeton, N. J., pp. 426-449.
Portes, A., M. Castells and L. A. Benton (eds) (1989) 'The Informal Economy: Studies in Advanced and Less Developed Countries', The John Hopkins University Press, Baltimore.
Powell, W. W. (1990) 'Neither Market nor Hierarchy: Network Forms of Organization', *Research in Organizational Behavior*, no. 12, pp. 295-336.
Primorac, Ž. (1996) 'Hrvatska poduzeća - godinu dana poslije in *Gospodarska politika Hrvatske - što i kako u 1997. godini?*, 4. tradicionalno savjetovanje, Hrvatsko društvo ekonomista, Opatija, 21. i 22. studeni 1996., pp. 122-136.
Pusić, Eugen (1995) 'Kvaliteta ljudi u upravi', *Financijska praksa*, vol. 19, no. 4, pp. 277-299.
Pusić, V. (1992) 'Vladaoci i upravljači', Novi Liber, Zagreb.
Radnić, A. i N. Ivandić (1996) 'Neslužbeno gospodarstvo u turizmu i ugostiteljstvu', *Financijska praksa*, vol. 21, no.1-2, pp. 231-240.
Ramljak, O. (1997) 'Za sanaciju 16 poduzeća - 2,1 milijarda kuna', *Slobodna Dalmacija*, 4. siječnja 1997.
Reljac, B. (1996) 'Neslužbeno gospodarstvo u međunarodnoj trgovini', *Financijska praksa*, vol. 21, no. 1-2, pp. 195-216.
Rose-Ackerman, S. (1994) 'Reducing Bribery in the Public Sector' in Trang Duc V. (ed) (1994), pp. 21-28.
Santini, G. (1995) 'Pretvorba', *Ekonomija*, vol. 1, no. 6-7, pp. 329-453.
Šajatović, M. (1997) 'Zakon savane', *Poslovni svijet, Večernji list*, 8 January 1997.

Štulhofer, A. (1996a) 'Sociokulturni aspekti neslužbenog gospodarstva – Između oportunizma i nepovjerenja' *Financijska praksa*, vol. 21, no.1-2, pp. 125-140.
Štulhofer, A. (1996b) 'Politička ekonomija neslužbenog gospodarstva u Hrvatskoj - sociokulturne dimenzije porezne evazije', *Financijska praksa*, vol. 21, no. 1-2, pp. 277-294.
Tanzi, V. (1983) 'The underground economy: The causes and consequences of this worldwide phenomenon', *Finance & Development*, vol. 20, no. 4, pp. 10-13.
Thomas, J. J. (1992) 'Informal Economic Activity', The University of Michigan Press, Ann Arbor.
Tokman, V. E. (ed) (1992) 'Beyond Regulation: The Informal Economy in Latin America', Lynne Rienner Publishers, Boulder & London.
Tokman, V. E. and E., Klein (eds.) (1996) 'Regulation and the Informal Economy: Microenterprises in Chile' and Jamaica, Boulder & London: Lynne Rienner Publishers.
Trang, D. V. (ed) (1994) 'Corruption and Democracy – Political Institutions, Processes and Corruption in Transition States in East-Central Europe and in former Soviet Union', Institute for Constitutional and Legislative Policy, Budapest.
*** (1996), 'Uredba o postupku nabave roba i usluga i ustupanju radova', *Narodne novine - official gazette of the Republic of Croatia*, no. 25, 29. March 1996.
*** (1995), 'Zakon o radu', *Narodne novine - official gazette of the Republic of Croatia*, no 38, 8. June 1995.
*** (1996), 'Zakon o trgovini', *Narodne novine - official gazette of the Republic of Croatia*, no. 11, 9. February 1996.

PART III
MEASUREMENT ISSUES

8 Electricity Intensity and the Unrecorded Economy in Post-Socialist Countries
MÁRIA LACKÓ*

Introduction

The underground economy is universal, it is present in any economic system, in developed market economies, in the socialist/post-socialist countries and in developing economies. In spite of such universality, the direct causes of the underground economies in the different systems are different.

In the developed market economies the main factors affecting the underground economy are high tax rates, the burden of regulation by the state, varying possibilities of employment in the official economy and low tax-morality. In the developing countries the causes are similar, though their weights are different: the major determinant is the lack of opportunities for the agents to participate in the official business and labor market.

The causes, emergence and perpetuation of the underground economy in socialist economies are quite different from those in market economies. In fact, the usual causes of underground activities in market economies could not be as significant in the socialist environment because of the extremely narrow scope of formal taxation and the absence of unemployment in the official labor force. Major factors triggering the expansion of the underground economy in socialist countries were the pressures of permanent shortages, the negligible size of the legal private economy, the low level of services provided by the state, and the lack of competition (Kornai, 1992).

In the post-socialist system, a gradual restructuring of the factors that trigger underground activities is taking place: the factors that were charac-

---

* Institute of Economics, Hungarian Academy of Sciences, Budapest, Hungary.
  E-mail: gacs@iiasa.ac.at
  The same paper will be published at Edwin Maskin and András Simonovits, *Planning, Shortage, and Transportation: Essays in Honor of János Kornai* (Cambridge, MA: The MIT Press, 1999).

teristic of the socialist system are losing importance, while those characterizing the market system are gaining ground. Major new developments, like the disappearance of shortages, the emergence of competition and a service market, and the growing role of the legal private economy (Kornai, 1995) all lead to the disappearance of the earlier causes of the underground economy, and give way to the traditional causes present in market economies. In the course of gradual restructuring, financial and tax discipline develops slowly.

'In the socialist system discipline was enforced by the bureaucracy itself, many times with arbitrary and brutal means' (Kornai, 1993:326). Distrust and indifference towards the state characterized the behavior of the citizens. In the early 1990s, in the course of the transition process, the means of enforcement have gradually changed to those of the constitutional state. However, to establish trust in the state takes a much longer time than changing the regulatory system (Kornai, 1992; 1993). As a consequence of economic liberalization and continuing distrust in the state, the scale of the underground has grown fast in these economies.

The size of the underground economy has taken a prominent place in the transition literature for several reasons. First, the size of the unrecorded economy has far reaching consequences for the actual, as opposed to officially registered rate of decline in output. Second, the pervasiveness of unreported activities determines the size of the missing revenues from the government budget in the times when endeavours at stabilization seek all possible sources of budgetary revenues.

As student and later as colleague of János Kornai I became acquainted with the characteristic features of socialist and the post-socialist economies. One of the general principles that I learned from him during these twenty years was that for the description, analysis and understanding of economic phenomena, measurement is indispensable, even in the case of arcane concepts such as the underground economy.

The measurement of the exact size of the underground economy has not been solved in any economic system, let alone in the post-socialist economies. Many estimation methods have been established and applied that have produced results supporting, complementing, but also at times contradicting one another. A consensus about reliable and acceptable approaches is far from having been established.

In this study I deal with methods of estimation of the underground economy which rely to a great extent on aggregate electricity consumption data. The application of these methods has become widespread, and results from this approach are frequently cited in the transition literature. Following the presentation of the method devised by Dobozi and Pohl (1995) and

Kaufmann (1995), I show why these methods are infeasible for measuring the underground economy in the post-socialist economies. At the end of the paper, I briefly present my own model, which relies on the development of residential electricity consumption as an alternative to aggregate electricity consumption.

The Dobozi and Pohl Method of Estimating the Change of Size of the Underground Economy

In 1995, two supplementary papers were published in the newsletter 'Transition' with talkative titles: 'Real Output Decline in Transition Economies - Forget GDP, Try Power Consumption Data!' (Dobozi and Pohl, 1995); and 'Electricity Consumption and Output Decline - An Update' (Dobozi, 1995). In these papers the authors claim that in the post-socialist countries, especially in the (FSU) countries, the statistically registered drop in GDP after 1989 exaggerates the actual decline, possibly by a very large margin. They assert that 'to measure overall economic activity in an economy, electric power consumption is usually the single-best physical indicator of economic activity. Overall economic activity and electricity consumption have been empirically observed throughout the world to move in lockstep — with an electricity/GDP elasticity close to one' (Dobozi and Pohl,1995). Data for post-socialist countries do not show the same pattern. Dobozi and Pohl suggest that the huge differences between figures for electric power consumption and GDP can most readily be explained by a rapid growth of the underground economies. These ideas have not been without their consequences, reappearing in subsequent writings (Transition Report EBRD, 1995) and at numerous conferences dealing with post-socialist transition.

In Table 8.1 we can see the relevant data for East European and Baltic countries and for the countries of Commonwealth of Independent States. In the period 1989-1994, in East European transition economies (with the possible exception of the Czech Republic) the cumulative decline in power consumption closely matches the drop in GDP, yielding an electricity-GDP elasticity of about 1 (meaning that 1 percent GDP fall was associated with about 1 percent drop in electricity consumption). As Dobozi and Pohl write: 'Even in those East European countries where the economic structure and product lines changed drastically, as in Poland, the correlation between power use and economic activity remained fairly close' (Dobozi and Pohl, 1995, p.10).

In most FSU countries however, the reported output declines are completely inconsistent with the power consumption trends; thus, according to

Dobozi and Pohl, the reliability of official statistics has seriously to be questioned. The gap between increasing electricity consumption and declining GDP can only be explained by gross underreporting of GDP. In the period 1989 and 1994, the output downturn in Russia and Ukraine may have been inflated by official statistics more than twofold, in Azerbaijan as much as threefold, and in Georgia, Kazakhstan, Latvia and Moldova by 50 to 90 percent. Several factors distort official statistics:

- the widespread underreporting of output in order to avoid high taxes,
- the overrepresentation of large state-owned industrial enterprises that are undergoing major retrenchment, and
- the shortcomings of data collection in capturing ever increasing private activities. (Dobozi, 1995)

Based on the above considerations, Kaufmann (1995) reported some concrete calculations concerning how, with what speed and to what size the underground economy grew in the Ukraine between 1989 and 1994. For the case of economies in transition, careful consideration of all special features such as very low initial electricity prices that are gradually adjusted upward; untapped potentials for efficiency improvement, and restructuring towards less electricity-intensive activities suggests that on balance, electricity efficiency per unit of overall GDP may increase somewhat over time. In this case, the electricity/GDP elasticity in transition countries may be less than unitary elasticity. While still being a good proxy, this means that the changes in electricity consumption may to some extent underestimate the changes in overall GDP.

By subtracting the official estimate of GDP from the electricity-based estimated value of overall GDP, we can arrive an estimate of the unrecorded economy. If the estimate of changes of overall GDP, approximated by the rate of change of electric power consumption, is somewhat underestimated, it means that the unrecorded economy will also be somewhat underestimated. Consequently, this estimate of the unofficial economy, if biased, is likely to be a conservative estimate (Kaufmann, 1995).

Table 8.1 Growth in power consumption and real GDP in East Europe and the former Soviet Union, %

East-Central Europe		1990	1991	1992	1993	1994	1995
Bulgaria	Power	-6.9	-14.4	-6.6	2.3	0.2	-23.7
	GDP	-9.1	-11.7	-7.3	-2.4	1.4	-26.4
Czech Republic	Power	-0,5	-8.9	-2.1	-0.5	3.1	-9.0
	GDP	0.2	-14.2	-6.0	-0.9	2.6	-18.3
Poland	Power	-2.4	-6.0	-6.8	-4.1	0.8	-17.3
	GDP	-3.5	-11.9	-3.0	-0.9	2.0	-16.6
Hungary	Power	-8.1	-2.4	-2.6	2.1	0.8	-10.1
	GDP	-11.6	-7.6	2.6	3.8	5.0	-8.7
Romania	Power	-15.8	-9.4	-8.9	-1.4	-4.0	-34.2
	GDP	-5.6	-12.9	-10.0	1.3	3.4	-22.5
Slovakia	Power	-0.8	-7.7	-4.6	-6.3	2.6	-16.0
	GDP	-0.4	-14.5	-7.0	-4.1	4.8	-20.4
Baltic Countries							
Estonia	Power	0.5	-3.0	-15.2	-10.1	6.1	-21.1
	GDP	-8.1	-11.0	-14.2	-6.7	6.0	-30.6
Latvia	Power	-0.3	-3.5	-19.8	-18.8	2.5	-35.8
	GDP	2.9	-8.3	-35.0	-15.0	2.0	-46.8
Lithuania	Power	-4.0	-0.8	-22.0	-25.3	-2.4	-45.8
	GDP	-5.0	-13.1	-37.7	-24.2	1.7	-60.4
Commonwealth of Independent States							
Armenia	Power	-14.3	-1.7	-12.7	-33.8	-10.2	-56.3
	GDP	-7.4	-10.8	-52.4	-14.8	5.4	-64.7
Azerbaijan	Power	-0.4	0.4	-15.0	-3.5	-7.9	-24.5
	GDP	-11.7	-0.7	-22.6	-23.1	-21.9	-59.2
Belarus	Power	1.3	0.4	-10.3	-10.0	-11.8	-27.6
	GDP	-3.0	-1.2	-9.6	-11.6	-21.5	-39.9
Georgia	Power	-2.0	-10.2	-20.5	-14.3	-26.0	-55.6
	GDP	-12.4	-13.8	-40.3	-39.0	-35.0	-82.1
Kazakhstan	Power	1.3	-3.1	-5.9	-7.9	-14.5	-27.3
	GDP	-0.4	-13.0	-13.0	-12.0	-25.0	-50.2
Moldavia	Power	6.5	-4.6	-14.9	-11.3	-12.6	-33.0
	GDP	-1.5	-11.	-29.0	-9.0	-22.0	-56.3
Russia	Power	-0.4	-2.3	-6.2	-5.5	-8.5	-21.2
	GDP	-4.0	-13.0	-19.0	-12.0	-15.0	-49.4
Ukraine	Power	1.0	-2.2	-6.2	-7.8	-11.7	-24.6
	GDP	-3.4	-12.0	-17.0	-17.0	-23.0	-54.9
Uzbekistan	Power	1.5	-3.7	-6.1	-3.5	-3.6	-14.6
	GDP	1.6	-0.5	-11.1	-2.4	-2.6	-14.6

Source: Transition Report 1995, European Bank for Reconstruction and Development.

As a starting point of estimating the size of the unrecorded economy in Ukraine, Kaufmann uses the results of the well-known Berkeley-Duke research on the Second Economy of the USSR (Alexeev at al., 1987) conducted during the late 1980's. These estimates roughly range between 8% and 16% of the total economic activity. Thus, for purposes of his calculation, Kaufmann uses the midpoint estimate of 12%, assuming that this share of all the economic activity was unrecorded in 1989. The next step in his calculation is to derive the figures for the overall GDP proxy, based on overall electricity consumption. He also computes the growth indices of official GDP.

The figures in Table 8.2 are Kaufmann's proxy variables for the calculations on the overall and official GDP, respectively. They incorporate the baseline 1989 estimate for the unofficial economy of 12%. Table 8.3 presents Kaufmann's calculations on the evolution of the Ukrainian unofficial economy during the period 1989-1994 in index numbers, starting with 12.0 in 1989 (since base index is 100 for the overall economy). The first and third rows come from the calculations in Table 8.2, while the second row (unrecorded economy) is the difference between the third and first rows.

Table 8.2 Changes in electricity consumption (As a proxy of overall GDP) and official GDP in Ukraine 1989-1994

	1989	1990	1991	1992	1993	1994
Growth rate in Electricity Consumption		0.0	-2.2	-6.2	-7.8	-11.7
Electricity Consumption Index (1989=100)	100.0	100.0	97.8	91.7	84.6	74.7
Growth rate in Official GDP		-3.8	-13.4	-17.5	-14.9	-24.5
Official GDP Index (Index 1989=88)	88.0	84.5	73.2	60.4	51.4	38.8

Source: Kaufmann (1995).

From Table 8.3 it can be seen that:

- by 1994 the unrecorded economy had tripled, while the official economy had contracted to less than half the size it was in 1989;

- the decline in the overall economy since 1989 was one-quarter, which while significant, is still less than half the decline derived from official statistics. The decline in the official economy was mitigated by the rapid growth in the unrecorded economy during the period.

Table 8.3   Evolution of the official and unofficial economy in Ukraine 1989-1994, %

	1989	1990	1991	1992	1993	1994
Official Economy Index	88.0	84.5	73.2	60.4	51.4	38.8
Unofficial Ec. Index	12.0	15.5	24.6	31.3	33.2	35.9
Overall Economy Index	100.0	100.0	97.8	91.7	84.6	74.7

Source: Kaufmann (1995).

On the basis of Table 8.3 Kaufmann calculates the relative shares of the official and unrecorded economies. According to, by 1994 the estimated share of the unrecorded economy in the overall Ukrainian economy was 48.1%. Kaufmann adds that this result is consistent with micro-survey estimates.

The above described estimation method of the unrecorded economy is very simple, and appealing. However, as the authors Dobozi and Pohl admit, there are people who are skeptical of this method.

> Although our article was generally welcomed as being on the right track to obtain more reliable - and certainly low-cost - estimates of the extent of output retrenchment during the systemic transition, some skeptics argued that while power consumption and economic activity tend to move in tandem in market economies, it may not be relevant for transition economies that are experiencing rapid and massive structural changes. Many argue, that the increase in electricity consumption may reflect structural movement toward higher electricity intensity in GDP. (Dobozi, 1995, p.19).

I am among the skeptics, despite the fact that I agree with an approach that uses indicators of electricity consumption for the estimation of the share of underground economy in GDP. My skepticism derives from several factors. The first kind of doubt arises when applying the same kind of analysis of the data that Dobozi, Pohl, Kaufmann and others employed. One can not avoid asking: how is it possible that according to the calculations of Dobozi and Pohl, the underground economy did not grow in Bulgaria, Romania or Uzbekistan during the years of transition, while in the other countries, the size of the underground economy seemed to grow rapidly? This problem also arises in the case of Hungary. Measurements based on other methods for estimating unrecorded income led to a uniform understanding that in Hungary there was a spectacular rise in the underground economy' share of GDP during the first years of the transition (Árvay and Vértes, 1994; Ékes, 1993; Sík ,1995; Lackó, 1995). This demonstrated growth in unrecorded income growth does not conform to the estimates obtained by the electrical consumption method.

The second kind of doubt derives from the examination of the case of Finland. In the early 1990s Finland, just like the East European economies, and to some extent due to similar factors, experienced a significant fall in GDP. Between 1990 and 1993 the GDP decreased by 13.6%, while electricity consumption, far from decreasing, increased by 5.5%.

The growth of electricity intensity in Finland in 1990-1993 was 22%, not much less than the average of 32% for the 18 post-socialist countries in 1989-1994, but far larger than the average of 8.3% recorded for the East European and Baltic countries in 1989-1994. Do the similarities suggest that just like in the transition economies, Finland's growth of electricity intensity can also be explained by a sudden jump in the underground economy? To see whether this might be true, let us carry out the same calculation for Finland that Kaufmann did for Ukraine. The initial share of the unofficial economy, which is relevant for 1990 (10.0%), was taken from my own estimation (Láckó, 1996).

According to this calculation, the share of the underground economy in Finland would increase from 10% to 27% in three years, i.e. its relative size would rapidly triple! We get a similarly surprising and unrealistic result if the starting share is 5% instead of 11%. In that case the share of the underground economy in 1993 would be 23%, which would mean an even more radical change, since the result would be more than four times the size of the starting value. The results cited above are astonishing, and given what we know about the actual Finnish experience, can not be true. The calculation therefore illustrates the questionable nature of the results based on this method.

Table 8.4 Relative shares of official and unofficial GDP in Ukraine 1989-1994, %

	1989	1990	1991	1992	1993	1994
Official GDP	88.0	84.5	74.9	65.9	60.8	51.7
Unofficial GDP	12.0	15.5	25.1	34.1	39.2	48.1
Overall GDP	100.0	100.0	100.0	100.0	100.0	100.0

Source: Kaufmann (1995).

In fact, the growth of electricity intensity in Finland is connected with the normal effects of recessions rather than the expansion of the unofficial economy. In recessions, electricity consumption does not decrease as much as the GDP because fixed (overhead) electricity use does not contract in proportion with the drop in general capacity utilization. Dobozi and Pohl also mention this effect when they discuss electricity intensity of countries in transition. However, they add: 'It is plausible to assume that the consumption-increasing effect of this factor was largely offset by the combined impact of higher electricity tariffs and shifts in the output mix away from heavy industry' (Dobozi and Pohl, 1995, p.18).

In the following section, I will show that in the 18 post-socialist countries under investigation, it is mainly the differences in the size of structural changes of the economy that determine the differences in changes of electricity intensity.

Analysis of Changes in Electricity Intensity in 18 Post-socialist Countries in the Period 1989-1994

It is obvious that at times of recession, due to smaller than usual capacity utilization, electricity intensity grows, as we saw in the Finnish case. In post-socialist countries, however, additional factors are also present. According to OECD experts (Electricity in European Economies in Transition, OECD, 1994), in individual countries of East Europe, but particularly in FSU countries since 1990, the industrial sector has largely maintained its level of energy consumption, despite the fact that industrial production, in value-added terms, has fallen substantially. Reasons for this included the following:

- the share of industrial output represented by energy intensive basic industries, including the power industry, has actually increased;
- inefficient plants have not been closed, but instead have operated at lower part-load efficiencies. According to Roxburgh and Shapiro (1996) in Russia, because of the Excess Wages Tax, which actually is an employment subsidy, unemployment is internal to the enterprise: this gives a strong incentive for the firm to retain excess workers on low wages rather than making them redundant. This kind of tax influences not only state-owned firms but also privatized ones. Moreover, it was found, that privatized firms made fewer workers redundant than state owned companies (Standing, 1994). According to the calculation made by Kaufmann (1995), the rate of the underground unemployment

in Ukraine is 35%. Internal unemployment most probably led to higher electricity intensity in the industry than there would be if unemployment were external;

- electricity price rises have been limited in real terms, and nominal price adjustments have often been accompanied by consumers' refusals to pay;

- few or no investments have been made in new plants to improve electricity efficiency;

- the decision-makers lack the ability to evaluate the energy use implications of their investment choices. Under the centralized economic system, decision on investments into fixed assets were based primarily on the available production capacity and plan targets for physical output, with little emphasis on productivity or efficiency. This legacy has produced industrial enterprise managers largely unfamiliar with cost accounting procedures.

Based on this list of specific factors that determine electricity use in post-socialist economies we may assume that it is the rate at which structural changes take place in the individual post-socialist countries that will mostly explain the differences in the growth of electricity intensity across these economies. In the sequel I investigate this problem with the help of a cross-sectional examination of 18 post-socialist countries. Although one can not exclude the possibility, that the growth of the underground economy influences the growth of electricity intensity, I do not believe that the approach employed by Dobozi, Pohl and Kaufmann is appropriate for the periods and the economies to which these authors have applied the method.

In the analysis that follows, I identify three different indicators of structural change Ind, d and u which are defined as follows:

1 Ind - the percentage change in the share of industry in the production of GDP between 1989 and 1994:

2 d - the percentage difference between the decrease of electricity consumption in industry and the decrease of total electricity consumption in 1989-1993:

3 u - The maximum percentage rate of unemployment between 1989 and 1994:

We assume that the larger structural changes that took place in a particular economy, that is, the faster the dismantling of socialist type industries, the less growth in electricity intensity occurred. More precisely:

- the more the value added of the industrial branches decreases compared to the official GDP, the less growth in electricity intensity occurs,
- the more the electricity consumption in industrial branches decreases in comparison to total electricity consumption, the more pronounced a shift there occurs from highly electricity intensive branches to branches with less electricity intensity, and therefore the less the electricity intensity of the economy grows;
- the higher the rate of unemployment, which is to a high degree structural unemployment, the larger structural changes happened in respect with the dismantling of industry of socialist type and therefore the slower the rise of electricity intensity in the economy.

The data used for the verification of these assumptions are presented in Table 8.5 and Table 8.6. Table 8.7 shows the average size of the individual structural indicators for the different groups of countries. In the last column the average change in electricity intensity is presented.

The table shows that for the East-Central European countries each indicator of structural change is 1.6 - 2 times as large as the average indicator of the full sample of 18 countries. The indicators for the Baltic Countries are similar to the total average, while the indicators for the countries off the CIS countries are half as large as the average indicators. In the last column of the table, it can also be noticed that in line with our assumption, the larger the structural change, the lower is the growth of electricity intensity.

The regularity which is suggested by the interrelations of the country group averages, i.e. that the development of electricity consumption is significantly influenced by the scale of structural changes, is now subjected to a more exact econometric analysis. Let us look first at the correlation between the indicators of the individual countries.

From Table 8.8 we can see that there is a close positive relationship between the change in electricity consumption and the change in the official GDP.

We find also an interesting relation between two indicators of structural change: the larger the decrease of the share of industrial branches within the official GDP, the larger the rate of unemployment.

The table also shows an important correlation between the change in the official GDP and the structural indicator measured by electricity consumption. The less the electricity consumption in industrial branches decreases in comparison with total electricity consumption, that is, the smaller the structural change in this field, the larger the fall that is experienced in the official GDP. We have to be careful with the interpretation of this result. If electricity consumption in the industrial branches contained an increasing share of unregistered elements compared to that contained in total electricity consumption, then it would give sufficient explanation for a larger decline in the official GDP. In this case the growth in total electricity intensity would indeed be caused by the growth of the underground economy. However this assumption is most probably not well founded: if the electricity consumption due to non-registered production were in the industrial branches large and growing then at least the same would apply to the total electricity consumption, since trade and service activities are much easier to keep unregistered.

From Table 8.8 it is evident that the growth of electricity intensity is correlated with the measure of structural changes related to electricity consumption in industry: the less the decrease in electricity consumption in the industrial branches compared to total electricity consumption, the more electricity intensity increases.

Table 8.5 Indicators of structural changes in transition countries

East-Central Europe	ind	du	u
Bulgaria	-23.5	-18.0	16.4
Czech Republic	-10.0	-23.0	3.5
Poland	-8.0	-26.0	12.3
Hungary	-19.4	-17.4	16.0
Romania	-19.3	-14.0	10.9
Slovakia	-14.9	10.0	14.8
Baltic Countries			
Estonia	-8.4	-18.0	3.5
Latvia	-13.1	-9.0	6.5
Lithuania	-3.3	-1.0	4.2
Commonwealth of Independent States			
Armenia	-22.5	-10.0	6.4
Azerbaijan	7.7	-12.0	0.9
Belarus	5.2	-15.0	2.5
Georgia	-21.3	-3.0	8.4
Kazakhstan	9.2	-11.0	1.6
Moldavia	1.8	-2.0	1.2
Russia	-11.1	-9.0	2.1
Ukraine	-3.5	-11.0	0.4
Uzbekistan	2.7	-14.0	0.3

Notes:
ind: the change of the share of industry in the production of GDP between 1989 and 1994.
d: the difference between the change in electricity consumption in the industrial branches and the change in the total electricity consumption.
u: the maximal rate of unemployment between 1989 and 1994.

Table 8.6 The changes in electricity intensity and its elements

East-Central Europe	de	dgdp	dint
Bulgaria	0.763	0.736	1.04
Czech Republic	0.910	0.817	1.11
Poland	0.827	0.834	0.99
Hungary	0.899	0.913	0.98
Romania	0.658	0.775	0.85
Slovakia	0.840	0.796	1.06
Baltic Countries			
Estonia	0.789	0.694	1.14
Latvia	0.642	0.532	1.21
Lithuania	0.542	0.396	1.37
Commonwealth of Independent States			
Armenia	0.437	0.353	1.24
Azerbaijan	0.755	0.408	1.85
Belarus	0.724	0.601	1.20
Georgia	0.444	0.179	2.48
Kazakhstan	0.727	0.498	1.46
Moldavia	0.670	0.437	1.53
Russia	0.789	0.506	1.56
Ukraine	0.754	0.451	1.67
Uzbekistan	0.854	0.854	1.00

Notes:
de: the change in electricity consumption between 1989 and 1994.
dgdp: the change in the official GDP between 1989 and 1994.
dint: the change of electricity intensity between 1989 and 1994.

Source: Transition Report 1995, European Bank for Reconstruction and Development.

Table 8.7 Mean values of the indicators of the structural changes and electricity intensity by group of countries

Group of countries	ind	d	u	dint
East-Central Europe	-15.9	-18.1	12.3	1.005
Baltic Countries	-8.3	-9.3	4.7	1.237
CIS Countries	-3.5	-7.0	2.6	1.550
Total	-8.4	-11.0	6.2	1.320

Source: own calculations.

Table 8.8 Correlation among the indicators of the countries

	de_i	$dgdp_i$	$dint_i$	ind_i	u_i	d_i
de_i	1.00					
$dgdp_i$	0.81	1.00				
$dint_i$	-0.50	-0.84	1.00			
ind_i	0.23	0.13	0.15	1.00		
u_i	0.10	0.45	-0.38	-0.75	1.00	
d_i	-0.47	-0.72	0.66	0.32	-0.39	1.00

Notes:
de_i the change in electricity consumption between 1989 and 1994.
$dgdp_i$ the change in the official GDP between 1989 and 1994.
$dint_i$ the change of electricity intensity between 1989 and 1994.
ind_i the change of the rate of industry within the GDP
u_i the maximal rate 1989 and 1994.
d_i the difference between the change in electricity consumption in the industrial branches and the change in the total electricity consumption (1989-1993).
i country.

Econometric Analysis

In this section we formulate our hypothesis as an equation and attempt to verify it with a cross-section econometric estimation.

Equation (1) expresses our hypothesis, that in addition to the changes in the official GDP, it is the scale of the three kinds of structural changes that determine total electricity consumption. With this, of course, we do not state that the growth of the unofficial economy does not influence electricity consumption or the growth of total GDP. We only state that the difference between the shifts in electricity consumption and the change in the official GDP is not all that mystic and underground, and it shows a strong relation to the scale of structural changes.

The equation is as follows:

$$de_i = \sigma_1\, dgdp_i + \sigma_2\, ind_i + \sigma_3\, d_i + \sigma_4\, u_i + \sigma_5 \qquad (1)$$

$$\sigma_1 > 0 \quad \sigma_2 > 0 \quad \sigma_3 > 0 \quad \sigma_4 < 0$$

where:
- de_i: the change in electricity consumption between 1989 and 1994.
- $dgdp_i$: the change in the official GDP between 1989 and 1994.
- ind_i: the change of the share of industry in the production of GDP between 1989 and 1994 ui: the maximal rate of unemployment between 1989 and 1994.
- d_i: the difference between the change of electricity consumption in the industrial branches and the change in total electricity consumption, 1898-1993.
- i: country indicator. The countries are: Bulgaria, Czech Republic, Hungary, Poland, Romania, Slovak Republic, Estonia, Latvia, Lithuania, Armenia, Azerbaijan, Belarus, Georgia, Kazakhstan, Moldova, Russia, Ukraine, Uzbekistan.

In Table 8.9 the results of the econometric estimations are shown. The estimations were carried out with the ordinary least squares method, based on cross-sectional data from 18 countries.

The estimation was carried out in different variants (see Table 8.9). The signs of the parameters are mostly as expected, and the indicators of fitting are acceptable. In the course of the estimation, three dummy-variables were used for the countries Romania, Georgia and Uzbekistan.

In estimation A1 we have not yet taken into account the differences in the scale of structural changes across the countries. According to the results obtained here a 1% decrease of GDP was accompanied on average by a 0.5% decrease in electricity consumption in the 18 post-socialist countries. In fact, this estimation does not help the analysis, it only describes the investigated event.

Table 8.9 Results of estimation of (1) function: dependent variable de_i

Independent variables	(A1)	(B1)	(C1)	(D1)	(E1)	(F1)
$dgdp_i$	0.5310	0.6535	0.7052	0.8542	1.002	0.0209
	(5.43)	(6.06)	(4.22)	(10.23)	(11.56)	(11.04)
ind_i		0.0047				-0.0010
		(2.46)				(-0.70)
d_i			0.0043		0.00402	0.00433
			(1.31)		(2.72)	(2.75)
$\ln u_i$				-0.0774	-0.0765	-0.0840
				(-5.65)	(-6.92)	(-5.42)
$du5$		-0.1405	-0.1930	-0.1479	-0.1639	-0.1699
		(1.91)	(2.31)	(3.18)	(4.32)	(4.27)
$du13$		0.044	-0.0340	0.1270	0.1556	0.1529
		(0.48)	(0.35)	(2.04)	(3.03)	(2.90)
$du18$		-0.0993	-0.0520	-0.2973	-0.3221	-0.3344
		(1.23)	(0.59)	(4.37)	(5.78)	(5.61)
constant	0.4055	0.3825	0.3643	0.3287	0.2839	0.2787
	(6.56)	(7.84)	(7.54)	(7.84)	(7.54)	(7.11)
aR^2	0.627	0.76	0.69	0.902	0.936	0.933
F	29.57	11.84	8.43	32.28	42.50	34.83
Standard error of regression	0.0845	0.067	0.078	0.0434	0.035	0.036
Mean of dependent variable	0.7236	0.7236	0.7236	0.7236	0.7236	0.7236

Source: own calculations.

In estimations B1, C1 and D1 we included the three different structural indicators individually. In all three cases the sign of the structural parameter showed up as expected; however, the significance of the parameter in estimation C1 is not appropriate. The reason for this is the multicollinearity caused by the close negative correlation between the variables gdp_i and d_i. The fitting of the equation improved in all three cases in comparison to estimation A1, with the most spectacular improvement in the case of the indicator of the rate of unemployment (estimation D1).

The parameter of the rate of unemployment is significantly negative. The negative sign is as expected, since we assumed that larger unemployment indicates a larger scale of structural changes, which, ceteris paribus, reduces electricity consumption.

The assumption of a negative sign here is not, however, evident at all: we could have assumed and obtained a positive sign likewise due to the widely known close relationship of the size of the underground economy and the level of unemployment. It is a tendency in developed market economies that the larger the rate of unemployment, the larger the size of the underground economy.

This process in which the pool of the unemployed strengthens the activities in the underground economy will most probably gradually become more pronounced in the Eastern European countries. Inactive members of the families start to participate intensively in the underground economy, and through this, contribute to the increase of electricity consumption and intensity. This growth of electricity intensity is blurred by the effect of the structural change, which is characterized by the reduction of the usual role of socialist heavy industry, and the subsequent cut in electricity intensity. According to our calculations, from the two effects in the period 1989-1994, structural changes turned out to be more powerful: this is shown by the significantly negative parameter in equations Dl, El and Fl.

In estimation El we found some genuinely interesting results. If there was no difference between the 18 post-socialist countries' speed of structural change, then GDP and electricity consumption would really move closely together (value of parameter belonging to variable $dgdp_i$: 1.00).

In estimation Fl all three structural indicators are presented. Here, due to the close negative relation between indi and ui, multi-collinearity arose.

Because of the multi-collinearity between $dgdp_i$ and d_i, equation (1) had to be reformulated and re-estimated. The new function, equation (2), the dependent variable, is the change of electricity intensity, which is a function of the indicators of structural change.

$$dint_i = \theta_1 \, ind_i + \theta_2 \, d_i + \theta_3 \, u_i + \theta_4 \qquad (2)$$

$$\theta_1 > 0 \quad \theta_2 > 0 \quad \theta_3 < 0$$

where
$dint_i$:   *the change of electricity intensity between 1989 and 1994*

Table 8.10 Results of estimation of (1) function: dependent variable $dint_i$

Independent variables	(A2)	(B2)	(C2)	(D2)	(E2)	(F2)
ind_i	0.0163				0.0091	-0.027
	(2.98)				(2.08)	(-1.04)
d_i			0.022	0.0129	0.00433	0.0133
			(4.58)	(5.59)	(2.75)	(5.71)
$\ln u_i$		-0.2102		-0.1559		-0.1735
		(6.98)		(-5.65)		(-6.78)
du5	-0.2538	-0.2195	-0.3832	-0.2419	-0.2887	-0.2548
	(1.10)	(1.61)	(2.15)	(3.22)	(1.75)	(3.36)
du13	1.4102	1.3572	1.003	1.2067	1.1657	1.1801
	(6.04)	(10.05)	(5.52)	(15.3)	(6.48)	(14.31)
du18	-0.4621	-0.8237	-0.2323	-0.6511	-0.3389	-0.6657
	(2.02)	(5.37)	(1.31)	(7.27)	(2.03)	(7.37)
constant	1.418	1.5706	1.5442	1.6442	1.5628	1.6498
	(20.52)	(30.17)	(21.9)	(52.3)	(24.68)	(51.98)
aR^2	0.71	0.90	0.81	0.97	0.85	0.97
F	11.4	37.32	19.53	105.75	20.52	88.96
Standard error of regression	0.213	0.129	0.171	0.07	0.15	0.07
Mean of dependent variable	1.3189	1.3189	1.3189	1.3189	1.3189	1.3189

Source: own calculations.

We did a couple of estimations for equation (2), the results of which are shown in Table 8.10. In these estimations the parameters proved to be significant and got the expected signs (except that of the variable ind_i in estimation F2 because of multi-collinearity). The most satisfactory result came out of estimation D2, where no multi-collinearity distorted the estimated parameters.

At the end of our econometric analysis we return to the case of Finland to check the applicability of our results to this specific country. Our question is the following: How big is the difference between estimation and reality, if we estimate Finland's change of electricity intensity with the estimation results of equation (2) (i.e. with the parameters that were estimated from the analysis of 18 post-socialist economies)?

During the recession of 1990-1993 in Finland, the rate of unemployment increased by 14.3 percentage points, electricity consumption in the industrial branches increased by 3.6%, while total electricity consumption increased by 5.7%; accordingly the value of the variable d_i is -2.1. If we put these numbers into equation (2), and use the parameters produced by estimation D2, we get an estimation of 20.2% increase of electricity intensity for Finland. The real increase of electricity intensity was 22.3%; the difference between real and estimated change is a lot smaller than the margin of error of the estimated function.

This result contradicts the concept initiated by Kaufmann for the post-communist countries. In our equation the growth of electricity intensity in Finland was explained by the forced structural changes rather then by the explosive growth of the underground economy.

The results of the statistical analysis and the econometric estimates in sections 5 and 6 confirm our hypothesis that it is the structural changes which take place in the countries with different speeds that are decisive in the development of electricity intensity. We do not exclude the possibility that the rapid growth of the underground economy also influences the growth of electricity intensity. We simply point out, that from the aggregate data, as usually employed, it is very difficult to draw conclusions concerning the growth of the underground economy.

Residential Electricity and Underground Economy – Description of a New Method

Since the underground economy is present in any economic system, underground activities play a role in each sector of the economy, including those of industry, trade, other services, and even households.

Lackó (1995, 1996) analyzes the size of underground activities present in households in a cross section of countries and uses these results for the estimation of the volume of underground activities at the national level. That model utilized data on residential electricity consumption, a part of aggregate electricity consumption.

In the following I briefly summarize this model. The method helps to establish the share of the underground economy in different countries in a given period (the calculations were made for 20 OECD economies and 4 post-socialist countries). The approach does not attempt to calculate the growth of the underground economy, and in this respect it is not directly comparable with the Dobozi-Pohl-Kaufmann calculations. The model would be capable of measuring unrecorded income growth too, but at this stage, the unavailability of the necessary data prevents this exercise.

An advantage of the model based on residential electricity consumption is that it relies on meso-level analysis, i.e. the investigation of the behavior of households. This allows it to ignore substantial differences in the macro-structure of the different economies, and the impact that shifts in this macrostructure have on the electricity consumption, and on the underground economy.

The use of households as the level of analysis is also beneficial for another reason. One characteristic feature of economic transition in Eastern Europe is the mushrooming of small private business, which is set up practically in a family-household framework. In this milieu this fast growing economic activity can easily operate mostly underground without being registered with the state.

The method is based on an econometrically tested model that uses data of developed market economies. Subsequently, the estimations of the size of the underground economy in the post-socialist countries needed some modifications according to the specificity of this system.

The first premise for the model was that in each country a part of the household consumption of electricity is used in the underground economy. We postulate that the electricity consumption of households in a country is determined not only by such visible factors as the size of the population, the level of development, the country's geographical location (climate and weather), the relative price of electricity, and access to other energy sources, but also by the extent of the underground economy.

In the model the underground economy is represented by three proxy variables: the tax/GDP ratio, the inactive/active labor ratio and the ratio of public social welfare expenditures to GDP. The first two proxies represent well-known relationships: the higher these ratios the higher the share of the underground economy. The third indicator is related to the enforcement of taxes: the higher the third ratio, the stronger the efforts that are made by the state to collect outstanding taxes.

The parameters of the model were estimated by a cross-section of the countries in different variants: (1) for 19 OECD countries in 1990, (2) for 19 OECD countries in 1989 and (3) through a panel data base made up of the data for 1989-1990. The estimated parameters were significant, the signs coincided with the expected ones. Accordingly, the results supported our assumptions about the determinants of household electricity consumption, including the impact of the underground economy.

After the estimation of the parameters of the model, residential electricity consumption could be decomposed into underground and official consumption showing the per capita household consumption of electricity related to the underground economy as a share of total per capita household electricity consumption. This calculation was carried out not only for 19 OECD countries but, following some necessary modification, also for four

East European countries (Hungary, Poland, Czech Republic and Slovakia). The parameters obtained for the developed market economies were applied to these four post-socialist economies to establish that part of household electricity consumption that was independent of the underground economy. After subtracting this part of the consumption from the actual electricity consumption we arrived at the share of household electricity consumption used in the underground economy in total household electricity consumption. As this sequence of calculations shows, the proxies characterizing determinants of the underground economy in developed market economies were not used here.

This exercise aimed to determine the contribution of the underground economy to GDP in the individual countries. However, without the knowledge of how much GDP is produced by one unit of electricity in the underground economy of each country, the share of the underground economy in the GDP can not be calculated. Since data for the per unit use of electricity in the underground economy are unavailable an indirect conversion method had to be used.

This method was rather rudimentary. The results of one of the estimations known from the literature was taken (a calculation carried out for a single country for the early 1990s), and the other countries' data (their index of underground economy expressed in terms of residential electricity consumption) were proportioned to this base country.

Table 8.11 summarizes the results of our estimations. According to the results of our investigations, in the early phase of transition, the size of the underground economy in some post-socialist countries (Hungary, Poland) is two times larger than in the average of developed market economies, and much larger than in the developed economies that have the largest underground part (Spain, Greece, Ireland, Belgium, Italy). The share of the underground economy in the Czech Republic and Slovakia was smaller, but in the latter it has increased steadily by the largest scale in the four countries.

Table 8.11 The shares of the underground economy in per cent of GDP

Country	1990	1991	1992	1993	1994
Poland	30.8	29.7	33.0	33.6	32.8
Hungary	26.7	32.4	34.8	32.8	31.0
Czech Republic	n.a.	15.2	19.9	14.4	15.4
Slovakia	n.a.	11.2	14.7	15.0	22.3
Spain	22.9				
Greece	21.8				
Ireland	20.6				
Belgium	19.8				
Italy	19.6				
Denmark	16.9				
Austria	15.5				
Australia	15.1				
Germany	14.6				
Portugal	13.8				
Netherlands	13.4				
Finland	13.3				
Japan	13.2				
U.K.	13.1				
France	12.3				
Canada	11.7				
Sweden	11.0				
USA	10.5				
Switzerland	10.2				
Norway	9.3				

Source: Lackó (1997).

Summary

This paper disputes the frequently presented and quoted statement, that in post-socialist economies data on power consumption are better indicators for aggregate output changes than official GDP. The development of electricity consumption allegedly reflects the combined growth of official and underground economies, and they tell the true story about decline of output in these countries between 1989 and 1994.

The authors Dobozi, Pohl and Kaufmann claim that the statistical drop in GDP after 1989 in post-socialist countries, especially in the case of countries of former Soviet Union, exaggerates the actual decline, possibly by a very large margin. They take it for granted that in market economies aggregate economic activity and electric power consumption usually move in lockstep (with an electricity-GDP elasticity close to one). Since the post-socialist countries do not show the same pattern, they claim that this feature can be explained rationally only by a rapid growth of the underground (unofficial) economy.

Testing the validity of this approach, the Kaufmann method was applied to Finland, a developed market economy that suffered an output decline in the early 1990s comparable to that in the post-socialist economies. The results were so unrealistic concerning the implicit growth of the underground economy in Finland that we had to question the underlying assumptions of the Dobozi-Pohl-Kaufmann approach.

This paper attempts to show that the variations in electricity intensity in post-socialist countries are not necessarily reflections of the growth of the unrecorded sectors of the economy. Statistical and econometric analysis of data for 18 post-socialist economies shows that the measured and registered structural changes are sufficient to explain the differences in the changes of electricity intensity in this region.

In the course of my investigations I have become convinced that using aggregate electricity consumption data and the assumption of constant electricity intensity is not the proper way to calculate the size or growth of the underground economy either in mature market economies or in economies in transition. I have become convinced, however, that other indices (like residential electricity consumption) and other assumptions lead to more satisfactory estimations of the size of the underground economy in developed market economies and post-socialist countries, as shown in my earlier work (Lackó, 1995,1996,1997).

References

Alexeev, M., G. Grossman, N. Malyshev, A.Sayer, V.Treml (1987) Studies on the Soviet Second Economy, *Berkeley-Duke Occasional Papers on the Second Economy in the USSR*, no 11.

Árvay, J. and A. Vértes (1994) A magánszektor és a rejtett gazdaság súlya Magyarországon. (The Magnitude of the Private Sector and Hidden Economy in Hungary). *Statisztikai Szemle*, no. 4 (7), pp. 517- 529.

Dobozi, I. and G. Pohl (1995) 'Real Output Declines in Transition Economies - Forget GDP, Try Power Consumption Data!', *Transition*, vol. 6, no. 1-2. Jan.-Feb.

Dobozi, I. (1995) Electricity Consumption and Output Decline - An Update Transition, vol. 6, no. 9-10, Sept-Oct.

EBRD (1995) Transition Report, Investment and Enterprise Development.
Ékes, I. (1993) Rejtett gazdaság – Láthatatlan jövedelmek tegnap és ma, (Hidden Economy Invisible Incomes of the Population), Budapest.
Freeman, C. and L. Soete (1994) Work for all or Mass Unemployment, Pinter Publishers London , New York.
IEA (1994) Yearbook.
Kaufmann, D. (1995a) On Ukraine's economy: A Glimpse at the past, Pausing at Present, Peering into the Future. Handout for Presentation at the IIASA Workshop on Ukraine- GATT/WTO, Laxenburg, Austria.
Kaufmann, D. (1995b) How Large is the Unofficial Economy in Ukraine: An Electrical Approach to Measurement, World Bank, mimeo.
Kornai, J. (1992) The socialist system: The political economy of communism, Princeton: Princeton University Press.
Kornai, J. (1992) The Post-socialist Transition and the State: Reflections in the Light of Hungarian Fiscal Problems, *American Economic Review*, Papers and Proceedings, May, vol. 82, No. 2, pp.1- 20.
Kornai, J. (1993) The Evolution of Financial Discipline under the Post-socialist System, Kyklos, Fall, 1993, vol. 46., No. 3., pp. 315-336.
Kornai, J. (1995) Eliminating the Shortage Economy: A General Analysis and Examination of the Developments in Hungary, *Economics of Transition* 3 (1), March, pp. 13-37.
Lackó, M. (1992) The Extent of the Illegal Economy in Hungary Between 1970 and 1989 - a Monetary Model, *Acta Oeconomica* 44 (1-2), pp. 161-190.
Lackó, M. (1995) Rejtett gazdaság nemzetközi összehasonlításban, (Hidden Economy in International Comparison) *Közgazdasági Szemle* 52(5), pp. 486-510.
Lackó, M. (1995) Hungarian Hidden Economy in International Comparison, Paper presented at the conference 'Hungary: Towards a Market Economy', Budapest, 20-21 October 1995.
Lackó, M. (1996) Hidden Economy in East European Countries in International Comparison, Paper made during the author's Phare-ACE Fellowship at IIASA in 1996.
Lackó, M. (1997) The Hidden Economies of Visegrád Countries in International Comparison: A Household Electricity Approach, in: L. Halpern and Ch. Wyplosz (Eds.): Hungary: Towards a Market Economy, Cambridge University Press (forthcoming).
OECD Paris (1995) Energy Policies of the Russian Federation 1995 Survey.
OECD Paris (1995) Energy Policies of Hungary 1995 Survey.
OECD (1994) Electricity in European Economies in Transition.
Roxburgh, I. and J. Shapiro (1996) Russian Unemployment and the Excess Wages Tax Communist Economies and Economic Transformation, vol. B., no. 1.
Sík, E. (1995) The Volume of the Second-to-Informal (STI) Economy in Hungary, mimeo.
Standing, G. (1994) Labor Market Dynamics in Russian Industry in 1993; ILO-CEET Reports, 1994, 2, Budapest, Hungary.
UN (1993) Economic Bulletin for Europe vol. 45.
UN (1995) Annual Bulletin for Electric Energy Statistics 1994 and 1995, New York.
World Bank (1993) Ukraine Energy Sector Review, 1993 Report.

9 Measuring the Underground Economy by the System of National Accounts

SANJA MADŽAREVIĆ* & DAVOR MIKULIĆ**

Introduction

The underground economy is a phenomenon that can be found in all political, social and economic systems in all phases of their development, but it appears in different proportions and with different intensity. It need not always be considered dangerous to a system. In some economic and political systems it is a necessity that supplements the legal economy and lessens social tensions. The unofficial economy is made easier by the existence of 'holes' in the legal and institutional framework, 'holes' which are unavoidable in the initial developmental phases of a new economic system (Kukar, 1995). The unreported economy has its negative and positive effects on the economy as a whole. The negative effects are, for example, tax and contributions evasion, which results in the need to distribute the obligation to finance public goods among legally registered economic entities. On the other hand, some of the positive effects are activating productive potential that would otherwise remain unused and satisfying needs that the legal economy is not able to meet at the moment. We might say that the unofficial economy in a way has a complementary effect in relation to the formal economy.

Estimation of the underground economy in Croatia is an extremely difficult task. The lack of statistical comparisons with international standards and the inadequate quality of monitoring the growing number of economic

---

* Department for Macroeconomic Analyses and Forecasts of the Ministry of Finance of the Republic of Croatia, Zagreb, Croatia, e-mail: Sanja.Madzarevic@mfin.hr
** Economic Institute, Zagreb, Croatia. E-mail: mikulic@ekist.eizg.hr
Authors wish to thank the following employees of the Central Bureau of Statistics - Ana Nedjeljković, Marijana Dragičević, Darko Jukić, Jadranko Križanac, Danka Ražnjević, Saša Madžarević - for their help and co-operation.

entities and transitional changes present an additional obstacle to its quantification. The unrecorded economy distorts the relation of national income and economic activity; quantification and research are necessary in order to establish economic, social and legal measures to reduce its negative impacts on the economy.

Measuring the Unrecorded Economy by the Method of Discrepancies in National Accounts

The first step in measuring the volume and economic significance of the underground economy is to determine what is to be measured. A wide range of different activities comes to be classed as the 'unofficial economy' and, accordingly, there is a whole range of methods for measuring them, which is shown in Figure 9.1. *For the purpose of this paper, the unofficial economy is understood to cover all production activities that are not part of the formal economy and all market transactions unrecorded or underestimated with the purpose of evading or diminishing taxes.*

The subject of this paper is measuring value added which is not recorded in national accounts and which can be measured by one of the indirect estimation methods of the underground economy - by determining the discrepancy between the sum of components on the income and expenditure side of the gross domestic product. This method does not provide the *absolute level* of the underground economy, but only the *difference* between the independent estimates of the income and expenditure side of the gross national product. Statistical recording of individual expenditure aggregates is subject to adjustments due to the scope and reliability of data sources. The largest component on the expenditure side of the gross domestic product is private consumption. Household budget surveys are often used as a mean of estimation. Depending on the choice of sample and on the survey quality, it can provide fairly reliable data on actual private consumption. In the case of income estimation, there is a strong inclination to conceal its actual value because of fear of the tax authorities and the survey method in this case gives rather unreliable results.

Economic statistics in Croatia are presently in a situation in which the old system of national accounts has been abandoned because of its theoretical and practical shortcomings without a new system having been introduced as yet. This paper will therefore as far as possible try to bring together the aggregates that used to be monitored according to the old concept of material production (MPS) and the SNA concept. A lot of time, effort and funds are necessary for full adjustment of statistics to the new SNA concept.

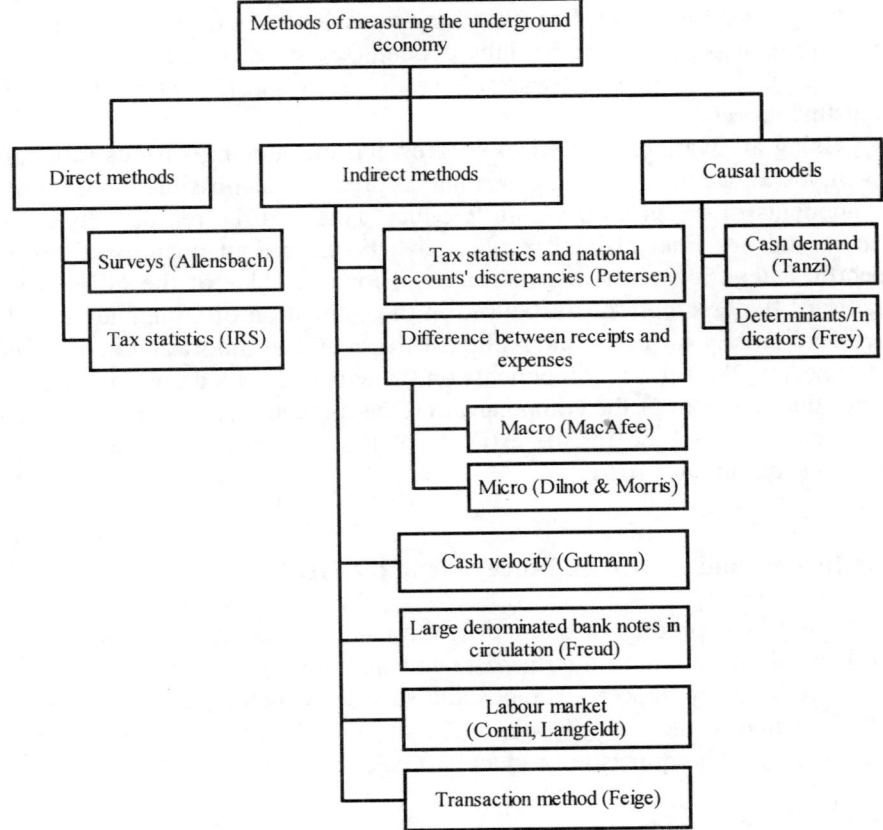

Figure 9.1 Methods of measuring the unofficial economy

Source: Smith, S. & S. Wied-Nebbelin (1986): The Shadow Economy in Britain and Germany, Anglo German Foundation, p. 28.

The last official estimate of the GDP in current prices according to the SNA concept was made for 1990 by the conversion method. For later years all we have is only the estimate in 1990 constant prices. This estimate does not seem to give satisfying results and is presently being revised. A system of national accounts that would incorporate various different interconnected tables, aggregates and classifications into a consistent and coherent set is still far from being available. However, there are some basic outlines on which the system of national accounts can be constructed, based on the obligation of legal entities to submit annual statistical reports to the Payment Agency. These reports cover only a part of the data needed to construct the whole system. Empirical data used for assessment of the unofficial economy in this paper therefore partially depend on the authors' estimate based on the opinions of experts aware of the direction and the intensity of the adjustments needed.

Using all available statistical sources and introducing various rational assumptions, we have tried to determine as precisely as possible the level of components of the gross domestic product. This was the reason why estimates, and not final official results, have been used in quantification of specific categories of the expenditure and income sides of the GDP. The reality of the assumptions introduced in the estimation of components will therefore largely influence the reality of the estimated unofficial economy. As expected, the sum of components on the expenditure side of the GDP is larger than the sum of the components on the income side, and their difference represents a base for the estimate of the total volume of the underground economy in Croatia.

The Income and the Expenditure Side of the GDP

Gross domestic product is defined as the sum of final uses of goods and services (all, except their intermediate consumption), measured in purchase prices, reduced by imports of goods and services which should at the same time be equal to the sum of primary incomes distributed by resident production units. The domestic product can be shown by the following equation:

$$C + I + G + E - U = W + O + T_{ind}.$$

The left side represents domestic product as a sum of final uses and the right side shows it as the sum of domestic producers' income. Private consumption is marked as C, government consumption as G, investments as I, exports as E, imports as U, net indirect taxes as T_{ind}, salaries and wages as W and gross operating surplus as O.

The Income Side of the GDP

The income approach to gross domestic product estimate represents the sum of value added as costs of all production plants in the country. These costs include net taxes on products, reumuneration of employees, fixed capital consumption and net operating surplus. Some data sources provide estimates for some of the components for all types of activities. Other sources provide estimates for several, or even for all components of one type of activity. A combination of several sources is usually used in practice in order to use the available data as fully as possible, as well as to perform cross checking wherever possible.

In estimating the income side of the GDP, the data from annual financial accounts by legal entities to the Payment Agency were used. For estimating the added value produced by economic entities that are not monitored by the Payment Agency, such as tradesmen and private agricultural producers, data obtained by the special Central Bureau of Statistics surveys were used. The adjustments made on this side had the purpose of bringing the aggregates nearer to those defined in the SNA. The estimated volume of hidden incomes was not added, although it should also be recorded according to the SNA concept, which resulted in the fact that this side shows the registered income - the base for estimating the volume of the underground economy. The results of statistical data processing are shown in Table 9.1.

Remuneration of Employees

Remuneration of employees include registered gross wages and salaries paid to persons employed, as well as those originating from independent professions, crafts and trades and free occupations, agriculture and forestry, property and proprietary rights, social receipts and remuneration based on temporary work (authors' fees). Compensation for holidays, sick leaves and other shorter leaves of absence are included in this category if employers pay them. Compensation for business trips or other expenses caused by business itself are not included in compensation of employees, but belong to intermediate consumption. Since a part of employee remuneration (for example, luncheon vouchers, local public transportation bonus, holiday cash grant, etc.) is recorded as a non-material expense and because it is a part of employee remuneration, by its nature and according to the SNA definitions, an adequate adjustment had to be made for this part of labor costs.

Subsidies and Taxes on Products and Services

Indirect taxes are tax levies for production, acquisition, sale or use of goods and services as well as import levies. Subsidies are a certain amount given by the state to producers in addition to their sales receipts. Transfers to state companies to cover losses which result from selling below production costs due to political decisions are also treated as subsidies. The amount of subsidies is often deducted from indirect taxes, and the category thus obtained is called net indirect taxes.

Taxes on products in Croatia are taxes on general sales of goods and services, excises and taxes on international trade and transactions. Until 1993, the same aggregates were estimated according to the annual financial accounts of the Payment Agency. The amounts for the last two years were estimated according to the tax statistics of local government, fund and central government budgets. The same sources were used in estimating subsidies as in estimating indirect taxes.

Operating Surplus

The net operating surplus of a production establishment is defined as the amount that remains after the deduction of intermediate consumption, net indirect taxes, fixed capital consumption and remuneration of employees from the gross production. The profit, as calculated in business accounts, can be a weak approximation of operating surplus. In the adjustment, the profit should be reduced by net property incomes (dividends, interest, etc.), capital transfers (which are to a certain extent already included in profit) and receipts resulting from sales of fixed capital. The category consumption profit of fixed capital should be taken into consideration because it is probable that it will be calculated differently in business accounts than would be necessary for national accounting. In addition, the changes in inventories must be taken into consideration; they are not included in measurement of profit, but should be included in measurement of the added value produced.

Operating surplus is estimated as a residual between business receipts, intermediate consumption, net indirect consumption, and gross remuneration of employees. In the government units (funds, ministries, education, health and non-profit institutions), according to the SNA definitions, there can be no net operating surplus.

The operating surplus of entrepreneurs should be adjusted for the imputed dwelling rents that represents the price at which the owners could rent their private apartments in the market. The income from the imputed dwelling rents is estimated according to the data of the State Institute for Macroeconomic Analysis and Forecasts (SIMAF). Since the imputed dwelling rents represents both an income and an expense for owners and users of apartments, it does not influence the volume of the discrepancy between the expenditure and the income side of the gross domestic product, but is used for the estimation of the total gross domestic product as a basis for representing unofficial economy volume.

The Expenditure Side of the GDP

An alternative way to reach the gross domestic product is by summing up final uses which are: government final consumption, households' expenditures for final consumption, gross capital formation and changes in inventories and net exports.

The value of the gross domestic product by the expenditure approach is estimated by combination of the data obtained from the Central Bureau of Statistics, the Payment Agency, the National Bank of Croatia, the Ministry of Labor and Social Welfare, Ministry of Finance, Croatian Red Cross and other available sources.

Private Consumption

The expenditures for private household consumption are defined as the expenses for final consumption of households in the domestic market increased by direct purchases of the resident household abroad and reduced by direct purchases of non-resident households in the domestic market. In the undeveloped statistics of the national accounts it is usual to estimate total expenditures for private final consumption as a residual after deduction of independent estimates of other final uses from the sum of gross domestic product (obtained by production or income approaches) and imports. However, this method should be avoided because it excludes the possibility of detecting statistical discrepancies. The very existence of independent estimates for all the components on the expenditure side, including private consumption, provides the base for estimating the volume of the underground economy. The data on expenditures collected by the household sampling method are used for making referential estimates of expense distribution for household consumption. However, even in developed statistic monitoring systems, such surveys are conducted in long-term intervals, and expenditures for the final private consumption must be estimated for the years in which the survey was not conducted.

The level of private consumption in the Republic of Croatia in 1990 is a result of the survey on household consumption for the same year. It provides rather useful, although probably underestimated, data on the funds used for household consumption. The non-existence of surveys on household budget until 1995 (Survey on Additional Household Jobs, CEMA,

1995) significantly limited estimates of household consumption for the following years.

Further efforts in research on household consumption for the following years were directed to the estimation of total supply of goods[1] in the domestic market through the data of the official statistics on domestic production adjusted for the change in inventories and in registered import and export of goods. Under the assumption of identical trends of private consumption and total supply in the domestic market, the data thus obtained were used as indicators of trends in household consumption.

The changes in domestic production were approximated by quantity indices of individual branches of industrial and agricultural production. The production was then adjusted for the changes in inventories. Reduction of inventories is, together with production, an additional source for satisfying private consumption. When inventories increase, the case is the opposite. An additional difficulty was the unavailability of data on inventories at product level. Since we do not know which part of inventories can become an object of private consumption, calculations were made with total change of stock in Versions 1 and 2, while Version 3 was calculated under the assumption that only 60 per cent of inventory change (i.e. approximately share of private consumption in the GDP) influenced the private consumption. Comparison of both versions of the adjusted domestic components shows that the difference between the two values was not higher than 5 percent in all the years.

The source for import and export data are customs declarations, which are submitted to the Customs Office by the shipping companies in the name of their clients at the moment of imposition of custom duties. Since some goods avoid the prescribed procedure with the purpose of evading tax charges, adjustments were made for the assumed value of unregistered import and export in Version 2. In Version 3, the values of the unregistered imports and exports were additionally adjusted. The adjustments are explained in one of the following sections entitled 'Balance of exports and imports of goods and non-factor services'.

Public Consumption Expenditures

The SNA defines public consumption expenditures as the value of gross production of government services reduced by the value of government sales and the value of any own investments included in the gross production. Public consumption expenditures correspond therefore with the value of goods and services produced by the state for its own current consumption.

Government consumption in Croatia is understood to be all current expenditures for goods and services of all units of local and central government, meaning expenditures for gross wages and salaries of persons employed in government service and other expenditures on goods and services. State investments are included in gross investments item. Until 1993, the data obtained from the Payment Agency on the consolidated general government were used. The last two years were assessed on the basis of the data obtained from the Ministry of Finance.

Gross Fixed Capital Formation

Gross fixed capital formation consists of two main components: gross investment into fixed capital and increase of inventories. Gross fixed capital formation consists of expenditures by production plants for acquisition of investment goods diminished by the sales of used investment goods. Inventories consist of producer-owned goods which were acquired for intermediate consumption, but have not been used yet, of goods intended for sales which have not been sold yet and of the production process itself. Gross investment in inventories does not include all inventories, but only changes relative to the previous period, which always bring along problems connected to changes in price.

Investment consumption is estimated on the basis of data obtained from the Central Bureau of Statistics on the realized gross fixed capital formation adjusted for changes in total inventories according to the annual financial statements of economic entities. Since the research of Central Bureau of Statistics on the realized fixed capital formation by legal entities does not cover all economic entities (targeted samples obtained from the Payment Agency - payments for the investments from the account of a legal entity), the data published underestimate the real investment level.

There is a further need for adjustments in private construction (with the share of about 30 per cent in total official fixed capital formation), which was an important investment activity during the war against Croatia. Its size is estimated by the Central Bureau of Statistics based on the data on changes in trade and construction. When an organized process of post-war reconstruction and building starts, with the state as the largest investor, it can be assumed that the level of official registering of investments is growing. The adjustment factors vary between 5 and 25 per cent of recorded fixed capital formation. The gross fixed capital formation thus obtained (shown in Table 9.5) was used for the estimation of the medium level of the size of the underground economy (Version 3).

It can be concluded that the changes in gross fixed capital formation were largely determined by the war, by negative gross fixed capital formation in 1991 and by drop in inventories during the three war years. The normalization of the situation and the revival of economic activities brought an increase in gross fixed capital formation in 1994. It is obvious that a high share of negative gross investments occurred only in the 1991 - 1993 period.

Balance of Imports and Exports of Goods and Non-Factor Services

Export of goods and non-factor services is one of the components of final demand. On the other hand, import is a source of goods and services supply. All acquisitions by extra-territorial entities, such as embassies, international organizations or foreign military forces, are considered as exports of the country where the transaction were made.

In addition to the official data obtained from the National Bank of Croatia on the exports and imports which were used in Version 1, in order to estimate the volume of the unofficial economy, it is also necessary to estimate humanitarian aid, trends in unregistered exports and imports of goods (shopping abroad) and unregistered export of services (mostly tourist). In estimating the unregistered import of goods in Version 2 (lower level of underground economy size), two elements were used: the entry of passengers into Croatia in motor vehicles with Croatian license plates[2] and the volume of possible spending abroad according to the changes in exchange rate and in real income (between US $ 60 to US $ 120). We should bear in mind that the number of passengers crossing the border is probably underestimated due to the method of monitoring applied, and the fact that part of such imports was used for further 'black market' sales in the domestic market. The goods thus 'relieved' of customs duties and taxes are cheaper and, regardless of quality, more competitive in the current conditions of the low standard of living. As a result of assumptions mentioned, the size of the unregistered import of goods dropped from about US$ 2 billion in 1990 and reached its bottom level in 1992, when it accounted for only one fourth of its 1990 value. It is assumed that unregistered imports have been increasing again during the last three years of the period observed due to the combined effect of the level of domestic market prices, real income and exchange rate appreciation. The size of 'local border traffic' imports last year was 13 per cent higher than its 1990 level.

The largest adjustments for the unregistered exports of goods in the same Version were made for 1991 and 1992 since the data of the National Bank of Croatia on individual aggregates of the balance of payments were just a rough approximation of their actual trends. The adjustments per item did not exceed 20 per cent of the registered export of goods. Also, a decreasing trend is obvious due to the improvement of the balance of payment statistics. The 1990 data on the imports and exports with the republics of former Yugoslavia were estimated based on the social accounts for 1990. It should be mentioned that the 1991 estimate of the international trade with Slovenia and other republics of former Yugoslavia was made on the basis of its 1992 value and that it is very probable that the intensity of exchange before and immediately after gaining the independence was higher.

In Version 3, the number of passengers who crossed the Croatian frontier in motor vehicles with Croatian registration plates increased by 20 per cent, while the assumed spending on goods imported remained the same as in Version 2. Total exports of goods was also additionally adjusted for the unregistered exports of goods (which was a consequence of 'soft' frontier with neighboring states), for the estimated consumption of the international military forces, for mis-invoicing of the registered exports and for money laundering, which has not yet been completely legally regulated.

In addition to the export of goods, Version 3 also estimates the unregistered export of services. The unregistered export of services was estimated according to the changes in the registered export of non-factor services, overnight stays, and estimated consumption of international military and monitoring missions. It is important to mention that the largest adjustments of the unregistered export of non-factor services were made for the 1990-1992 period because of the international exchange statistics with the states of former Yugoslavia. The items did not exceed the level of 20 per cent of the total registered exports. As final result of this adjustment, the 1995 value of total export of non-factor services, unregistered and registered, is equal to the level of 1991. The 1992-1993 period is characterized by a considerable decrease (about 70 to 80 per cent of the 1991 level). The following year, however, started bringing some of the effects of a peacetime situation and an increase in tourist services.

It should be stressed that the amounts of the estimated consumption abroad, as well as of all other adjustments in the export of goods and services, are not a result of any more complex research or surveys (as neither in fact exist), but that they are primarily based on the estimates by the authors. The unregistered imports of goods would be much easier to estimate if there was a survey on the consumption of domestic residents abroad. As far as a more precise quantification of the exchange with the republics of former Yugoslavia in the 1990-1992 period is concerned, it would become possible if an input-output table for at least one of the years mentioned was made. (The relationships of 1987, which is the last year when such a table was made, have undergone significant changes). On the export of goods side, the adjustments were made based on unregistered export that was a consequence of the consumption by international military forces in Croatia. However, no exact indicators of their intensity and trends were available. It would be highly useful to examine various sources (including also military formations as much as possible), in order to obtain at least some indications of the volume of their expenditure in Croatia. In our opinion, such adjustments are closer to the actual trade flows than the officially recorded ones.

Comments on the Results Obtained

The following Tables show the results of the aforementioned research. The share of the unofficial economy is expressed as the share of the differences in the GDP (without imputed dwelling rents) according to the expenditure and income approach in the gross domestic product obtained by the income approach (including also imputed dwelling rents) and which is assumed to correspond to the officially registered GDP.

Version 1 shows the components of the gross domestic product according to the expenditure approach obtained by using only official data, together with an estimate of the private (household) consumption explained in one of earlier sections of this paper. Since there are justifiable doubts that the official statistics cover all economic transactions, which is confirmed by the statements of statisticians, additional assumptions on trends of unregistered exports, imports and gross fixed capital formation were introduced in Versions 2 and 3. Table 9.7 shows that there was a significant increase of the underground economy present in the 1990-1993 period, varying between 26 per cent in 1990 to approximately 38 per cent in 1993. During the following years, its share in the GDP calculated by the income method dropped to 32.6 per cent.

With medium assumptions on the volume of the unregistered exports and imports in Version 2, the share of the underground economy in the registered gross domestic product varied between 17.81 per cent in 1990 to 29.7 per cent in 1993 and 22.72 per cent last year.

Underground economy dynamics in this Version approximately correspond to the dynamics obtained by the use of only the official data, but the level is significantly lower. It is a little surprising that the incorporation of the assumptions about the unregistered transactions (imports and exports), which are also a form in which the underground economy operates, makes the volume of the total underground economy lower. The explanation is found in the method of discrepancies in national accounts applied, which provides only differences in the estimates of the gross domestic product calculated by the income and expenditure approach. This results in a situation when simultaneous adjustments of exports and imports for the value of the unofficial transactions lower the share of the underground economy, while the real level of the unregistered transactions is indeed higher.

The estimate of a medium level of the size of the underground economy in Version 3 is a result of further adjustments of the components on the expenditure side of the gross domestic product. Due to the earlier mentioned problems, the level of investments has been adjusted. The flows of international trade were also additionally adjusted, especially export of services, which resulted in the increased share of the volume of the underground economy in the GDP.

The share of the underground economy in the registered gross domestic product in this Version varies between 22.84 per cent in 1990 and 33.72 per cent in 1993. The same trend that was obvious in the earlier mentioned two Versions is also seen here. The next two years, as expected, brought a decrease in the share of the underground economy to 32.8 per cent and 24.24 per cent respectively.

The growth of the share of the underground economy in the registered domestic product until 1993 should be viewed in the light of the drop in real incomes, high inflation and the existence of a 'parallel' currency (German Mark) for domestic transactions, high tax burden and war. Since the government did not allow financial transactions to be carried in parallel currency throughout the whole inflationary period, we can assume that a considerable number of domestic transactions in foreign currency remained unregistered in the regular flows. The share of the informal economy started decreasing in the following year and this was continued more strongly in 1995, which was in a significant measure stimulated by the stabilization program and greater confidence in government institutions. It is assumed that tax relief on consumption from the initial rate of 50 per cent in 1993 to 20 per cent in 1994, and reduction of income and profit tax rates in 1994, additionally caused a part of the 'gray zone' in the economy to switch into official economic flows.

In order to illustrate real trends of individual components of the gross domestic product, Table 9.11 shows the GDP according to the basic components (obtained by the *lower margin* version) in 1990 constant prices. Nominal values were deflated by the retail prices index, which is not an exact deflator for individual components in practice.

Since presently there is no official value of the gross domestic product in Croatia for the 1991-1995 period, and since the only available 'GDP estimate in 1990 prices is nothing more than a rough approximate' (de Leeuw, 1994, p 15), comparison with the alternative estimates of the GDP trends would not provide reliable conclusions. Changes in the real GDP estimated by the expenditure method, which includes also imputed dwelling rents, has been increasing during the last two years of the period observed, varying between 2.27 per cent in 1994 and 3.75 per cent in 1995.

Table 9.10 shows the GDP structure estimated by the expenditure method which includes dwelling rents. It can be assumed that the significant growth of the private (household) consumption share in 1991 was a consequence of the pre-war psychosis when the greater part of income was spent on inventories of primary goods. A high share of private consumption in 1995 can be explained by real appreciation of the exchange rate, by growth of real incomes, and by people's need to increase the standard of living to its pre-war level. Table 9.10 shows also a strong negative gross investment process in 1991, while the growth of the gross investments during the three following years was a consequence of trends in inventories. A stronger current account deficit than recorded in the balance of payment of the National Bank of Croatia is a consequence of the assumptions used in Version 2. The growth of government consumption remains as a residue since its value remains unchanged in all the three Versions.

The results obtained are just guidelines for further research. Such approximations, however, do show the dynamics of the underground economy of Croatia to be dynamic, although its level is probably underestimated because of the available statistics and assumptions mentioned above. More comprehensive and higher quality research is necessary for certain aggregates of the gross domestic product (economic activity of tradesmen and private agricultural producers, gross fixed capital formation, statistics of international trade flows) and the adoption of the UN system of national accounts (SNA). The size of private consumption will be easier to estimate after the survey on household budget intended for next year. Also, a more detailed research into the share of the underground economy in individual economic sectors and calculation of the gross domestic product by organizational principle would provide another 'control point' for further adjustment of the method of discrepancies in national accounts. Revival of economic activities, increased labor demand in the formal sector, increase of efficiency of employees and the economy of scale will most certainly cause a part of the informal sector to switch into the formal economic flows. It can be assumed that the decrease of the share of the underground economy in the economy as a whole occurring in the last two years is partially a consequence of such trends.

Summary

This paper measures the added value that is not recorded in the Croatian national accounts, using one of the indirect methods of evaluating the underground economy, namely, the discrepancy between GDP income and expenditure. This method does not yield the absolute level of the underground economy but only the difference between independent measures of GDP income and expenditure. The discrepancy arises because households tend to conceal or underreport their incomes to a greater extent than they conceal or underreport their expenditures. Income underreporting is a form of tax evasion. The economic statistics system in Croatia has abandoned the previously used system of national accounts in favor of the material production system (MPS), hence in this paper we have tried as far as possible to bring individual parameters closer to the system of national accounts. We have endeavored to determine the levels of individual components of GDP as accurately as possible by using all the available statistical data and by introducing a series of rational assumptions. The validity of these assumptions introduced in order to determine individual components of GDP influences to a large extent the reliability of the estimates of the underground economy. As we expected, total GDP expenditure is higher than total GDP income. The difference between the two is the basis for estimating the size of the underground economy in the Republic of Croatia.

The size of the underground economy is expressed as the difference between GDP income and expenditure (excluding residential property rent) as a proportion of GDP measured by the total income method, which includes residential property rent and which we assume corresponds to the officially registered GDP. In some versions additional assumptions were introduced concerning unregistered exports, imports and gross investments (lower limit), which can also be considered part of the underground economy. This was done due to justified suspicions that the official statistics do not include all the economic transactions in their entirety, a suspicion confirmed by statements from official statistical analysts. We have used the national account discrepancy method, and present lower and upper limit estimates of the discrepancy. Since the discrepancy only measures the degree to which expenditures are understated by less than income, the true level of the unrecorded transactions is in fact higher than the estimated discrepancy.

The growth of the underground economy in relation to the registered GDP up to 1993 is a consequence of falling real incomes, high inflation, and the existence of a 'parallel' currency for domestic transactions, the high tax burden and the wartime circumstances. During 1994 and 1995, efforts were made to reduce the underground economy. The stabilization program, growing trust in government institutions and the recovery of overall economic activity certainly contributed to these efforts. The results obtained are merely guidelines for further research. However, approximations of this type show the dynamics of the underground economy in Croatia. Despite our use of all the available statistical data, we suspect that our estimates still understate the true magnitude of unrecorded income in the Croatian economy.

Notes

1. Because of the lack of adequate quantitative indices of services, we assumed that the consumption of services has the same dynamics as the consumption of goods.
2. The number of passengers crossing Croatian border in motor vehicles with Croatian licence plates was obtained from the Central Bureau of Statistics.

References

CEMA (1995) 'Dodatni poslovi kućanstava u Hrvatskoj', veljača/ožujak 1995, Zagreb.
de Leeuw, F. (1994) 'Croatia: Report on the National Accounts - Statistic Mission (July 11-29, 1994), Zagreb.
Kukar, S. (1995) 'Siva ekonomija v Sloveniji: Razlogi za njen razvoj in ocene njenega obsega', *IB Revija*, no. 1-2-3, pp. 16-25.
Smith, S. and S. Wied-Nebbeling (1986) 'The Shadow Economy in Britain and Germany', Anglo-German Foundation, London.
UN (1993), *System of National Accounts 1993*, Commission of EU, IMF, OECD, UN, WB, Washington, DC.

Table 9.1 Gross domestic product (income approach), current prices (in Kunas)

	1990	1991	1992	1993	1994	1995
Gross remuneration of employees	172.553.071	253.689.560	1.176.742.157	16.239.450.912	34.833.399.412	43.942.586.026
Gross operating surplus	56.192.376	109.948.895	1.039.261.053	12.485.086.544	21.459.865.134	15.927.797.314
Net indirect taxes	31.206.520	32.048.129	346.499.932	5.930.449.851	17.170.868.951	19.875.398.000
Gross domestic product (without imputed dwelling rents)	259.951.967	395.686.584	2.562.503.142	34.654.987.307	73.464.133.497	79.745.781.340
Gross domestic product (with imputed dwelling rents)	278.874.967	440.171.584	2.923.630.142	42.042.366.000	85.725.495.000	95.036.820.000

Table 9.2 Index of changes in private consumption (Version 1), in Kunas

	1990	1991	1992	1993	1994	1995
Adjusted domestic production, 1990 prices	208.907.955	211.180.738	164.965.263	132.521.078	119.199.931	124.331.158
Imports, 1990 prices	58.101.790	42.874.834	49.958.292	52.261.352	58.565.800	84.107.607
Exports, 1990 prices	45.504.486	37.268.749	52.046.575	44.193.725	48.230.204	52.444.847
Supply in the domestic market, 1990 prices	221.505.259	216.786.823	162.876.980	140.588.705	129.535.527	155.993.918
Supply in the domestic market, current prices	221.505.259	483.434.615	2.780.415.913	38.819.038.822	70.675.710.648	86.813.871.996
Indices of changes in supply in the domestic market	100,00	218,25	575,14	1396,16	182,06	122,83

184 *Underground Economies in Transition*

Table 9.3 Index of changes in private consumption (Version 2), in Kunas

	1990	1991	1992	1993	1994	1995
Adjusted domestic production, 1990 prices	208.907.955	211.180.738	164.965.263	132.521.078	119.199.931	124.331.158
Imports, 1990 prices	80.633.156	51.190.861	58.004.242	60.472.216	76.649.268	105.533.622
Exports, 1990 prices	45.508.919	50.053.393	62.492.372	45.611.397	49.080.117	52.527.541
Supply in the domestic market, 1990 prices	244.032.192	212.318.206	160.477.133	147.381.897	146.769.083	177.337.239
Supply in the domestic market, current prices	244.032.192	473.469.598	2.739.448.970	40.694.759.778	80.078.488.899	98.691.875.530
Indices of changes in supply in the domestic market	100,00	194,02	578,59	1.485,51	196,78	123,24

Table 9.4 Index of changes in private consumption (Version 3), in Kunas

	1990	1991	1992	1993	1994	1995
Adjusted domestic production, 1990 prices	208.907.955	199.870.150	154.472.441	132.221.427	120.463.972	124.110.912
Imports, 1990 prices	85.139.429	54.754.872	59.613.432	62.114.389	78.066.584	108.740.699
Exports, 1990 prices	50.011.462	41.746.090	53.832.223	47.115.529	51.899.216	55.741.969
Supply in the domestic market, 1990 prices	244.035.923	212.878.932	160.253.650	147.220.287	146.631.340	177.109.642
Supply in the domestic market, current prices	244.035.923	474.720.019	2.735.633.978	40.650.136.339	80.003.335.094	98.565.212.963
Indices of changes in supply in the domestic market	100,00	194,53	576,26	1.485,95	196,81	123,20

Table 9.5 Investment consumption, in Kunas, current prices

	1990	1991	1992	1993	1994	1995
Total investments in fixed capital	38.456.032	58.836.444	363.051.661	6.027.590.680	13.552.116.887	13.613.546.253
Change in inventories	19.710.202	-79.414.511	-164.372.007	-752.830.388	6.507.131.046	2.955.982.870
Gross fixed capital formation	58.166.234	-20.578.067	198.679.654	5.274.760.292	20.059.247.933	16.569.529.123
Adjusted gross investments	62.011.837	-5.868.956	289.442.569	6.781.657.962	22.092.065.466	17.250.206.436

Table 9.6 Exports and imports of goods and non-factor services, in Kunas, current prices

	1990	1991	1992	1993	1994	1995
Version 1						
Registered exports	195.558.259	126.965.077	1.508.871.188	19.412.330.855	39.191.691.970	37.767.580.659
Registered imports	189.491.062	123.335.916	1.423.454.076	18.659.201.278	40.428.703.023	49.495.807.258
Version 2						
Adjusted exports	195.562.692	155.474.834	1.687.187.739	19.803.775.353	39.655.411.626	37.813.601.829
Adjusted imports	212.022.428	141.880.655	1.560.803.684	20.926.366.636	50.295.200.767	61.419.831.924
Version 3						
Adjusted exports	210.250.818	163.415.245	1.714.527.325	20.474.047.806	42.090.662.521	40.467.780.028
Adjusted imports	216.528.701	149.828.401	1.588.273.605	21.379.799.708	51.068.500.315	63.204.636.857

Table 9.7 The underground economy estimate (Version 1), in Kunas, current prices

	1990.	1991.	1992.	1993.	1994.	1995.
Gross investments	58.166.234	-20.578.067	198.679.654	5.274.760.292	20.059.247.933	16.569.529.123
Total private consumption	198.036.824	432.214.820	2.485.831.433	34.706.169.839	63.187.633.997	77.615.960.551
Government consumption	69.876.232	103.790.000	649.336.255	9.969.023.862	23.542.640.000	28.284.490.000
Registered exports	195.558.259	126.965.077	1.508.871.188	19.412.330.855	39.191.691.970	37.767.580.659
Registered imports	189.491.062	123.335.916	1.423.454.076	18.659.201.278	40.428.703.023	49.495.807.258
GDP - expenditure approach (w/o imputed dwelling rents)	332.146.487	519.055.914	3.419.264.454	50.703.083.569	105.552.510.877	110.741.753.075
GDP - income approach (w/o imputed dwelling rents)	259.951.967	395.686.584	2.562.503.142	34.654.987.307	73.464.133.497	79.745.781.340
GDP - income approach + imputed dwelling rents	278.874.967	440.171.584	2.923.630.142	42.042.366.000	85.725.495.000	95.036.820.000
Underground economy (% registered GDP)	25,89%	28,03%	29,30%	38,17%	37,43%	32,61%

Table 9.8 The underground economy estimate (Version 2), in Kunas, current prices

	1990	1991	1992	1993	1994	1995
Gross investments	58.166.234	-20.578.067	198.679.654	5.274.760.292	20.059.247.933	16.569.529.123
Total private consumption	198.036.824	384.229.698	2.223.115.600	33.024.581.330	64.985.236.032	80.090.357.772
Total private consumption	69.876.232	103.790.000	649.336.255	9.969.023.862	23.542.640.000	28.284.490.000
Exports	195.562.692	155.474.834	1.687.187.739	19.803.775.353	39.655.411.626	37.813.601.829
Imports	212.022.428	141.880.655	1.560.803.684	20.926.366.636	50.295.200.767	61.419.831.924
GDP (expenditure approach)	309.619.553	481.035.809	3.197.515.563	47.145.774.201	97.947.334.824	101.338.146.799
GDP - income approach (w/o imputed dwelling rents)	259.951.967	395.686.584	2.562.503.142	34.654.987.307	73.464.133.497	79.745.781.340
GDP income approach + imputed dwelling rents	278.874.967	440.171.584	2.923.630.142	42.042.366.000	85.725.495.000	95.036.820.000
Underground economy (% registered GDP)	17,81%	19,39%	21,72%	29,71%	28,56%	22,72%

188 *Underground Economies in Transition*

Table 9.9 The underground economy estimate (Version 3), in Kunas, current prices

	1990	1991	1992	1993	1994	1995
Gross investments	62.011.837	-5.868.956	289.442.569	6.781.657.962	22.092.065.466	17.250.206.436
Private consumption	198.036.824	385.238.549	2.219.985.723	32.987.864.258	64.923.254.777	79.986.345.892
Government consumption	69.876.232	103.790.000	649.336.255	9.969.023.862	23.542.640.000	28.284.490.000
Exports	210.250.818	163.415.245	1.714.527.325	20.474.047.806	42.090.662.521	40.467.780.028
Imports	216.528.701	149.828.401	1.588.273.605	21.379.799.708	51.068.500.315	63.204.636.857
GDP (expenditure approach)	323.647.009	496.746.436	3.285.018.266	48.832.794.180	101.580.122.449	102.784.185.499
GDP (income approach)	259.951.967	395.686.584	2.562.503.142	34.654.987.307	73.464.133.497	79.745.781.340
GDP income approach + imputed dwelling rents	278.874.967	440.171.584	2.923.630.142	42.042.366.000	85.725.495.000	95.036.820.000
Underground economy (% registered GDP)	22,84%	22,96%	24,71%	33,72%	32,80%	24,24%

Table 9.10 The GDP structure by the expenditure approach (Version 2), per cent

	1990	1991	1992	1993	1994	1995
Gross investments	17,7	-3,9	5,6	9,7	18,2	14,2
Private consumption	66,0	81,6	72,6	74,1	70,0	81,8
Government consumption	21,3	19,7	18,2	18,3	21,4	24,3
Net exports	-5,0	2,6	3,6	-2,1	-9,6	-20,3

Measuring the Underground Economy by the SNA 189

Table 9.11 Estimation of the GDP size and underground economy share in 1990 - constant prices (Version 2)

	1990	1991	1992	1993	1994	1995
Gross investments	58.166.234	-9.227.833	11.638.670	19.103.299	36.764.897	29.773.419
Total private consumption	198.036.824	172.300.313	130.230.284	119.603.248	119.105.938	143.912.585
Government consumption	69.876.232	46.542.601	38.038.168	36.104.247	43.149.312	50.823.772
Exports	195.562.692	69.719.657	98.835.588	71.722.207	72.681.047	67.946.421
Imports	212.022.428	63.623.612	91.432.001	75.787.832	92.181.816	110.363.932
GDP (expenditure approach)	309.619.553	215.711.125	187.310.710	170.745.169	179.519.378	182.092.265
GDP expenditure approach + imputed dwelling rents	328.542.553	235.659.556	208.465.557	197.499.619	201.992.190	209.568.393
GDP (income approach)	259.951.967	177.437.930	150.111.633	125.507.996	134.646.191	143.293.423
GDP income approach + dwelling rents	278.874.967	197.386.361	171.266.480	152.262.446	157.119.003	170.769.551
Underground economy (% registered GDP)	17,81	19,39	21,72	29,71	28,56	22,72

Table 9.12 Underground economy (% of recorded GDP)

1990	1991	1992	1993	1994	1995
17.8 - 25.9	19.4 - 28.0	21.7 - 38.2	29.7 - 38.2	28.6 - 37.4	22.7 - 32.6

10 Assessment of the Underground Economy in Agriculture, Industry and Trade

DAVOR MIKULIĆ[*] & SAŠA MADŽAREVIĆ[**]

Introduction

In every economic system, part of production, income and employment falls outside the monitoring range of official statistics. There are several causes for the non-registration of economic activities: intentional registration of data that do not correspond to the real situation; intentional non-registration of all activities; situations in which there is no legal obligation for economic entities to report their economic activities at all. As such, an unrecorded economy may have a significant influence on the economy as a whole, especially in the field of public income and the labor market. Its quantification, therefore, is essential in order to provide insights into real trends of economic activities and to make possible correct and successful assessment of any economic system and policy implementation.

An economic policy that is only geared to dealing with the official sector is in control of neither the positive nor the negative effects resulting from the existence of the unrecorded sector. In addition to quantifying the size of the underground economy, it is useful to assess its components and know the changes in specific economic activities that comprise the unrecorded economy. Only then can we determine those activities where official statistics are less reliable and do not offer a solid basis for economic analysis and the implementation of economic policy.

There are several classifications and definitions of the underground economy. For the purpose of this study, the underground economy is understood as unreported or unregistered income. Unrecorded income is any income produced by an economic activity that should, according to national

---

[*] Economic Institute, Zagreb, Croatia, e-mail: mikulic@ekist.eizg.hr
[**] Senior Adviser, Budget Preparation and Consolidation Department, Ministry of Finance, Zagreb, Croatia, e-mail: Sasa.Madzarevic@mfin.hr

income accounting conventions, be included in national accounts, but is not included. (Feige, 1990). Some authors broaden the notion of the underground economy to include productive activities which do not fall within production limits according to the existing SNA methodology, but which could nevertheless be considered as economic activities because of their characteristics (Kukar, 1995). Such activities are those which increase the well-being of an individual or a household, but are not considered production activities according to the existing methodology. Some examples of such activities are services intended for consumption within a household itself, like bringing up the children or cooking.

According to SNA, production limits cover production of all goods (physical products), whether they are sold, exchanged or used for private final consumption, and services intended for other users. Among the services intended for private consumption, only the use of private apartments and the services for which staff is paid fall within the above mentioned production limits.

According to the 1993 SNA, production limits also include illegal production, or the production of goods and services the selling, distribution and possession of which is illegal, as well as production activities which are usually legal, but which become illegal when performed by unauthorized producers. Because there are no statistics in Croatia concerning illegal production and distribution, our study will concentrate on the assessment of the underground economy in the more limited sense.

A great deal of this study is based upon the data obtained from official Croatian statistics, with full knowledge that these data are themselves inadequate in many ways. Often they are not consistent with international standards, they suffer from inadequate monitoring of small business enterprises and entrepreneurs, and use large but biased samples. The very definition of the underground economy requires that we base our study on official data. In order to define the unrecorded economy, we must use the data on that part of the economy that is recorded in the official statistics, from which we can then draw conclusions about economic activities which are not so recorded.

Since the official data on registered gross domestic product is given in current prices for 1990,[1] this study will stay within a relative presentation of the underground economy in value indicators. It should be pointed out that the Central Bureau of Statistics (Državni zavod za statistiku) is expected to continue to use the same methodology as before (using data obtained only from the formal sector) in its future data processing. The data on the underground economy will also refer to these hypothetical values.

The estimation methods used to assess the size of the underground economy can be classified into the following two groups:

1. Methods using the data in surveys already completed;
2. Methods processing authentic data gathered with the primary purpose of assessing the underground economy.

Since there has not yet been a survey whose primary purpose was to assess the volume of unrecorded economic activity in the Republic of Croatia, this study will rely upon existing investigations conducted by the Central Bureau of Statistics. Alternative sources will also be used, like the CEMA survey on the additional business in households.

Assessment of Underground Economy in Agriculture

Total agricultural production can be classified into production by agricultural companies and co-operatives, and production by private producers and households. Private producers provide almost two thirds of total agricultural production. The business activities of legal persons are monitored through their annual financial statements. Since the companies in question are mostly large, with no real reason for any significant income hiding or income evasion, this study will concentrate on establishing the volume of unregistered income realized by private producers.

According to the Law on Income Tax, income from agriculture is any cadastral income established and regulated by special legal regulations. Consequently, private agricultural producers are not bound to report the real level of their income. This has resulted in the lack of any relevant source of information for keeping track of income made in this way. The net value of agricultural production achieved by private producers (according to the methodology given for agricultural social product — private sector, 1990) is a matter of the Central Bureau of Statistics experts' evaluation. The last year processed was 1992 and the information following approximately the same methodology for 1993 and 1994 has been assessed by means of quantity indices and prices of specific groups of products.

The Croatian Central Bureau of Statistics data on areas under cultivation, production and home processing (production of wine, brandy, jam, etc.) by private producers have been obtained by estimation mainly carried out by agricultural producers and experts associated with statistical offices and familiar with particular areas. Estimators used their own knowledge of the area, and cadastral information, as well as various records, data from earlier years and information obtained from agricultural experts and producers (1995 Statistical Yearbook).

The data on the quantities of agricultural products produced by private producers gathered in this manner were used to estimate the gross and net production values. The quality of data on income realized by private producers, therefore, depends on the quality of quantitative data gathered. If the estimated quantity is underestimated, the registered income will be also underestimated. However, since the estimations in the great majority of cases were made by experts using all available information to make their best estimates of quantities produced, we consider the conclusions reached and data obtained to be of a rather high quality.

The gross value of agricultural production is calculated on the basis of these statistical data, on the quantities produced and producer prices. According to the notes on methodology about the definition of social product for private producers, producers' prices for agricultural products are purchase prices adjusted for occasional quality incompatibility of products purchased and for the direct selling of a part of products at higher prices at farmer's markets.

Comparison between the gross social product in agriculture and quantities produced confirms that producers' accounting prices do not deviate significantly from purchase prices.

According to the 1993 SNA concept, all non-commercial production, including production for own final usage, should be evaluated according to basic prices (net value of the producer) at which the products could be sold in the market. Since it is certain that private producers do sell a part of their products at prices higher than purchase prices, it can be concluded that agricultural production as recorded so far is underestimated.

The rules for measuring non-commercial production indicate that both the part of production that is sold directly at market places and the products used for personal consumption should be evaluated according to the average (higher) market prices. An average market price should, thus, be a measured weighted average of purchase and retail prices.

The production gross value can be adjusted if the prices according to specific groups of agricultural products are added to the difference between purchase and retail prices, which will be implemented to the assumed share of retail sales.

In the absence of any systematic survey of the quantities of agricultural products sold on the market places, we have assumed that the value realized in this manner varies between 15 and 25 per cent of the purchase value. This assessment is based on an evaluation by statisticians. However, since the volume of the underground economy largely depends on these assumptions, we believe that a systematic survey of quantities sold at farmer's markets would be most useful.

Our assumption has been implemented only in relation to the production of fruit and vegetables, cattle, honey, milk and home processing. Other groups, like cereals, industrial crops and agricultural by-products have not been adjusted. The extent of adjustment was established according to the difference between purchase and retail prices. Two different versions are offered in this study, taking into account the range in prices according to products in specific groups. It should be pointed out that products where larger quality deviations may occur, resulting in larger deviations between purchase and retail prices, have not been taken into account while establishing the price difference.

In vegetables, the biggest difference was noticed for carrots. The ratio between retail and purchase price was 2.1. The smallest difference was found for red onions (1.4). In fruit and viticulture, the smallest difference was found in apples (1.2) and the biggest in pears (1.6). The price ratio for hens' eggs in retail and purchase was 1.2. For milk, depending on the year, it varied between 2.4 and 2.7 and for honey between 2.9 and 3.3.

In the products of home processing, the smallest difference was found in the price of brandy (with retail prices being almost twice as high as purchase ones). Wine in retail sale was almost five times more expensive than wine offered at purchase.

According to a moderate version, the price for vegetables was thus adjusted by the adjustment factor of 1.6; for fruit and wine production by 1.3; for cattle by 1.2; for milk by 2.5; for honey by 2.9; for eggs by 1.2 and for home-processing by 2.2.

Our second version took into consideration larger price differences, resulting in the following adjustment factors: for vegetables 1.9; for fruit and wine production 1.6; for honey 3.3 and for home processing 3.0. The rest of the adjustment factors remained unchanged.

In the absence of any elements to allow assessment of the reproduction material costs, it was assumed that the relation between gross production value and material costs remained unchanged with regards to official statistics. Any more precise quantification of intermediary consumption requires knowledge of technical input and output relation for each of the products.

The assumption of the unchanged relation between gross production and material costs also means that the added value, or private producer's income, is exactly as underestimated as is the production gross value.

Table 10.1 shows assessment of the lower and the upper limit of unrecorded income in agriculture.

The Table shows that, with the assumptions introduced, the accounting for the production of private producers conducted by the Central Bureau of Statistics influences underestimation of production gross value and added value of between 6 and 19 per cent for the period mentioned. If cadastre income based on the data obtained from the Central Bureau of Statistics is taken as the tax base, it is probable that it will also be underestimated. The change of underground economy estimations depends on the product composition. If the share of products with greater differences between their purchase and selling prices increases, the share of non-registered income will also increase.

It is interesting to note that the 1995 CEMA survey on additional business shows that almost a third of all households (approximately 120,000) engaged in additional business carry out agricultural activities. Such a high percentage share can most probably be explained by the fact that these households are mainly either agricultural or mixed households which engage in mutual labor exchange. Since official statistics do not assess total output and income, such mutual exchange does not influence the total level of realized income, but only its redistribution within the population sector.

Assessment of Underground Economy in Industry

The Central Bureau of Statistics collects industrial statistics through monthly, yearly and other regular reports. Industrial and non-industrial firms that have plants used for industrial production complete the reports. A monthly survey is conducted on a sample composed of economic entities with more than 20 employees. Yearly surveys include economic entities with 10 to 20 employees and also some smaller firms if their production is significant for the industry they are engaged in.

Table 10.1 Assessment of lower and upper limit in underground economy (Kunas, current prices, % underground economy)

Year		Field Crops	Fruits and Vegetables	Stock-raising	Home Processing	Gross Production	% Underg. Econ.
1990	Official Statistics	8.139.670	8.397.431	8.898.306	2.744.210	28.179.617	
	Lower Limit Assessment	8.139.670	8.987.954	9.654.825	3.238.168	30.020.616	6,5
	Upper Limit Assessment	8.139.670	10.011.443	10.231.253	4.116.315	32.498.681	15,3
1991	Official Statistics	12.260.256	12.819.218	11.485.839	5.751.301	42.316.614	
	Lower Limit Assessment	12.260.256	13.670.646	12.546.480	6.786.535	45.263.918	7,0
	Upper Limit Assessment	12.260.256	15.199.707	13.356.968	8.626.952	49.443.882	16,8
1992	Official Statistics	88.887.639	140.868.773	106.054.170	69.246.348	405.056.930	
	Lower Limit Assessment	88.887.639	149.824.020	115.505.669	81.710.691	435.928.019	7,6
	Upper Limit Assessment	88.887.639	166.359.342	122.707.372	103.869.522	481.823.875	19,0
1993	Assessment Official Statistics	1.410.594.242	1.266.602.703	1.754.996.865	600.290.390	5.032.484.200	
	Lower Limit Assessment	1.410.594.242	1.352.330.926	1.894.366.517	708.342.660	5.365.634.345	6,6
	Upper Limit Assessment	1.410.594.242	1.504.478.278	2.000.388.863	900.435.585	5.815.896.967	15,6
1994	Assessment Official Statistics	2.813.523.301	2.656.392.214	3.412.944.560	1.384.810.452	10.267.670.527	
	Lower Limit Assessment	2.813.523.301	2.851.002.582	3.668.113.653	1.634.076.334	10.966.715.869	6,8
	Upper Limit Assessment	2.813.523.301	3.179.972.243	3.861.715.027	2.077.215.678	11.932.426.249	16,2

The trends according to monthly data do not deviate in any significant way from the trends established in yearly surveys. This fact, confirmed in almost 100 per cent of samples, indicates that industrial production is well covered and that the data reflect the real situation.

According to the published surveys conducted in developed countries and according to theoretical assumptions, the level of hidden activities in industry drops with the increase of economic entities in specific industrial activities (Franz,1985). The surveys also confirm that the underground economy in industry is more pronounced in industries which are closer to their final consumers.

One of the characteristics of industrial production in the Republic of Croatia is that the majority of industrial products is manufactured in large firms. Of the total number of industrial workers, less than 13 per cent is employed in firms with less than 50 employees. The contact with final consumers, therefore, is not direct, but is realized mainly through the network of wholesale and retail distributors (in part also for intermediary consumption and exports). In view of all this, it can be expected that the underground economy level in industry will be lower than that in other lines of business.

The data obtained from the Payment Agency (Zavod za platni promet) indicate that the average net pay in large companies is almost 50 per cent higher than the report on net pay filed by small industrial firms. Under the assumption that the productivity in small and medium-sized enterprises is not lower (but is probably even higher) than the productivity in large companies, the income of employees in small and medium-sized industrial enterprises and of those in large companies have been equalized (assumption 1). Our second assumption was that the income of employees in small firms is larger than the income of employees in large companies (net pay of kn 2.500 in 1994 and net pay of kn 3.000 in 1995). The results of these two assumptions are shown in Table 10.2.

Our assumption about the equal or larger productivity in smaller firms during this period of transition can be justified by the higher flexibility of smaller firms, enabling them to adjust to the changing situation, which compensates for the smaller effect of economy of scale in large companies. It can be assumed that in a period of significant structural changes, the productivity in smaller firms is at least equal to that in big companies. The gross pay in smaller firms was, therefore, also equal or even higher.

It can be assumed that the difference between the unpaid net wages, tax and contributions is shown in the form of material costs (paid through student service organizations, consumer coupons, entertaining, per diem expenses and business trips expenses). The profit realized by such firms is automatically reduced by the same amount and the required income tax is not paid.

The above mentioned adjustments refer only to small and medium-sized enterprises. Most probably, large companies also hide a part of their income, but there is no sufficient data to allow us to arrive at valid conclusions. Any further survey should take this direction and would be a great deal easier if the balance sheets of specific companies were open to inspection.

Table 10.2 Assessment of underground economy in industry

Type	Simulation I All companies equal incomes 1994	Simulation I All companies equal incomes 1995	Simulation II Small companies Income 2500 kn 1994	Simulation II Small companies Income 3000 kn 1995
Share of non-registered net pay in registered pay	7,8%	8,3%	16,3%	15,9%
Unpaid tax and contributions in wages - % of tax and contributions paid	10,2%	11,9%	17,9%	20,5%
Share of non-registered income in added value in industry (percent underground economy)	5,5%	7,7%	10,7%	14,0%

As Table 10.2 indicates, the underground economy in industry shows a lower level than in other economic activities. This result was to be expected since industrial activities are mainly performed in large companies with fewer direct contacts with their final consumers.

The Assessment of Economy in Trade

According to data obtained from the Central Bureau of Statistics, the real volume of retail trade has shown a considerable drop ever since 1990. In 1995, it showed only 47.7 per cent of the sales volume of 1990. The lowest level of real sales volume was recorded in 1993 at 37.4 per cent of the volume of 1990.

Although this was a period of a decrease in economic activities and real incomes, the index of registered trade most probably underestimated the real level. It is hard to believe that the index of real trade is so far below the gross social product, which in 1995 reached approximately the level of 70 per cent of 1990.

The assumptions, therefore, that part of trade remains outside the reach of official statistics and that the index of real retail turnover is underestimated are rather justifiable. These assumptions are even more confirmed by the appearance of numerous sellers who offer their goods in market places and fairs. Most certainly, the greater part of their sales volume remains unregistered.

Attempting to assess the volume of the underground economy in trade, we shall use the assumption of a constant share of merchandise going through the trade network in net offer. This assumption will be the more justifiable the more disaggregated the data are. This follows from the fact that a certain part of goods is intended exclusively for personal consumption and that there is a rather high probability that the share of such goods going through the trade network does not change significantly. It should be stressed that our assumption could have been less severe if we had an input-output table which allowed a more precise definition of total offer share that usually does not go through the trade network (like, for example, the greater part of investment goods and governmental expenditure). The latest such table in the Republic of Croatia was for 1987. In the meantime, huge structural changes have occurred and we estimate that this table not reliable any more for the purpose of research.

The application of the weighting method based on retail trade turnover will only somewhat ease the problem of non-registration of goods that do not go through the trade network. The application of a weighting system based on the composition of goods sold in retail trade and disaggregation will considerably lessen the possibility of the appearance of any significant deviations due to changes in composition of net offer with regards to final purpose. It was decided, therefore, to analyze net offer according to groups of goods. Further disaggregation (analysis at the level of products themselves and not the groups of products) would certainly offer even better information and insight and is advisable for further study. Also, some components of net offer were obtained at a sufficiently low aggregate level and others only at the level of the economy as a whole.

Domestic production, import and export, therefore, were used disaggregated into groups of goods, while the data on changes in commodity stockpiles and the non-registered import of goods were used only as an aggregate referring to the whole economy. Some deviations, even to a more significant extent, are to be expected here; this was unavoidable because of the lack of relevant data (since information about commodity stockpiles is given only according to specific industries).

The net offer of certain goods on the domestic market consists of domestic production increased by import and diminished by export of the same goods. In order to eliminate the influence of accumulation or activation of commodity stockpiles, the net supply resulting from such activities should be adjusted by the amount of the changes in stockpiles. If stockpiles increase, the net supply should be reduced by the amount of the rise in stockpiles in order to obtain real supply which represents the basis for trade activities. In the case of a drop in stockpiles, the situation would be reversed.

Currency changes and insufficient control have resulted in the phenomenon of very widespread selling of imported goods in market places, goods which have not been registered in foreign trade statistics. For the purpose of this study, such unregistered imports were estimated on the basis of the data obtained from the Central Bureau of Statistics on the number of travelers entering the Republic of Croatia in cars with domestic number plates who were assumed to have spent the sum of U$ 60 to U$ 120 per person.[2] The import of humanitarian aid was not taken into account in total imports because, under the assumption of fair distribution, it should not be a sales item.

A Model

Let us suppose that the trade added value realized by selling a certain product (DV_i) equals the product of multiplication of trade margin (a_i), product price (P_i) and quantity sold (Q_i):

$$DV_i = a_i * P_i * Q_i.$$

Total added value in trade equals the sum of added values by products:

$$DV_t = å * Dv_i.$$

Let us further suppose that the same share of net supply of a certain product goes through the trade network, i.e.,

$$Q_i = b_i * S_i, \quad b_i = \text{const.}$$

The net offer, or trade basis (S_i) equals domestic production (D) increased by imports (U) and diminished by exports (E), adjusted for the changes in commodity stockpiles (DZ):

$$S_i = D_i + U_i - E_i - DZ_i.$$

The change in net supply can be shown in the following manner:

$$\frac{S_{it}}{S_{i0}} = \frac{D_{it} + U_{it} - E_{it} - \Delta Z_{it}}{S_{i0}}$$

From the available data, the real increase in domestic production, imports and exports (based on values expressed in US$) and changes in stockpiles (only aggregatively) can be computed. The above expression can now be written as

$$\frac{S_{it}}{S_{i0}} = \frac{D_{it} * D_{i0}}{D_{i0} * S_{i0}} + \frac{U_{it} * U_{i0}}{U_{i0} * S_{i0}} - \frac{E_{it} * E_{i0}}{E_{i0} * S_{i0}} - \frac{\Delta Z_{it} * \Delta Z_{i0}}{\Delta Z_{i0} * S_{i0}},$$

where the ratios of the second members of a fraction are, in fact, weightings of individual components which will be defined on the basis of the share of each supply component in the total net supply of that particular product.

The total added value computed on the basis of the above mentioned assumptions and the registered added value can now be put into the following relation:

$$\frac{DV_{itu}}{DV_{itr}} = \frac{a_{it} * P_{it} * Q_{itu}}{a_{it} * P_{it} * Q_{itr}} = \frac{b_i * S_{it}}{Q_{itr}} = \frac{b_i * S_{i0} * (\frac{S_{it}}{S_{i0}})}{b_i * S_{i0} * \frac{Q_{itr}}{Q_{it0}}} = \frac{\frac{S_{it}}{S_{i0}}}{\frac{Q_{itr}}{Q_{it0}}}.$$

The aggregate expression of unreported trade will be derived from the computation of weighted averages, where the weightings of a specific group were allocated on the basis of its share in the retail trade in the base year.

The results of this model's application are shown in Table 10.3. They should be understood as the relationship of unregistered retail and registered, but not aggregate, sales.

As has already been mentioned, the model is based on the assumption that the whole retail sales in the base year was recorded. It should also be mentioned that the model does not allow for the possibility of selling at prices different from those reported. It is assumed that sellers will try to report lower income by filing reports presenting smaller quantities sold.

Also, the possibility of filing reports with higher purchase prices and increased intermediary costs intended to present diminished net income has not been explored. This would also be an excellent subject for further surveys in order to obtain better and more accurate assessment of unregistered incomes in trade.

The same results are shown in Table 10.4, but based on the assumption that the unregistered quantity sold in 1990 was 20 per cent, which corresponds approximately with the unregistered income assessment for the same year at the level of the whole economy (Madžarević and Mikulić, 1996).

Table 10.3 Assessment of the underground economy in trade, assuming that there were no unregistered retail sales in 1990

	1990	1991	1992	1993	1994	1995
Index of domestic supply	100,0	74,2	62,3	61,0	59,4	59,8
Index of import supply	100,0	69,3	111,0	106,3	124,4	183,3
Index of import	100,0	93,2	159,2	140,6	136,1	134,8
Index of net supply without adjustment	100,0	71,7	56,9	59,9	58,6	67,0
Index of sales volume changes	100,0	-164,8	-38,3	-10,8	42,6	19,2
Index of unregistered import	100,0	52,7	35,7	36,4	72,1	91,1
Index of net supply with adjustment	100,0	89,0	62,6	63,4	61,1	73,1
Index of registered trade	100,0	72,9	44,1	37,4	42,4	47,7
Underground economy - percentage	0,0	22,1	42,0	69,6	44,2	53,2

As both Tables show, there is no doubt that there is a substantial difference between the total net supply, reflected in the trade base itself and recorded trade. It can therefore be concluded that there is still a considerable gap, largely caused by the underground economy, even though the amount of the goods going through the trade network has somewhat diminished.

It is interesting to notice that the underground economy trend grew until 1993, when, according to our results, almost as many goods remained unreported as were registered in statistical monitoring. In 1994, the underground economy volume showed a certain drop, to increase again the following year.

Table 10.4 Assessment of the underground economy in trade, assuming that 20 per cent of retail sales in 1990 were unregistered

	1990	1991	1992	1993	1994	1995
Index of domestic supply	100,0	74,2	62,3	61,0	59,4	59,8
Index of import supply	100,0	69,3	111,0	106,3	124,4	183,3
Index of import	100,0	93,2	159,2	140,6	136,1	134,8
Index of net supply without adjustment	100,0	71,6	56,9	59,9	58,6	67,0
Index of sales volume changes	100,0	-164,8	-38,3	-10,8	42,6	19,2
Index of unregistered import	100,0	52,7	35,7	36,4	72,1	91,1
Index of net supply with adjustment	120,0	106,8	75,2	76,1	73,4	87,7
Index of registered trade	100,0	72,9	44,1	37,4	42,4	47,7
Underground economy – percentage	20,0	47	70,4	103,5	73,1	83,9

The method applied gave very high, almost unbelievable, underground economy rates in trade. They are, however, confirmed by an alternative assumption, which will be presented only as an example, due to the incompleteness of available data (no accurate number of craft- and tradesmen and workers working for them, no data about the time spent in additional business in trade).

According to the data from annual financial statements collected by the Payment Agency, in 1995 there were 29,800 employees employed in large companies engaged in retail trade, 12,287 employees in medium-sized enterprises and 24,621 employees in small firms. The average net pay reported by small entrepreneurs amounted to about 60 per cent of the pay reported by large companies (kn 1,023 as compared to kn 1,627). As it is difficult to believe that small firms are so much less efficient and that their employees earn such small wages, it can be concluded that their reported wages have been considerably underestimated in order to reduce income tax. Let us, therefore, stay with the conclusion reached that the underground economy in small firms is considerable. Should we care to compare the total number of employees in the companies which have submitted their annual financial statements (66,708) with the official information by the Central Bureau of Statistics about the number of workers employed in retail trade (about 73,000), we can conclude that a certain number of firms has not submitted their annual financial statements at all. According to the statistical experts, those are mainly small companies. We assume that the underground economy is present to a greater extent in those companies as well. If we further assume (though no accurate records exist) that at least half of the total number of craftsmen registered under 'Other' in the Health Insurance Fund, is engaged in trade, we would get an additional 25,000 workers who can justifiably be assumed to be hiding a good deal of their activities.

All this would seem to indicate that there is a considerable amount of underground economy even in trade, which at least partially operates within the existing institutionalized framework. The results of the CEME survey can be added here, confirming that an additional 56,000 people are engaged in trade as additional business (13 per cent of 560,000 inhabitants engaged in additional business, i.e. those who work, but are not employed either in firms or with tradesmen). The figure of 83.9 per cent of underground economy in 1995 seems to make sense after all.

The growth in volume of the underground economy in the period mentioned can be assigned to several factors: insufficient financial control (which can in turn be justified by the war and the coming into being of the new state which had only just begun to develop its institutions, including tax administration) and the drop in production and real incomes, leading more and more people to turn towards the informal trade sector.

The development of informal trade is even stronger during the transition period through which the Croatian economy is passing. The drop in the number of workers employed in the so-called formal sector, which is usual and expected during privatization and reconstruction processes, has led to a drop in the real income of the whole population. In order to slow down the drop of their standard of living as much as possible, people have been turning towards alternative and cheaper supply sources. On the other hand, a considerable number of people have lost their full-time employment, with small chances of finding new jobs in the formal sector. They are also forced to seek new sources of income in the informal sector.

There are several factors influencing the decrease in the underground economy in 1994. With no imminent danger of war any more, government bodies could increasingly concentrate on the strengthening of financial control, considerably increasing the risks of informal business. Also, the gradual cut of tax rates led a section of the underground economy to switch to the formal economy. Large chains of stores managed to reconstruct their business, leading to a decrease in price differences. Real income also showed a slight increase, which, combined, resulted in partial substitution of the formal for the informal sector. Although it is often stated that monetary policy was very restrictive, the data obtained from the National Bank of Croatia show that money supply increased to a certain extent. A part of this increase, reflected in higher incomes, went to the population, directly influencing the rise in demand for goods and services.

Since firmer tax control (realized through numerous actions of the appropriate authorities, like Štibra, which was repeated several times) and a moderate growth of real income continued in 1995, the renewed rise of unregistered trade comes as something of a surprise. It should be considered in the light of the high rate of personal consumption in 1995 (Madžarević and Mikulić, 1996), which was largely satisfied through retail trade and prompted by the two military actions of liberating the occupied territories of the Republic of Croatia.

With the appreciation of the kuna and the increase of income, the population in Croatia felt that its purchasing power had also grown, primarily in regard to imported goods. At the same time, domestic goods became relatively more expensive, resulting in the fact that more and more domestic personal consumption was satisfied by imported goods, leading to a considerable increase in the trade deficit.

Another reason for the rise in personal consumption is partially of a psychological nature. In a large number of Western countries after the Second World War, the population tried to make up with a sudden rise in personal consumption for consumption lost during the war. The war in Croatia influenced the rise in personal consumption in the same way.

Since some significant structural changes also occurred in consumption, the rise of the underground economy can be explained by its greater flexibility.

During the war and because of smaller real wages, permanent goods like cars, furniture or technical equipment, were probably[3] only used and not bought new. With relatively higher incomes, it seems that such goods are more in demand and that a greater part of this demand is satisfied from informal sources. The most obvious example is found in the imported second-hand car market.

Conclusion

As shown in the assessment of the volume of the underground economy (relation between unregistered and registered income) in the economic activities described, depending on the years and the way of measurement, its share varied in agriculture up to 19 per cent in 1992, in industry up to 14 per cent in 1995 and was by far the highest in trade, with 103.5 per cent with regard to reported income.

The level of the underground economy in agriculture and industry is lower with regard to the assessment for the whole economy. Trade, on the other hand, is a highly profitable activity where non-reported activities and tax evasion are still very profitable, due primarily to low fines and still high tax rates.

In conducting research at the level of the informal economy in the three economic activities mentioned, we have encountered several difficulties. One of them was insufficient and incomplete statistical monitoring of changes in the formal economy of these activities. Also, there were no alternative data sources. The methods applied could be further developed, but the range of such development largely depends on the improvement of the quality of the statistical basis upon which the research is founded.

The major goal of this study was quantification of the underground economy in the three economic activities mentioned. Causes and changes were only partially and marginally touched on. The reasons why the underground economy exists, its effects and the measures to be taken against it are still open to further research.

Summary

In addition to efforts to quantify the overall size of the underground economy, it is very useful to evaluate the extent and growth of individual sectors of unrecorded activity in order to identify those sectors where the formal statistics are less reliable and therefore cannot be a good basis for economic analysis and economic policy. Since different activities can have completely different characteristics, including the branch structure by company size and proximity to the end consumer, different estimation methods are often necessary in different activities.

Estimating the extent of the unregistered income in agriculture has been reduced to establishing the difference between the methods of evaluating output for personal use in domestic statistics and evaluating this type of output according to the UN methodology (SNA). There are justified reasons for believing that the official statistics cover amounts of individual agricultural products well and that deviation from the SNA methodology is reduced to the use of wrong prices. The official statistics evaluate the entire output based on wholesale prices (there are only minor corrections for assumed sales of produce at market places, which have almost no effect on the average price). However, according to the SNA methods it should be evaluated based on average market prices. Since market place prices are much higher than wholesale prices, an average market price is calculated.

This price is the average of the market place price and the wholesale price. The entire output should be valued according to this price. Depending on the assumed market place sales and the years, the underground economy was between 6% and 19% in the period from 1990 to 1995.

Data obtained from the Payment Operations Bureau suggest that the registered average salary in large industrial companies is 50% higher than the registered net salary in small companies. In addition to the assumption that productivity in small companies is not lower than productivity in large companies, it was assumed that the average income earned by a unit of labor (which consists of net salary and contributions) is constant regardless of company size. A further assumption was that productivity and hence added value is higher in smaller companies. Based on these assumptions it was concluded that the underground economy in industry was between 5.5% and 14% from 1994 to 1995.

The simplifying assumption of a constant proportion of goods passing through the trade network in the net supply on the domestic market was used in estimating the underground economy in trade, The net supply of a certain good consists of the domestic output increased by exports and reduced by imports with necessary corrections for activation or increases of stocks. This model leads to the conclusion that from 1990 to 1993 the underground economy increased by almost 70% of the total trade income. In other words, if the level of the underground economy was 20% in 1990 (according to some estimates this was the level of the underground economy in the overall economy), then in 1993, that percentage (the ratio of unregistered and registered income) increased to over 100%.

Since it is very difficult to measure the underground economy because individuals attempt to conceal it from the tax authorities and official monitoring, it was necessary to introduce the above mentioned assumptions and the reliability of all the estimates depends on their reliability. The primary goal of this work was to quantify the underground economy in the stated economic branches while the cause of its existence and dynamics were only partly discussed.

Notes

1. The last official gross domestic product according to the SNA concept was obtained by the method of conversion and refers to 1990. For the following years, the Croatian Central Bureau of Statistics has only the GNP estimations in constant prices obtained by the usage of quantitative indices and added value from 1990. As this estimation does not seem to give reliable results, it has been abandoned. New estimation procedures, however, have not been established yet. The Central Bureau of Statistics is currently engaged in adoption of the SNA concepts according to which the underground economy will also enter within production limits and it seems quite possible that the data on final gross domestic product will include also that kind of activities. Their extent, however, cannot be known until the final results are published.
2. The assessment of non-registered import is in more detail explained in a section of the project by Madžarević and Mikulić, *The Assessment of Informal Economy Using the System of National Accounts* (1996).
3. Neither any available data nor this study can establish the quantities sold and the supplies of the population in specific products for the 1990-1995 period. This might be improved by the announced survey on household consumption, which is to be conducted by the Central Bureau of Statistics of the Republic of Croatia.

References:

Blades, D. W. (1982) 'The Hidden Economy and the National Accounts', *Economic Outlook, Occasional Studies*, OECD, Paris.

Centar za istraživanje marketinga (CEMA) (1995) 'Dodatni poslovi kućanstava u Hrvatskoj', Zagreb, veljača/ožujak 1995.

Državni zavod za statistiku Republike Hrvatske, 'Društveni proizvod poljoprivrednih djelatnosti - individualni sektor', 1995.

Državni zavod za statistiku Republike Hrvatske, Statistički ljetopis, 1996.

Feige, E. L. (1990) 'Defining and Estimating Underground and Informal Economies: The New Institutional Economics Approach', *World Development*, vol. 18, no. 7, pp. 989-1002.

Franz, A. (1985) 'Estimates of the Hidden Economy in Austria on the Basis of Official Statistics', *Review of Income and Wealth*, vol. 31, no.4, pp. 325-336.

Kukar, S. (1995) 'Siva ekonomija v Sloveniji: Razlogi za njen razvoj in ocene njenega obsega', *IB Revija*, no. 1-2-3, pp. 16-25.

Madžarević, S. and D. Mikulić (1996) 'Mjerenje neslužbenog gospodarstva sustavom nacionalnih računa', *Financijska praksa*, vol. 21, no. 1-2, pp. 141-156.

Miljenović, Ž., et all. (1996) 'Razvoj i organizacija hrvatskog energetskog sektora, Energetski institut 'Hrvoje Požar', Zagreb, pp. 37.

UN (1993) *'System of National Accounts 1993'*

11 Measuring Employment in the Unofficial Economy by Using Labor Market Data

SANJA CRNKOVIĆ–POZAIĆ*

Introduction

The unofficial economy is present in every society that has developed to the extent that its economic activities must be standardized in order to continue to operate normally and in an unhindered way. An economic system consisting of self-employed and relatively independent producers lies at the end of an economic range in which there is the least need for the formation of an unofficial economy. The development of interdependency in production, division of labor and interaction between different sectors of the economy requires that economic relations among those involved in product, labor and capital markets be organized so as to produce a transparent system. Although the benefits of such a system do not need to be specially stressed, the greatest of them, as far as the economy is concerned, is business efficiency. The institutional and legislative framework within which an economy operates, however, is a product of historical development. This necessarily means that it reflects not only previous economic but also political conditions and is not subject to quick and short-term changes.

The question that arises is whether the institutional framework is neutral, or whether it exercises positive or negative effects on the process of economic development. If it *is* neutral, changes in economic systems are needless and the issue of whether a greater amount of social product is generated in the formal or in the informal sector is not important. If it is *not* neutral, the direction and the extent of its influence needs to be estimated, with questions being answered about the volume of the unofficial economy, about what kind of relationship there is between the formal and the informal economy and whether these two sectors behave as substitutes or com-

---

* Head of the Croatian Employment Agency, Zagreb, Croatia.
   E-mail: crnkovic@hzz.hr

petitors in the process of economic development. The consequences of the answers to these questions are comprehensive and universal. If segmentation of the economy does not influence development negatively, what are its consequences for the development of the society as a whole?

One of the aims of economic development is the attainment of more even income distribution and an equal access to work, education, health and decent living conditions. Do segmented labor markets give rise to certain groups in society which do not have equal access to those rights as do groups in the formal sector? This is something that exceeds purely economic discussion and is reflected in questions such as human resource development, equality, exclusion of particular groups, the legitimacy of the state and its ability to influence the process of economic development. The informal economy creates its own power systems, the epitome of which is the illegal economy as established by, for example, the Mafia in Italy or the narcotics cartel in Columbia.

When we think about the unofficial economy, it is important to bear in mind that people engage in economic activities at all times, regardless of the formal institutional system which attempts to standardize them. Demand will create its own supply in any system and the character of legal regulations will decide whether the demand will be satisfied legally or illegally. If the legislative framework is rigid and allows only very restrictive forms of supply, parallel systems are bound to start developing. As a rule, rigid systems only create deeper illegality and never lessen the phenomenon itself. The whole wisdom lies in choosing the kind of institutional framework that will direct and set norms for economic activities, that does not stifle initiative and the attempts of individuals to achieve the well-being of society in general.

Some common individual behavioral patterns in normative frameworks should also be taken into consideration. The Swiss stereotype is well known, where people find their own personal liberty in a system where all the norms of conduct and all regulations prescribed by law are respected. In this case, obeying the rules by everybody ensures the liberty of all individuals. In such a value-system, individuals will try to stick to the rules of conduct in order to realise their own freedom without interfering with others. The Balkan stereotype is somewhat different. Due to historical circumstances, there have been frequent changes of power resulting in varied legislative frameworks and in difficult living conditions for the average person. The imposition of rules from 'above' and individuals' feeling of helplessness to change the system in which they must work, results in an unwillingness to accept such rules of conduct. Also, due to insufficient development, government itself has been lax in controlling the behavior of economic agents, not wishing to stir up rebellion among those denied 'a piece of the cake'. In conditions of such weak control, many areas of economic activity have flourished unhindered in the unofficial economy.

The aim of this study is to define in a more precise manner the concept of the unofficial economy in the labor market in Croatia and also to try to quantify its total volume and to single out the economic activities where it is strongest. The study will make use of the existing literature on the subject and of some established methods of evaluation.

The Unofficial Economy in the Labor Market: The Definition

The definition of the unofficial economy in most existing literature is largely non-standardized. Usually, it refers only to the object of research, often causing the results of analysis to be applicable only to the specific cases in question. For example, a taxonomy of the unofficial economy has thus developed that is applicable mainly to the labor market of developing countries (Portes, 1994). In such definitions, the unofficial economy is seen as inseparable from poverty. It is carried out in small production units at a low level of labor productivity and is characterized by work-intensive production on old-fashioned machines. Production itself and work resources are closely connected to the nuclear or extended family, unpaid family labor, etc. This perception of the unofficial economy is dominant among experts in the International Labor Organization (ILO) and it actually does explain the greater part of the unofficial economy in developing countries. In most cases, these activities are not illegal, but simply remain unregistered, due to lack of interest on the part of the legislative institutions in setting norms for them. Some authors believe that this part of the unofficial economy is the 'point of entry' to the formal economy and that its initial non legalized status is essential in the course of the original development of economic units. Others claim that this kind of unofficial economy lacks any positive developmental prospect because it operates on the margins of the formal system and its participants remain forever in a vicious circle of poverty.

Besides this definition, the relevant literature also offers a variety of other definitions which are all to a greater or lesser extent applicable to our situation. Institutional economists, who can be considered the successors of development economists, focus their attention on the relationship between the 'rules of the game' and economic development, considering that institutions are not neutral, but that they can substantially stimulate or hinder the process of economic and overall development (Feige, 1990). They believe that obeying the rules of the game entails staying within the formal sector, with all of its advantages and disadvantages, and that not obeying the rules of the game opens up the door to the informal sector. Each of the sectors has different transformation costs of production^1 and transaction costs^2, which, according to the institutional economists, boosts economic development. Through their empirical research, they aim to estimate which difference between these costs between the two sectors results in the highest rate of economic growth. The formal sector participants, operating within the system and abiding by the given rules of the game, have different transformation and transaction costs from those operating in the informal sector. For the institutional economists, the basic determinants of the economic development of a society can be found by the establishment of these costs and measurement of the scope of the unofficial economy.

Authors who have studied the unofficial economy in developed countries (Feige, 1989, 1990; Portes, 1994; Franz, 1995) define this sector as activities carried out by economic units which do not follow the institutionalized rules and are, consequently, not protected by them, or as all economic activities which are not regulated by the state, but which are carried out in the area where the same activities have a set of norms (Portes, 1994).

This definition is much more general than that offered by Hart, one of the founders of the unofficial economy concept, who mainly analysed developing countries (Portes, 1994).

The definition by Feige suggests that the unofficial economy consists of:

- production and distribution of legally prohibited goods and services;
- activities unreported for the purpose of tax evasion;
- unregistered or unrecorded activities, which are not statistically monitored in a satisfactory manner.

Figure 11.1 shows an extension of Feige's definition with hierarchical relations between various types of the unofficial economy. The circles shown should be understood as cross-sections and not as unions of sets. In other words, each particular phenomenon is defined from the borderline of one circle to the borderline of another. The dotted *C* circle shows all non-economic activities that are not subject to analysis in this study. Activities like housework, raising children, various hobbies and volunteer work greatly contribute to socioeconomic development, but the measure of their value has yet to be defined.

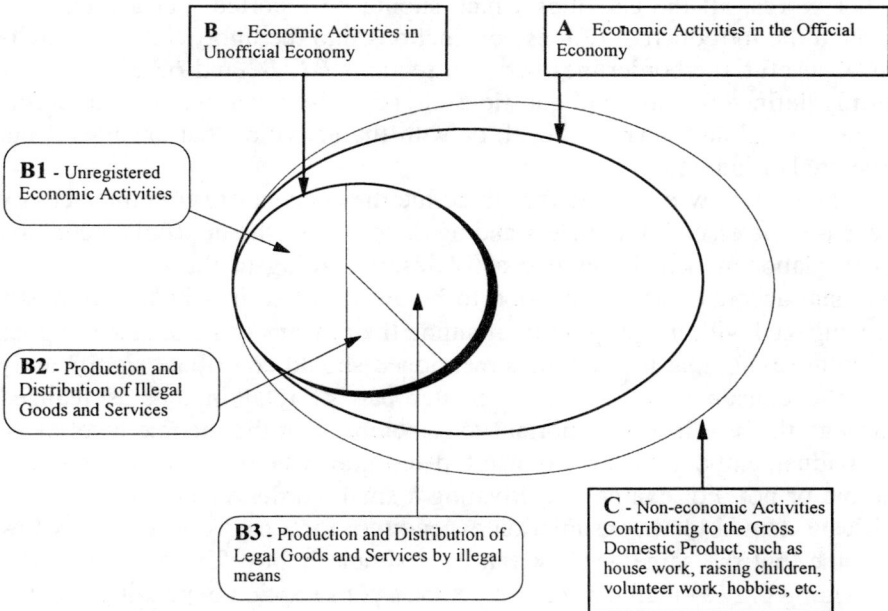

Figure 11.1 Relation between official and unofficial economy

Inside this circle, section *A* represents all the economic activities in a particular society in the official economy. Circle *B* shows the economic activities in the unofficial economy. All the activities inside this circle are 'invisible', but can be classified into three groups. The first group, represented as a part of the circle *B1*, consists of unregistered legal activities, like the work of private producers in agriculture, the employment of particular groups of usually inactive persons (housewives, students, retired persons) or the above mentioned underemployment in the informal sector of developing countries. The main characteristic of this part of the unofficial economy is that, often due to ideological reasons, it is not covered by official statistics.

Sections *B2* and *B3* represent illegal economic activities, where section *B2* represents the production and distribution of illegal goods and services *per se* and section *B3* is the production and distribution of legal goods and services conducted in an illegal way. Some examples of *B2* activities are prostitution, the production and distribution of drugs, selling foreign currency on the black market. *B3* activities refer to black marketeering, moonlighting, performing private business during working hours with or without using production equipment derived from one's main occupation or, in other words, all the activities which should be reported, but are not. Although the introduction of these distinctions into the unofficial economy is rather useful, the borderlines between sections *B1*, *B2* and *B3* are not very firmly defined. Doubts and questions already arise when we want to define what is legal and what is illegal, or with the activities that are illegal but tolerated or ignored.

This study will first attempt to define the concept of economic activity because it is essential in understanding the extent of the unofficial economy in the labor market. Economic activities, according to the UN system of national accounts, are understood to be all activities in which individuals are engaged with the purpose of attaining their means of sustenance. It goes without saying that the activities mentioned should contribute significantly to total consumption, or that a greater part of total income is realized through them. It is also important to remember that the income level of an individual, and not the activity itself, determines whether an activity is economic or not. For example, cultivating a small garden can be a rather significant item in total consumption expenditure for a person with a very low income, but the same activity can be a simple hobby for somebody else, providing only a small part of that person's consumption expenditure. In the former case, therefore, the activity should be considered an economic activity and not in the latter.

Besides the usual economic activities, this category also includes production for own needs (subsistence agriculture); labor exchange (helping a neighbor to build a stable, a house, a fence or to do the sowing or harvesting), which is an activity generally not paid, but a favor traditionally expected to be returned as needed; working for payment in kind; and helping on own estate, farm, independent profession (lawyers, artists and entertainers, freelancers, etc.) or engaging in activities by which a household earns its means of sustenance, without being compensated for it in any way (unpaid family workers).

Unregistered and Unreported Economic Activities

It is obvious that many of the activities defined so broadly will not feature in statistics. In other words, they are among the earlier mentioned legal unregistered activities. Apart from private sector agriculture just mentioned, which is ignored by official statistics, this sector also includes activities carried out by small enterprises and family businesses, which exhibit great fluctuations in the period of transition. None of the existing information sources can follow up the multitude of births and deaths of businesses. Many of these employ only the owner himself and often represent an attempt at developing an additional activity. Activities nearing the borderline of legality are also important to mention here, such as the provision of intellectual services, transcription, babysitting, cleaning of rooms and offices and a lot of other activities the supply of which has considerably increased during the last several years. Persons engaged in black-market activities, street shoeshine boys and car windscreen washers at crossroads can also be included in this group. All of these activities should be reported, but there are no control mechanisms to supervise them nor can such activities be registered as businesses or crafts, though it would seem logical to enlist them as independent professions. The quasi-legality of such activities is confirmed by the legal sale of the advertisement paper *Plavi i zeleni oglasnik (Blue and Green Advertiser)*, which handles supply and demand on the secondary market, thereby facing no competition from the Employment Agency, which makes no effort to mediate in the kind of jobs offered there. This study is an attempt to quantify this area of unregistered activities using the results of a pilot labor force survey, the results of which should, however, be taken only as indicative.[3] The measurable part of these activities is the work of particular groups which enjoy the formal status of retired persons, housewives, students or unemployed persons, and also additional activities by employed persons.

Illegal Economic Activities

The production and distribution of illegal goods is a part of the informal economy which is almost impossible to quantify from administrative sources or surveys simply because of the impossibility of getting honest answers to questions about activities and occupations in illegal activities. This segment should, therefore, be measured by other, for example monetary, methods of measurement of the unofficial economy.

Possible Sources of Work in the Unofficial Economy in Croatia

The unofficial economy has various causes. For example, the production and/or distribution of illegal goods and services is always present and always sink deeper underground when sanctions get stricter. But neither the harmful effects of such production nor prohibition are sufficient to lessen the demand for these goods. The extent of the occurrence of illegal production and distribution depends on the efficiency of sanctions. In the absence of any sanctions, such activities are likely to spread from strictly criminal to other population groups. For example, farmers in South America grow hemp, opium poppy and other opiates in the same way farmers in other countries grow industrial crops. This is possible only in conditions of extreme poverty and the non-existence of adequate sanctions.

On the other hand, with the illegal production and distribution of legal goods and services, the cause should primarily be sought in the individual standard of living and, within it, in the functioning of the state under conditions of limited wealth. A poor society is not able to generate enough funds to finance the state, and during periods when individuals' standards of living drop, both the individuals and the state strive to retain their former positions. Individuals evade their tax obligations and engage in black market activities, while the state increases its fiscal burden in those segments which cannot easily retreat into the unofficial gray zone. As a result, society as a whole is the loser. Services provided by the state constantly decline in quality, which is, in turn reflected on individuals, and not even significant acquisition of wealth in the gray zone can compensate for the decrease social of standards. (One cannot buy a whole street and bring it in line with one's personal standard of living, nor remove beggars at will). In such a situation, the legitimacy of the state becomes ever more questionable. The fact that wealth is gained in the unofficial economy without any real hindrance (the state cannot drastically move against such behavior because it would mean cutting off the only means of livelihood for many individuals living near the poverty line) continues to erode peoples' morals and generates mistrust of the state. The income distribution pattern is very important in this situation. If wealth is concentrated in a small number of very rich persons or groups, the power wielded by such wealth may be used to dictate the spreading of the fiscal burden over a large number of mainly poor inhabitants. This will, in turn, force many of them to perform activities in the invisible sphere.

According to Wiles (1987: 22), all economic systems are based on practical morals that co-exist with the broader theoretical ideology. In the socialist world, the gap between practice and ideology largely influenced the formation of a double life and morality. The deeper the gap became, the more activities that were earlier de facto illegal (if only on paper) became legalized. The institution of socially owned property was the major basis for illegal activities. The non-existence of legal owners made possible the utmost and extreme misuse of socially owned possessions for private purposes, the broad distribution of costs and privatization of profit. The attitude towards *nobody's property* blunted disapproval and even sanctioned the act of stealing at almost any level thereby undermining the moral strength of the society (Bićanić, 1987). As this system stimulated idleness, an impoverished society with rich individuals developed and social standard was the area which suffered most. Due to the low standard of living, the demand for basic needs was often much greater than the supply, soon leading to even greater contraction or narrowing of possibilities for many people. To put it simply, an increasing number of people had to satisfy their needs from an increasingly smaller piece of cake. Parallel systems started springing up everywhere. The system of family connections and the network of acquaintances and friends was the only thing that ensured special treatment for those who were not high enough in the hierarchy. A drop in the standards did not change the situation much. Although, for example, Skolka, 1995 claims that the area for development of the unofficial economy is very restricted because only work of low complexity entailing low qualifications can be carried out in this sector, the extent of the unofficial economy was very widespread, at least in the former socialist countries.

The third element that gives rise to the unofficial economy is restricted and low quality supply by the official economy. Supply composition was least adequate in various types of household services, but other types of services were not much better. The flourishing of the unofficial economy can thus be regarded as a consequence of insufficient control and the *laissez passé* approach on one hand, and of economic necessity and the lack of availability of a whole range of products and services in the official economy, on the other.

Methods of Measuring Employment in the Unofficial Economy by Using Labor Market Data

This study will use two methods of measuring employment in the unofficial economy. The first makes use of secular activity rates and the second is based on the results of the labor force survey. Each has its strengths and weaknesses. Criticism of both methods is well known; the attitude prevails that surveys attempting to quantify employment in the unofficial economy tend to overestimate it because it is often overly represented in the sample design (Barthelemy, 1988).

The basic assumption of the activity rate method is that there are long term trends in the rates mentioned, which depend on the level of economic development and on the type of economic structure. These two elements are inseparably connected because structural changes induced by differential gains in production technology initiate growth and gradually also economic development.[4] Thus countries at a low level of development have typically high activity rates and almost all working age persons are included in the production process. Economic development and growth make it possible for a section of the working age population to stop working and turn to other activities which expand their quality of living, but are not considered economic activities. In a historical context, this period corresponds with the period of industrialization, with the greatest expansion in activities like industry and mining, construction, transport and communication, etc. and with the decrease of agricultural activities. Decrease in the share accounted for by agricultural activities also results in a significant drop in activity rates and, consequently, today the countries with a relatively high share of agriculture have, *ceteris paribus*, higher activity rates. The post-industrial period is characterized by a drop in industrial activities and the development of tertiary and quaternary activities. These structural changes, which take place on a higher level of development, are followed by higher activity rates. Graph 11.1 shows the trends in activity rates in Croatia from 1971 to 1996.

A gradual drop of activity rates was noted up to 1981, followed by a small increase up to 1991, which would most probably have continued had the recession not occurred in the mid 80s and then been followed by the war. This was the period when Croatia was slowly entering the period of de-industrialization, with the simultaneous development of the tertiary sector. These changes increased the specific activity rates of women, which contributed to the increase in total activity rates. However, instead of growing after 1991, activity rates showed a constant drop and it seems that a pronounced contraction of the labor force is currently taking place. Statistical data from official sources indicate that both a drop in employment and a drop in unemployment causes the decrease in the labor force. Parallel movement of employment and unemployment in the same direction is theoretically unacceptable, but there is empirical evidence to show that in periods of entering or exiting from recession that is exactly what happens. In the recovery phase, with the provision of new jobs, the unemployed find employment. Also, that part of the population that has a certain connection with the labor market becomes active, but leaves it again in a period of recession. Those people, called discouraged workers, either find employment or register as unemployed persons with the Employment Agency, which causes employment during this period to increase at the same time as unemployment. The opposite situation is found when entering a period of recession and especially when recession lasts for a more extensive period and vacancies are rare, as is the situation in Croatia today. Employment decreases and certain individuals withdraw from the unemployment register, because they do not really expect to find employment through the Employment Agency.[5] After an unsuccessful job search, they give up and withdraw from the official labor market. However, for many family breadwinners this only means the beginning of the search for jobs in the informal economy. The two segments of the labor market generate different labor costs, security of employment, employment durability and rights that can be realized on the basis of employment. A considerably lower level of protection, but sometimes a higher price of labor in the unofficial economy is counterbalanced by lower incomes, but also security of employment and guaranteed rights in the official economy.

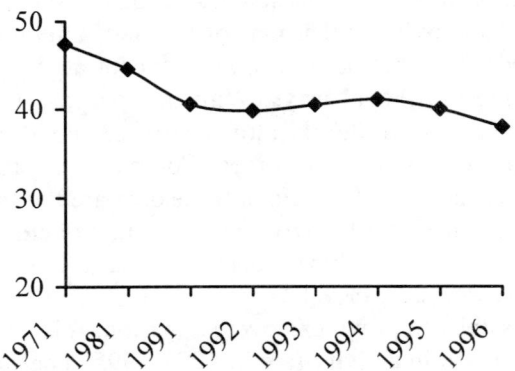

Graph 11.1 1971-1996 Activity (%)

Source: Statistical Yearbook, selected years; for the period after 1991, data obtained from Health Insurance Fund (Zavod za zdravstveno osiguranje) for employment and from the Employment Agency (Zavod za zapošljavanje) for unemployment, which, when combined, give the labor force.

Aside from this behavior of participants in the labor market, the drastic decrease of the labor force in Croatia can partly be attributed to the inadequacy of official statistics. The existing instruments for data collection on employment are largely organized to the monitor changes that used to occur in the former social, and now state-owned, sector. For example, monthly data on employment collected by the Central Bureau of Statistics are obtained from a 70 per cent sample of all those employed in every branch of activity. The sample was formed by systematically monitoring companies with the largest number of workers in order to satisfy the percentage required while monitoring the smallest number of companies. It is this procedure that is the cause of underestimation of the employment rate in the country, because the largest companies discharge the largest number of workers and new jobs are found in small companies which are completely outside the scope of official monitoring. What we have today is an excellent statistical picture of a system falling apart, and very bad monitoring of new trends on the labor market.

As well as having these shortcomings, official sources do not monitor employment in the police force, the army or the private agricultural sector. Comparison with other sources reveals that approximately 400,000 employed workers are missing from the official statistics. If we try to use these data without any adjustments, the difference as a whole could very well be ascribed to the unofficial economy, which would not be incorrect with regard to the *B2* definition mentioned earlier. Using other sources of information, however, we have reduced that part of the unofficial economy referring to unregistered economic activities and concentrated primarily on legal activities performed in illegal ways. With this purpose in mind, we decided to use the data from the Health Insurance Fund (*Zavod za zdravstveno osiguranje*) on its active insurees. Compared to other sources (Pension Fund, Central Bureau of Statistics), these data are the highest and, in spite of some double counting which to a certain extent overestimates the number of employed workers, we have decided to use this source as the maximum number of employed workers.[6]

Regardless of possible employment overestimation, this source of information shows a decrease in activity rate in 1991-1995. The same period was also characterized by a fall in GDP per capita of 11 per cent in the 1991-1992 period and of 0.85 per cent in 1992-1993. The next two years showed an increase of 0.6 and 1.7 per cent respectively. The GDP trend was followed by changes in employment. From 1991 to 1992, employment fell by 9.3 per cent and by 9.5 per cent in the following year. During 1994-1995, the number employed increased by 2.2 per cent and in 1995-1996 by 0.08 per cent. During the whole period, except for the last year, the number of unemployed workers also decreased, which combined to account for the decrease of the labor force up to 1994. After that period, the number of active workers increased. The activity rate as calculated below shows an increase only in the last year monitored and amounts to 4/5 of the 1991 rate level.

The theoretical assumption we introduced in the calculation of the volume of the unofficial economy was that the decrease in the development level resulted in an increase, and not a decrease, of activity rates, as the official statistics might lead us to believe. The difference between the activity rate as it was in 1991 and that measured during the next five years may be considered an indirect measure of the unofficial economy in Croatia.

The activity rate can be defined as the relation between persons who are or want to be employed and all persons of working age:

$$S_{ACT} = \frac{(\text{employed} + \text{unemployed population})}{\text{working age population}}$$

The sum of employed and unemployed workers is synonymous with the labor force, total labor supply or total active population. Alternately, activity rates can be represented by the ratio of labor supply and total population, which is what we are doing in this study. The main reason for doing this lies in the fact that it is much more difficult to estimate trends in the working age population than in the total population.

In order to measure total labor supply between 1991 and 1996, we estimated the change of total population in the country and multiplied the figure obtained by the activity rate from 1991. Table 11.1 shows all the aggregates that have been used.

The de facto active population (DE FACTO ACT) was obtained by adding the numbers of employed and unemployed workers. Besides the already mentioned problems with the number of employed workers obtained from this source, it should also be mentioned that the data on unemployed workers are very questionable. However, without a proper labor force survey, there are no instruments of sufficient quality to demonstrate the real situation.[7]

Table 11.1 Elements for estimation of employment in the unofficial economy

	1991	1992	1993	1994	1995	1996
Total population	4,499,049	4,495,289	4,492,469	4,490,589	4,488,710	4,479,733
De facto active	2,132,492	2,002,191	1,823,281	1,788,209	1,817,659	1,841,614
Activity rate	47.4	44.54	40.59	39.82	40.49	41.1
Hyp. active (SACT91=const.)	2,132,492	2,130,767	2,129,430	2,128,539	2,127,649	2,123,393
Hyp.active - De facto active.	0	-128,570	-306,133	-340,311	-309972	-285,359
% De facto active	0	6.42	16.79	19.03	17.05	15.53
Unemployed	227,399	274,972	259,454	245,694	241,484	264,124
Total employed	1,905,093	1,727,219	1,563,827	1,542,515	1,576,175	1,577,490
Economic units	1,555,458	1,395,401	1,253,885	1,217,936	1,238,900	1,228,663
Crafts and independent professions	128,255	121,227	126,868	142,983	166,638	182,388
Private agriculture production	221,380	210,591	183,074	181,596	170,637	166,439
1990 GDP constant prices	221,494.9	196,878.5	195,198.7	196,383	199,655.7	196,348.6

* Economic units are understood to be all companies regardless of their ownership, institutions, trade companies, firms and institutes. Special attention has been drawn here to crafts, independent professions and private agricultural producers.

Note: *GDP in 1990 constant prices was calculated for the Central Bureau of Statistics by the Economic Institute Zagreb. Data on employment were obtained from the Health Insurance Fund and refer to the situation in March of the years represented. They include some categories of the employed which are not covered by the Central Bureau of Statistics data. This choice has resulted in bringing into the open, in the visible zone, private agricultural producers, police, defense and many small enterprises which are not statistically monitored by the Central Bureau of Statistics.*

The number of active population in period t calculated by applying the activity rate from the $t-1$ period to the total population in the country is called hypothetical active population (*HYPACT*). This calculation was based on the estimate of total population from the 1994 Statistical Yearbook. Estimates for 1995 and 1996 were made on the basis of natural increase of population. Such estimations are very delicate, especially in the post-war period, because demographic methods that do not take into account population migrations are not as effective as demographic methods in peace time. The assumption here is that the total number of population has not changed significantly and that the number of those who came and those who left during the last 5 years is approximately the same. The credibility of this assumption will be tested and checked against the results of the first labor force survey which is to be conducted in November 1996.

Comparison of the de facto and hypothetically active population resulted in an employment measure of the unofficial economy, which was then compared with the de facto active population. As can be seen, the share of employed population in this part of the economy increased from 6.42 per cent in 1992 to 16.42 per cent in 1993. In 1994 it rose to 19.03 per cent of the active population. After that, it started to decrease and this year it dropped to below the 1993 level, to 15.3 per cent.

The growth of the unofficial economy is on one hand caused by a series of bankruptcies in the 1991-1993 period and by the inability of the private sector to generate a sufficient number of jobs in the official economy.

Graph 11.2 reveals an interesting correlation between the number of persons employed in the official economy (empl.), the unemployed population (unempl.) and the population employed in the unofficial economy (unoff. ec.). First, unemployment is positively correlated with employment in the official economy (with the correlation coefficient of 0.75). In the period when the drop of employment in the official sector is greatest, unemployment also drops. Second, employment in the unofficial sector is strongly and negatively correlated with employment in the official economy (correlation coefficient of -0.991) and negatively with unemployment (correlation coefficient of -0.82 per cent). This fact clearly shows that the unofficial economy is a shock-absorber for changes occurring in the official economy: when employment or unemployment increases, the unofficial economy decreases and vice versa.

This conclusion is of great importance for those responsible for economic policy because it brings into direct connection the visible and the invisible economic sphere. In other words, increase of employment in the official sector causes the volume of the unofficial economy to drop, while repressive methods can only lead to an ever increasing withdrawal into underground activities. According to this, repressive measures are not enough to reduce the unofficial economy, but should be accompanied by other economic policy measures aimed at stimulating employment.

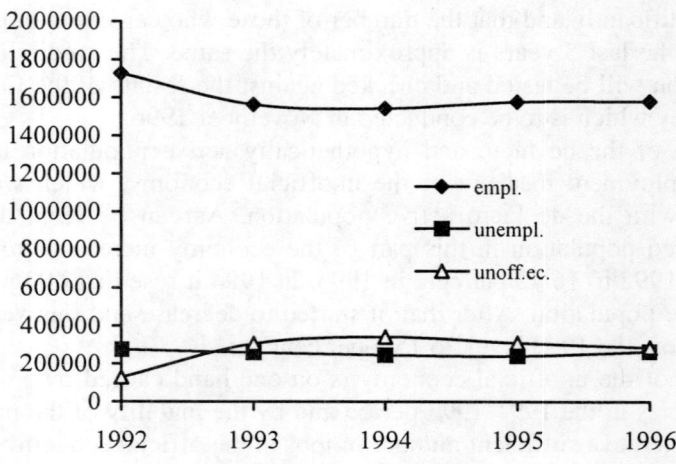

Graph 11.2 Changes in Employment, Unemployment and the Unofficial Economy

Estimation of Employment in the Unofficial Economy by Labor Force Survey

The labor force survey is a good information source on employment in the unofficial economy due to the fact that the measurement unit is a household and all the individuals in it. This brings the study into a context where individuals make their decisions about entering the labor market and where the pre-work and post-work contingents and employed, unemployed and inactive population are actually present. A household is, therefore, an ideal source for studying all events, not only in the labor market, but in all fields influencing the life of an individual.

At the end of 1995, a pilot survey of the labor force was conducted in four counties, covering a total sample of 1,492 households. Its results will be used in a limited way. In other words, they cannot be applied to the whole of Croatia, referring to the territory of the four counties surveyed[8] only. The relatively large sample will make the use of the survey results possible in calculating specific ratios and relationships between various categories and not total values of variables.

The survey makes it possible to gain an insight into the behavior of certain population categories that have never been the subject of monitoring in administrative, official statistics before. The participation of these categories in the labor market becomes more significant during periods of a decrease in the standard of living. These categories also represent an area where the attempt at self-employment is rather pronounced. International standards, which understand employment as work for at least one hour in the reference week, and their application in the survey will point to just these, so far invisible, categories. The reasons for focusing our attention on them are numerous. These categories operate on the margins of the formal sector; working hours are longer, and the effort made is more strenuous than usual, yet income, in spite of the labor involved, is insufficient for normal living. This is only one side of this kind of work. At the same time there are also some individuals who, through their multiple activities, achieve a high standard of living and do not belong to the marginal strata of the society.

The survey results are shown in the following Tables. It should be stressed that the calculation did not make any use of the data on private agricultural producers' activity, which was included in Table 11.1, due to the fact that it is not part of the unregistered or the unofficial economy, being adequately covered by the data on the health insurance of the producers in question.

The target categories selected for the survey are:

- persons having an additional activity besides their main job;
- unpaid family workers on the family land, craft enterprise, independent profession or company;
- persons engaged in various activities in order to earn their means of sustenance, like shoe cleaning, baby-sitting, offering various services like transcription, teaching languages or school subjects, selling their own or other people's products in markets or working as travelling salesmen. The common name for this category is own-account workers. Their activity is characterized by the fact that it ceases when they stop performing it and that their production equipment is very limited;
- persons whose prevailing status is different from the status they presently have, mainly including housewives, students, pupils, retired persons and persons who do not usually work and persons who cannot be classified into any of the above mentioned categories.

The first estimation method used in this study did not allow us to estimate the first of the above mentioned categories, which is of primary interest here. Some insight was shed on the rest of the categories by the population census which also numbered unpaid family workers and own-account workers. All the categories surveyed worked at least one hour during the reference week (November 1995) or were absent from work to which they could return.

Table 11.2 Persons employed in the unofficial economy, total and by occupation (labor force survey)

		\multicolumn{9}{c}{Major groups}
		1	2	3	4	5	6	7	8	9
Total employment	100									
Unofficial economy	25.79									
Unofficial economy	100	100	100	100	100	100	100	100	100	100
Employed workers with an additional job	24.20	6.23	60.00	41.67	29.17	10.00	22.22	19.14	33.33	33.33	33.33
Unpaid family workers	39.70	10.23	0.00	0.00	16.67	20.00	16.67	58.59	4.76	16.67	13.33
Other independent business activities	8.90	2.30	0.00	25.00	25.00	20.00	22.22	0.78	42.86	16.67	13.33
Housewives, students, unemployed workers, retired persons	27.20	7.02	40.00	33.33	29.17	50.00	38.89	24.15	19.05	33.33	40.00

Explanation of major groups of occupation according to the National Classification of Occupation based on the ISCO-88 international European classification:
  1 – Directors and managers of economic and similar organisations
  2 – Scientists and similar top experts
  3 – Technical and similar experts
  4 – Clerks
  5 – Salesmen and other service occupations
  6 – Occupations in agriculture, forestry and fisheries
  7 – Production services and individual products production
  8 – Production machine operators, transport machinery and vehicle operators and product assemblers
  9 – Elementary occupations

Table 11.2 shows work frequencies in the unofficial economy according to occupation at the highest aggregate level. According to this source, the level of the unofficial economy is 25.79 per cent of total employment. Among the categories, 6.23 per cent of the population surveyed are engaged in additional business activities, 10.23 per cent are unpaid family workers, 2.3 per cent are own-account workers and 7.02 per cent are housewives, students, retired persons and usually unemployed persons. The employment composition in the unofficial economy reads as follows: 39.7

per cent are unpaid family workers, 27.2 per cent are prevailingly inactive groups, 24.2 per cent are persons engaged in additional business activities and 8.9 per cent are own-account workers.

The employment composition in the unofficial economy shows that type 1, covering directors, managers and foremen, consists of employed workers with additional jobs in 60 per cent of cases and of usually inactive groups. The reason for this can be found in the fact that prevailingly inactive groups most frequently find self-employment in family businesses or as own-account workers. By employment status, however, they are treated as being equal to the managers of the largest companies.

Type 2 covers almost all the occupations for which a university qualification is required, such as engineers, architects, economists, system engineers, teachers, scientists, etc. Within this occupation group, employment in the unofficial economy is found mostly in the form of additional employment (41.67 per cent), but the work of prevailingly inactive groups (33.3 per cent) and own-account workers (25 per cent) can also be found here.

Unpaid family workers are typically characterized by their employment in occupation Type 6, i.e., in agriculture, forestry and fisheries (58.59 per cent). They appear, however, also as clerks, sales persons and other service occupation workers and as production machines and transport devices operators. They do not typically engage in activities requiring higher education or highly skilled working ability.

Own-account workers are mostly engaged in Type 7 occupations, i.e., production services and individual product production. The greatest variety of activities is covered by this category as, for example, making various wax, wood or textile products.

It is interesting to notice that housewives, students and retired persons are the most numerous in Type 7 occupations, covering clerks (59 per cent), and the jobs they engage in refer to office and clerical occupations.

Table 11.3 offers another insight into employment in the unofficial economy. It deals with the status in employment, in other words, whether a person is self-employed, an employee or an unpaid family worker. Self-employed persons have been represented as owners or co-owners of companies, crafts and trades, independent professionals and freelancers on one hand and, and as own-account workers on the other. Employees are distinguished by the ownership sector in which they are employed, and unpaid family workers stand by themselves. We cross-referenced status in informal employment with the individuals' activity status.

Table 11.3 Status in employment of persons working in the unofficial economy (per cent)

	Total	Additional job	House-wives, students	Unpaid family workers	Own-account activities
Owners of companies, crafts enterprises and similar professions	21.33	14.14	65.52	0.00	0.00
Workers employed in state-owned or mixed sector	17.54	67.68	6.03	0.00	0.00
Workers employed in the private sector	11.14	14.14	28.45	0.00	0.00
Unpaid family workers	40.76	3.03	0.00	100.00	0.00
Own-account workers	9.24	1.01	0.00	0.00	100.00
Total	100.00	100.00	100.00	100.00	100.00

Among persons working in the unofficial economy, the most numerous are unpaid family workers (40.76 per cent). This group is followed by the category of owners or co-owners of companies and independent professions or agricultural holdings with 21.3 per cent. Employees working predominantly in the state-owned or mixed ownership sector make up 17.54 per cent, and 11.14 percent are engaged in additional activities in the private sector. The remaining 9.24 per cent are own-account workers. If we want to compare the status in employment of these groups, we shall see that 67.7 per cent of persons having additional jobs are employees in the state-owned or mixed ownership sector and 14.14 per cent are company owners or co-owners. On the other hand, of predominantly inactive groups, 65 per cent are company owners, followed by persons employed in the private sector (28.5 per cent). Only 1.01 per cent of persons having additional jobs are own-account workers and 3.03 per cent in the same business activity are unpaid family workers.

This study has also attempted to show employment structure in the unofficial economy by sector of activity. However, the results have, for several reasons, turned out to be unreliable. One of the main reasons is the composition of individuals answering the questions about their additional activities. It seems that persons whose additional jobs are in agriculture were much more ready to talk about their additional activities than the interviewees in cities. This would indicate that over 70 per cent of persons employed in the unofficial economy was engaged in agriculture, forestry and fisheries, which is highly unlikely. A conclusion that persons engaged in black market activities tended to withhold information is probably much closer to truth, which has consequently left them under-represented in the survey, and this fact has considerably influenced the employment composition by activity.

Concluding Remarks on Measuring Employment in the Unofficial Economy by Using Labor Market Data

Two methods of measuring employment in the unofficial economy have been used in this study, in both cases using labor market data. Both methods have some advantages and some disadvantages. The method using historical activity rates has the advantage of not depending so much on the existing data on the number of the active population, which is generally considered unreliable. On the other hand, it relies on estimations of total population based on the demographic method of natural population increase, completely disregarding migration that took place during the last five years. According to this method, the number of persons employed in the unofficial economy varied between 6 per cent and 20 per cent of total labor force.

The labor force survey took into consideration categories that were not present in the official statistics and, combined, they made up as much as 25 per cent of the labor force in 1995. We are more inclined to accept the higher rate, largely because it takes into consideration population categories which are usually not covered by statistical monitoring and whose activity has increased several times over during the years of recession and war. The results of the next survey conducted a year later (November this year) will make possible much more reliable conclusions based on the same method. The survey will also offer more elements from which to draw conclusions on other characteristics of unrecorded work.

Coming back to our original questions, we should now be able to answer the question whether the presence of the unofficial economy at the present economic moment in Croatia is useful or harmful. The existence of the unofficial economy has both positive and negative aspects, both from the standpoint of economic units and from the standpoint of the state, which sets the rules of conduct. The unofficial economy is an advantage for economic units only up to the point when social underdevelopment becomes detrimental to individual wealth. Anarchy and merciless competition introduce a high degree of uncertainty in business operations. Also, it is very possible that a good quality supply cannot be maintained for longer periods of time in the absence of proper rules of conduct. For the state, on the other hand, the unofficial economy is an unavoidable evil in periods when various groups are below the poverty line, and would otherwise have to depend on the state for their means of sustenance in a system with a strict set of rules. By allowing black market activities, the state 'allows' these groups to take care of themselves.

Another advantage of the unofficial economy for economic units as well as for the state is its role as a 'point of entry' into the official economy. This argument rather resembles a protective policy towards the newly developed domestic industries that are temporarily protected from competition from abroad and is based on the hypothesis that the level of competition is higher in the unofficial than in the official economy. Economic units that manage to cross over from the unofficial into the official economy are the most successful ones and those responsible for economic policy have an interest in retaining such a filter.

However, regardless of some momentary advantages that the unofficial economy might offer to all employed in the economy, in the long run it eventually becomes harmful for all parties concerned. From the standpoint of workers, black labor means uncertainty about their employment and income and the loss of their basic rights. Resorting to black labor is more than anything else a necessity in a period when long-term interests are sacrificed for short-term gains. The loss of its fiscal revenues puts the very existence of the state in question, and by letting the unofficial economy flourish, the state loses its legitimacy and its raison d'être. Practical problems, however, always seem to bring about their own solutions and periods of stagnation seem to call for the establishment of a balance between the needs of the state and the needs of its citizens. The adjustment mechanism is the unofficial economy.

If the unofficial economy indeed *is* a negative phenomenon, how can it be reduced? The solution may be found in the statement that a state is as rich as its citizens. By giving up its income from the segment where sources of saving and investment are generated, the state could be a key factor in stimulating growth in general. In other words, a reduction of income and other taxes levied by the state would mean that a larger share of gross wages would be reward for the work performed. The fiscal burden can be reduced only if a reform of pension and health insurance is successfully carried out, which would make possible a gradual transition to types of insurance which would largely be under the control and care of the insured themselves.

These changes would stimulate employment in the official sector, or they would legalize black labor. Checks by inspection services should also be more frequent to make people understand that they cannot remain undiscovered any more if engaged in black market activities.

The only real remedy, however, against the flourishing of the unofficial economy is the growth of the economy itself and the development of society as a whole. Providing new jobs in productive activities will render more than one aspect of the unofficial economy needless. The need for additional jobs will disappear and, consequently, an individual's productivity in his or her main occupation will increase. Also, the number of persons working exclusively in the unofficial economy will decrease. Wage increases and higher secondary income transfers will reduce labor market pressure by prevailingly inactive groups and groups of persons who have been forced to work in the black market through economic necessity.

Appendix: The Unofficial Economy and Sectors of Economic Activity

Similar procedures were applied in estimating the unofficial economy in sectors of economic activity as were used for the total economy. The number of employed[9] and unemployed[10] persons by sectors of economic activity, combine at a certain moment to form the active population in a given sector. The activity rates for each sector were calculated by dividing the active population in a certain sector by the total number of the population in the country. The activity rate in time period t (1993) was applied to the total population in $t+1$ and the activity rate in time period $t+1$ was applied to the total population of the $t+2$ period. The difference between the de facto active and the hypothetically active population indicates the direction of structural adjustment in a given sector. If the hypothetically active population is bigger than de facto active one, a decrease of activity rate has occurred. In the opposite case, the activity rate has increased. The activity rate trend depends mostly on differential changes in employment and unemployment. In certain sectors, employment drops at the same time as unemployment and the activity rate decreases. In other activities, both employment and unemployment increase and, consequently, the activity rate increases. In other cases, opposite trends in employment and unemployment occur, which is the theoretically expected trend, and the direction of change of activity rates will depend on the relative fall or rise in employment and unemployment.

The graphs given below show several typical cases. The *A* Type represents sectors where the fall of activity rate decreased in both periods, resulting in labor supply reduction as workers attempted to find employment in other activities, either in the official or in the unofficial economy.

In Type *A* activities, the activity rate decreases and the hypothetically active population is larger than the de facto active one. The data shown in Appendix 1 indicate that both the number of unemployed persons who used to work in this sector of economic activity and the number of employed persons decreased simultaneously in the 1993-1995 period. Since the number of persons employed in industry and mining in the period mentioned was smaller by 23,083 employed persons, while the number of unemployed persons dropped by 5,901, these numbers, when added up, indicate the potential participants in the unregistered economy. Table 11.1, showing total decreases and increases of employment and unemployment for the two periods can be used for rough calculation of the level of all activities. In the 1993-94 period, employment dropped by 324,134 persons, while in the same period only 11,102 persons found employment. The resulting difference of 21,311 persons, who did not manage to find a job, partly joined the unemployed, but only 2,683 persons. This means that in the same period the remaining 18,628 persons joined those who disappeared from the Employment Agency register, there being 7,501 of them. This results in a total number of 16,129 persons as potential black labor candidates. The number of retired persons who did not seek any further employment should however, reduce this number, but unfortunately, such data are not available.

During the following period (1994-1995), employment decreased in certain sectors by 28,172 persons, but it increased in other activities by 45,679 persons. That increase was sufficient to absorb all the persons left unemployed from the previous period. At the same time, an increase in unemployment of 2,997 persons was also discerned. One of the reasons for this favorable trend in employment is the fact that the information source used also covers persons employed in the army and police force, who accounted for a major part of employment in 1995 when the military action *Storm (Oluja)* took place. In 1996 a decrease was recorded in employment and an increase in unemployment, which coincided with the process of demobilization.

Activity rate increase was noticed in sectors of type *B*. In most sectors, it took place in the 1994-1995 period, while the activity rate decrease was still present in the previous period. As the graphs indicate, all sectors represented show that the de facto active population was larger than the hypothetically active one, at least in the second period.

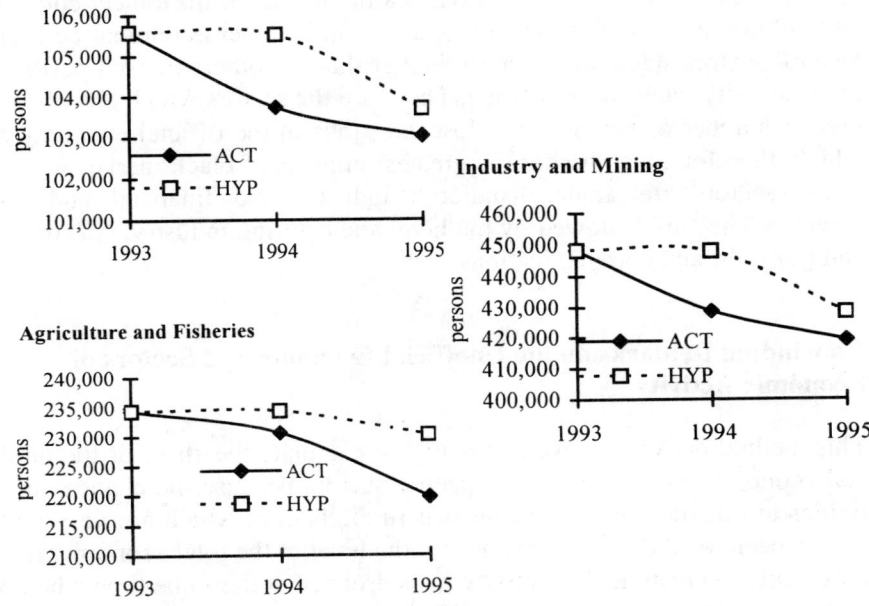

Graph 11.3 Type A activities

Table 11.4 Total changes in employment and unemployment

	1993-94	1994-95
Employment decrease	-32413	-28172
Employment increase	11102	45679
Difference	-21311	17507
Unemployment decrease	-7501	-5078
Unemployment increase	2683	8075
Difference	-4818	2997

*Source: Employment - Health Insurance Fund.
Unemployment - Employment Agency.*

It seems safe to conclude that employment, both in the official and the unofficial economy, takes place in the sectors that show an increase in activity rates because they reflect total labor demand.

It is also obvious that black market labor cannot develop so freely in sectors such as state administration, health and social insurance, education and culture and water management as it can in other economic activities. Several sectors stand significantly higher than all others in both periods as far as activity rates are concerned. These are the sectors which absorbed the greater number of persons who lost their jobs in the official economy and which, therefore, also harbor the greatest number of black market workers. These sectors are: trade, handicraft industry and financial and other services. They are followed by the hotel and catering industry, construction and transport and communications.

Concluding Remarks on the Unofficial Economy and Sectors of Economic Activity

This method does not make it possible to calculate the share of the unofficial economy accounted for by specific sectors because the changes in activities are themselves caused by structural changes which are very turbulent, especially at the present time.. At the level of the total economy, it was unrealistic to presume that activity rates dropped at the same time when *per capita* income dropped. The same, however, cannot be claimed at the level of specific activities because it is impossible to tell whether a particular activity share in the social product is going to increase or decrease. For that reason, the estimates in this study should be complemented by estimates based on macroeconomics aggregates by sector. The method used in this study made it possible to identify those activities which registered an increase in activity rates and, among them, those where employment in the unofficial economy is greatest, thus allowing future studies to concentrate mainly on them.

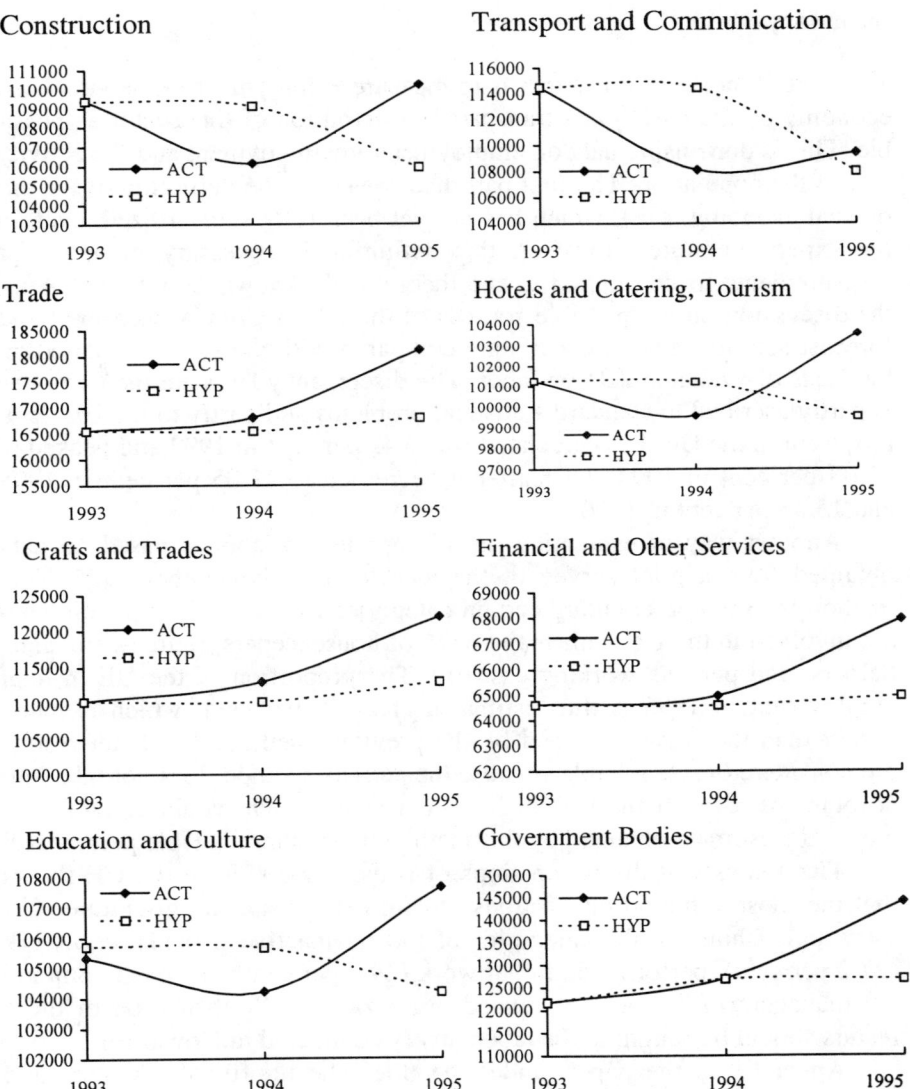

Graph 11.4 Sectors of Economic Activities - Type *B*

Source: Active population - Health Insurance Fund, Employment Agency, Hypothetically active population - Calculated on the basis of the activity rate in the previous period and estimation by the author of the total population for 1993, 1994 and 1995.

Summary

The central theme of this paper is to measure employment in the unofficial economy on the basis of as transparent a definition of this sector as possible. This is done using data on employment, unemployment and the activity rate of the population. The first part discusses only the definition of the unofficial economy (UE), which has not yet been fully standardized, even in the expert literature. However, this definition is necessary in order for measurements to be applied to the theoretically known population. After the discussion on the possible sources of the UE in Croatia, measured and forecast activity rates in Croatia are compared with the rates calculated on the basis of available data on labor. The discrepancy between the two rates is partly ascribed to standard statistical problems and partly to the UE: Employment in the UE thus calculated was 6.42 per cent in 1992 and peaked at 19.03 per cent in 1994. Thereafter it decreased to 17.05 per cent in 1995 and 15.53 per cent in 1996.

Another way of estimating the UE applied to labor is based on data obtained from a pilot survey of the workforce in November 1995. This method is based on counting certain categories of the work of people who are involved in the UE. This is the work of housekeepers, retirees, students, helpers, and persons working casually. The proportion of the UE in total employment in 1995 is thus estimated at 25.79 per cent, which is much higher than the figure obtained by the previous method. The latter results are considered more reliable because the activity method does not take into account the level of the UE in the initial year, which would certainly increase the estimate obtained by this method by an unpredictable percentage.

The analysis of the occupations of persons working in the UE shows that the most common occupations among helpers are in agriculture, forestry and fishing. In the categories of mostly inactive persons who work (27.2 per cent), perform additional work (24.2 per cent), the most common are managers in business or related organizations. Confirmation of these results should be sought in the labor survey conducted in November 1996.

Appendix to the paper, under the title 'The unofficial economy and economic activities', attempts on the basis of the rate of activity method to measure the size of the UE in individual branches. Two major groups of activities are identified according to trends in the rate of activities: those in which the rate of activity is increasing and those in which the rate of activity is decreasing. The assumption is that the UE is present in those branches where the rate of activity is increasing. The rate of activity is decreasing in the manufacturing industry, mining, agriculture, fishing, health and social insurance. On the other hand, the rate of activity is increasing in construction, transport, trade, independent trades, etc. In fact, it is impossible to reach conclusions using this method because it is a difficult to ascertain whether the change in the rate of activity is due to structural changes or increases and decreases of employment in the unofficial economy. The employment data obtained from the thorough survey of the workforce conducted in 1996 will be much more indicative in this respect.

Table 11.5 Data on activity composition, social product and labor productivity by sector of economic activities

	1993	1994	1995	1993-1994	1994-1995
Industry and Mining					
Act.	448214	428770	419230	−19444	−9540
Hyp. act.		448161	428223		−19938
ACT-HYP		−19391	−8993		
Unemployed	56939	52280	51038	−4659	−1242
Employed	391275	376490	368192	−14785	−8298
GDP	41211.3	40134.3	40224.1	−1077	89.8
GDP/ Employed	109.5	109.0	109.2	−0.46	0.24
S(ACT)	9.98	9.54	9.33	−0.43	−0.21
Agriculture and Fisheries					
Act.	234406	230623	219678	−3783	−0945
Hyp. act.		234408	230270		−4137.9
ACT-HYP		−3785	−10592		
Unemployed	6273	6798	7282	525	484
Employed	228133	223825	212396	−4308	−11429
GDP	19124.1	18505.3	18635.4	−618.8	130.1
GDP/ Employed	83.83	82.68	87.74	−1.15	5.06
S(ACT)	5.22	5.13	4.89	−0.08	−0.24
Forestry					
Act.	11254	11598	11869	344	271
Hyp. act.		11264	11581		317.00
ACT-HYP		334	288		
Unemployed	850	992	1034	142	42
Employed	10404	10606	10835	202	229
GDP	1909.6	2149	1988.3	239.4	−160.7
GDP/ Employed	180.05	198.34	183.51	18.29	−14.83
S(ACT)	0.25	0.258	0.264	0.01	0.01

240 Underground Economies in Transition

	1993	1994	1995	1993-94	1994-95
Water Management					
Act.	5072	4650	4912	−422	262
Hyp. act.		5074	4668		−406
ACT-HYP		−424	244		
Unemployed	306	323	341	17	18
Employed	4766	4327	4571	−439	244
GDP	774.8	780.3	785.9	5.5	5.6
GDP/ Employed	179.06	170.71	171.93	−8.355	1.225
S(ACT)	0.113	0.104	0.109	−0.009	0.005
Construction					
Act.	109377	106151	110233	−3226	4082
Hyp. act.		109121	105934		−3187
ACT-HYP		−2970	4299		
Unemployed	12937	12982	13402	45	420
Employed	96440	93169	96831	−3271	3662
GDP	5073.5	5048	5166.7	−25.5	118.7
GDP/Employed	65.59	52.13	53.36	−13.46	1.23
S(ACT)	2.43	2.36	2.46	−0.07	0.10
Transport and Communications					
Act.	114487	108100	109429	−6387	1329
Hyp. act.		114439	107998		−6441
ACT-HYP		−6339	1431		
Unemployed	8626	8411	8253	−215	−158
Employed	105861	99689	101176	−6172	1487
GDP	12100.4	12112.7	12447.5	12.3	334.8
GDP/ Employed	133.78	119.72	123.03	−14.06	3.31
S(ACT)	2.548	2.406	2.436	−0.14	0.03
Trade					
Act.	165436	168019	181185	2583	13166
Hyp. act.		165367	167878		2511.0
ACT-HYP		2652	13307		
Unemployed	14003	15957	19835	1954	3878
Employed	151433	152062	161350	629	9288
GDP	28775.6	29602.5	31957.9	826.9	2355.4
GDP/ Employed	211.21	183.47	198.07	−27.74	14.60
S(ACT)	3.683	3.740	4.033	0.06	0.29

	1993	1994	1995	1993-94	1994-95
Hotels and Restaurant Industry					
Act.	101253	99556	103564	−1697	4008
Hyp. act.		101211	99515		−1696
ACT-HYP		−1655	4049		
Unemployed.	22697	22190	22240	−507	50
Employed	78556	77366	81324	−1190	3958
GDP	5466.6	7209.1	6476.7	1742.5	−732.4
GDP/ Employed	101.60	88.65	79.64	−12.95	−9.01
S(ACT)	2.254	2.217	2.307	−0.04	0.09
Crafts and Trades					
Act.	110234	112993	121918	2759	8925
Hyp. act.		110188	112946		2758
ACT-HYP		2805	8972		
Unemployed	12442	12304	14047	−138	1743
Employed	97792	100689	107871	2897	2897
GDP	8752.2	9168.1	9624.9	415.9	456.8
GDP/ Employed	352.09	84.99	89.23	−267.1	4.2
S(ACT)	2.454	2.516	2.716	0.1	0.2
Housing and Other Public Utility Services					
Act.	29370	28591	29681	−779	1090
Hyp. act.		29368.5	28593.1		−775.4
ACT-HYP		−777	1088		
Unemployed	2644	2557	2768	−87	211
Employed	26726	26034	26913	−692	879
GDP	23828.5	23895.7	24048.5	67.2	152.8
GDP/ Employed	915.28	887.89	893.56	−27.397	5.678
S(ACT)	0.654	0.637	0.661	−0.017	0.025
Financial and Other Services					
Act.	64609	64967	67948	358	2981
Hyp. act.		64574.7	64951.6		377.0
ACT-HYP		392	2996		
Unemployed	3626	3499	3641	−127	142
Employed.	60983	61468	64307	485	2839
GDP	7683.8	7383.9	7632.2	−299.9	248.3
GDP/ Employed.	128.11	114.82	118.68	−13.28	3.86
S(ACT)	1.438	1.447	1.514	0.01	0.07

	1993	1994	1995	1993-94	1994-95
Education and Culture					
Act.	105331	104208	107672	−1123	3464
Hyp. act.		105663.6	104183.0		−1480.6
ACT-HYP		−1456	3489		
Unemployed	5639	4177	5264	−1462	1087
Employed	99692	100031	102408	339	2377
GDP	15379.9	15462.8	15366.8	82.9	−96
GDP/ Employed	155.66	150.99	150.05	−4.67	−0.94
S(ACT)	2.345	2.321	2.399	−0.02	0.08
Health Care and Social Services					
Act.	105586	103724	103032	−1862	−692
Hyp. act.		105529	103689		−1840
ACT-HYP		−1805	−657		
Unemployed	6137	5831	5509	−306	−322
Employed	99449	97893	97523	−1556	−370
GDP	14689.9	14489.1	14228.2	−200.8	−260.9
GDP/ Employed	150.06	148.57	145.90	−1.49	−2.68
S(ACT)	2.350	2.310	2.295	−0.04	−0.01
Government Bodies					
Act.	121729	126972	144118	5243	17146
Hyp. act.		126814	126919		105
ACT-HYP		158	17199		
Unemployed	9412	8105	7432	−1307	−673
Employed	112317	118867	136686	6550	17819
GDP	10428.7	10442.4	11072.5	13.7	630.1
GDP/ Employed	87.73	76.40	81.01	−11.337	4.610
S(ACT)	2.824	2.828	3.210	0.004	0.382

Note: Activity rates are expressed with regard to total population for the given year.

Source: - Employed - Health Insurance Fund *(March 1993, 1994, 1995).*
 - Unemployed - Employment Agency Yearbook, *same years.*
 - GDP - *estimate, Economic Institute.*

Notes

1 Transformation costs refer to the costs of basic factors of production in the process of economic development according to the neoclassical development model. These factors are combined in any one of the production function forms in which the variables are land, labor, capital and technology.

2   Transaction costs are the costs of exchange of goods produced.
3   The pilot survey was conducted by the Central Bureau of Statistics in October 1995, surveying 1,420 households in 4 counties (the City of Zagreb, Istria, Križevačko-koprivnička county and Splitsko-dalmatinska county).
4   Growth is understood to be exclusively the growth rate of GDP, while development is measured in terms of growth rates *per capita*. According to this, growth does not necessarily also bring about development, if there is great inequality in income distribution among the population, but it is its basic prerequisite.
5   When asked, during the ARS/95 pilot labor force survey, whether they believed that the Emplyment Agency could find a suitable job for them, 80 per cent of the unemployed workers answered 'No'. The Employment Agency Bulletin shows that approximately the same number of unemployed workers are struck off the records each month as the number of those do who find employment through the Agency. Since usually the names of those who do not report to the Agency for two consecutive months are struck off, it can be presumed that they either gave up because the time during which they were entitled to certain rights had expired or because they had found jobs elsewhere.
6   The Health Insurance Fund records exclusively employment in the official economy because every insured is registered by his employer or is the insurance holder himself. The advantage of this source is its coverage with regard to the official sources.
7   There are many categories of unemployed in Croatia today which do not correspond with international criteria defining unemployment. Besides the well known fact that some persons registered with the Employment Agency are in fact employed, there are also people registering with the Agency in order to obtain certain rights like pension and health insurance, social welfare, kindergarten free of charge, etc. On the other hand, there are unemployed persons who are not registered with the Agency. The results of the pilot survey conducted show the contingent of the real unemployed population as approximately 40 per cent smaller than the present one shown. This figure was obtained by comparison of the number of persons surveyed stating to be registered with the Employment Agency with the number of unemployed persons according to international criteria.
8   The City of Zagreb and the following three counties: Koprivničko-križevačka, Splitsko-dalmatinska and Istarska.
9   For the needs of this analysis, employment in crafts and trades was allocated to the relevant sector activity. This procedure is relatively incorrect because it makes possible monitoring crafts and trades only in four occupations and in four independent professions. For example, employment in trade and construction has not been represented separately in the data on crafts and trades and the greatest increase of employment was noticed exactly in these occupations.
10 The data on unemployment by activity for past years was available only for three years, which limits this analysis to the 1993-1995 period. Unemployed persons who were unemployed before that time were not included in the calculations.

References:

Barthelemy, P. (1988) The Macroeconomic Estimates of the Hidden Economy: A Critical Analysis, Review of Income and Wealth, series 34, no. 2. June.

Bićanić, I. (1987) The Inequality impact of the unofficial economy in Yugoslavia, in Allessandrini et. all. pp. 323-336.

Feige, E. L. (1990) Defining and Estimating Underground and Informal Economies: The New Institutional Economics Approach, World Development, vol. 18, no. 7, pp. 989-1002.

Feige, E. L. (1989) The Underground Economies: Tax Evasion and Information Distortion, Cambridge etc,. Cambridge University Press.

Franz, A. (1995) Schatzungen der Hidden Economy in Osterreich auf der Basis Officieller Statistiken, u Skolka 1995., pp. 83-89.

Portes, A., and Castells, M., Benton, L. (1989) The Informal Economy: Studies in Advances and Less Developed Countries, Baltimore and London, The Johns Hopkins University Press.

Skolka, J. (ed.) (1995) Die andere Wirtschaft: Schwartz und Do-it-yourself in Osterreich, Wien, Signum Verlag.

Wiles, P. (1987) The Second Economy, Its Definitional Problems, in Alessandrini, S. and Dallago, B.

12 Hidden Labor in Poland
MAŁGORZATA KAŁASKA* & JANUSZ WITKOWSKI**

The phenomenon of hidden labor is not directly statistically observable and so indirect methods should be used to estimate its size. A major source of information for the estimates in question are findings of the labor force surveys (LFS) which have been conducted by the Labor Division of the Central Statistical Office for three years. However the data on hidden labor provided by these surveys were limited to the total number of employed exclusively in the underground economy so it was necessary to carry out a special module survey. This was a survey in which participation in and income gained from hidden labor was analyzed from both the supply and the demand sides.

Introductory Remarks

One of the characteristic features of the contemporary labor market in Poland is the widespread use of hidden labor, often referred to as 'moonlighting', 'black jobs' or employment in the underground economy. The significant dimensions of the hidden labor phenomenon are not uniquely specific for Polish conditions. This phenomenon also appears, that is, in other countries, irrespective of the level of economic development and the living conditions of the population. In case of Poland we can speak, though, of essential changes in the features of this phenomenon in the period of systemic transformation.

From the point of view of an individual person, hidden labor may signify the only kind of professional activity or it may be additional to the registered (official) job. The second kind of hidden labor was quite common in the previous socio-economic system, providing additional source of income for low-paid employees (so-called 'side jobs'). This additional work in the underground economy also exists in our country now, in the period of formation of the bases for the market economy. There are, however, no

---

*   Head of the Labor Division in the Central Statistical Office, Warsaw, Poland.
** Professor, vice-president of the Central Statistical Office, Warsaw, Poland.
    E-mail: j.witkowski@stat.gov.pl

premises for the drawing of conclusions about whether this phenomenon is now less common than under the command economy, or more frequent (there are no reliable data on its dimensions in the past).

On the other hand, we can reasonably expect that having only a job in the underground economy is nowadays much more common. This is not equivalent to stating that such jobs must as a rule have a permanent or full-time character. They may be temporary, undertaken with a number of employers, but always without the appropriate employee's rights and privileges. Furthermore, such a job is not necessarily the only source of income, since the situation considered frequently concerns persons registered as unemployed and entitled to receive unemployment benefit. Likewise, this situation may involve retired persons and pensioners, who receive other kinds of regular pay.

The distinction of unregistered work as additional or primary is essential from the point of view of the diagnosis of the labor market. A large number of persons working additionally in the underground economy may mean that the actual demand for definite professional skills is higher than the number of persons with such skills. This kind of information might be an important prerequisite for the modernization of the educational policy and the transformation of the system of occupational training. Then, a high number of persons working exclusively (mainly) in the underground economy would mean that the actual number of jobs in the national economy is bigger than the one registered by the official labor market statistics. In both cases neglect of information on the persons working in the underground economy significantly limits the possibility of reaching the correct conclusions about, and elaboration of the correct opinions on, the labor market situation.

Having in mind the difficult situation on the Polish labor market in the transformation period, and especially the appearance of mass unemployment, it is especially important for the decision makers to know how many persons are employed exclusively (or mainly) in the underground economy. The estimates may mean that the actual number of jobless is lower than that shown by the respective registers, while the actual number of persons employed is higher than that established on the basis of official statistical reporting and questionnaires. That is why the first attempts at estimating the size of the hidden labor force in Poland, carried out by the Labor Statistics Division of the Central Statistical Office (GUS), concerned only main jobs.

Information Sources and the Methods of Estimation of the Number of Persons Employed in the Underground Economy

The phenomenon of hidden labor is difficult to observe statistically. Until now there have been no direct sources of information describing this phenomenon. Our knowledge had to be limited to information obtained through specially elaborated estimates. In the practice of CSO to date. two methods of estimation of the number of persons employed in the underground economy have been applied, these methods using three kinds of information sources, namely: (1) the analysis of the labor force survey (LFS), carried out through the households, (2) the employment statistics, based on the records of enterprises, as well as (3) the data on registered unemployment, obtained from the Labor Offices.

The possibility of obtaining the estimates mentioned only came when the labor force survey was carried out, for the first time in Poland, in May 1992; since then it has been conducted on a quarterly basis. Theoretically, the estimates of the number of persons employed in the underground economy can be obtained four times a year. This is of essential cognitive importance, for the chances of finding an unregistered job fluctuate significantly with the seasons of the year.

From the point of view of our considerations, the LFS methodology is decisive for the estimates of the number of persons working in the underground economy. The first, extremely important feature of this study is the obtaining of information from households. It is also important that on the basis of this survey the current professional activity of all the members of the households at the age of 15 and over is analyzed. Nevertheless, to be able to perform such an analysis, it is crucial to understand the definitions of the basic categories of the population in the labor market; the definitions of employed and unemployed person being the most important.
According to ILO recommendations persons treated as employed were those (of 15 and more years of age) who, in the reference week:

– did for at least 1 hour work bringing compensation or income, i.e. were employed as a salaried person, worked in their own (or rented) farm, or conducted their own economic activity outside agriculture, helped (without compensation) in the running of the family farm or of the family business outside agriculture,

– did not execute work (due, for instance, to sickness, vacation, interruption of the firm's activity, difficult weather conditions, strike etc.), but formally were employed either as salaried persons or as working on their own account.

Thus, the category of employed was assigned to all persons who in the reference week actually executed, or were formally engaged in, work, irrespective of the working hours and the formal character of the employment or labor contract or other kind of legal guarantee. This means that persons who work without any contract, and therefore - in accordance with our definition – are working in the underground economy, are treated as employed.

On the basis of the LFS we cannot, though, directly discern the persons who work on unregistered jobs, since questions on formal employment status are not asked. That is why it is necessary to useother sources of information on the working population as well.

The first method of estimating the number of employed in the underground economy consists of comparing the number of employed according to the LFS, which — conforming to the assumptions — covers all those employed (including hidden labor) with the number of employed reported from enterprise statistics which, on the other hand, encompass — due to obvious reasons — only persons formally employed. The number obtained through the LFS should be higher, the difference representing the number employed in the underground economy.

Application of this procedure, though, is in practice very complicated. This results primarily from the different subject domain of the two sources of information. First of all, the source survey concerns exclusively private households. This means that a part of the working population, living in collective households, is excluded from the survey. This applies first of all to the residents of workers' hostels, who ought to be included in the working population. The second group of persons living in collective households is constituted by pupils and students, who more and more often undertake remunerated jobs in order to supplement their budget. In the LFS they are treated as employed if in the reference week they were engaged in this type of work. At present, only the pupils and students who live in private households and satisfy certain criteria are classified as employed. Others are not covered by the survey, and therefore they are not included into the working population.

The LFS does not include persons employed abroad by Polish employers, these persons being accounted for in the official statistical reporting in the domain of labor. That is why the results of the LFS are somewhat underestimated as compared to the official reporting.

Thus, the very first task in the estimation of the number of persons employed in the underground economy using the method considered is to bring both sources of information to comparability with respect to subject scope. In practice to date, corrections are made to the number of employed after the LFS, since we dispose of the empirical basis for making such estimates. It is only the thus established number of employed, following the criteria of the LFS, that is being compared with the data deriving from the official reporting. The difference is interpreted as the number of persons employed in the underground economy.

The first estimate of the dimensions of hidden labor was carried out in 1993 according to the method described above. It turned out that this number amounts to a mere 365,000 persons. Let us recall that we are speaking of persons working exclusively (or mainly) in the underground economy, and not of those who work there in addition to having an official job. The number mentioned did not cover foreigners and children of less than 15 years of age, and referred to non-agricultural activity. Considering these circumstances, it was admitted that the number obtained was the lower bound on unregistered employment in Poland in August 1993.

Analogous estimates were also made for the years 1994-1995 on the basis of respective results of the LFS for August. The choice of this month was meant to secure full comparability with the results of 1993, through elimination of seasonal fluctuations. It was assumed that on this basis it will be possible to draw conclusions on the trends in unregistered employment. Calculations carried out for the latter years turned out to conform more to the social perception of the phenomenon, since employment in underground economy was estimated at 840,000 persons in 1994 and 755,000 persons in 1995. This means that in 1994 an essential increase of unregistered employment occurred, to decrease somewhat in 1995. It is probable that 1994 was a turning point: the magnitude of hidden labor then attained its maximum level. This level is altogether, though, not as high as has been suggested by the results of sample studies and the pronouncements of some analysts. It should suffice to emphasize that the number of persons employed in the underground economy, estimated according to the method outlined, was between 5% and 5.5% of the total official employment in Poland.

The second method of estimating the number of persons employed in the underground economy results from the quite common conviction that a part (perhaps even the majority) of the unemployed registered in the labor offices are in fact employed as hidden labor. Let us recall that according to the legal regulation in force an unemployed person can work and still remain on the register (together with the possibility of getting the unemployment benefit) if the income from work does not exceed 50% of the minimal wage. Thus, in a way by virtue of law an unemployed person may be in fact employed (one could attempt to define these persons as partly employed or partly unemployed), this not being allowed for by the LFS methodology.

The persons who are considered in the estimation of hidden labor by the second method are the jobless. In the LFS these persons are defined in a different manner than in the Law on Employment and Unemployment now in force, this law being the basis for registering the unemployed persons in the local labor offices. According to ILO recommendations, applied commonly in market economy countries, a person must satisfy three criteria in order to be considered unemployed:

- cannot carry out any remunerated and income-bringing work, nor help in the conduct of the family business during the week in question,
- must be seeking a job actively, that is - during the last four weeks (the week in question included), undertake some concrete action aiming at finding a job,
- must be ready (able) to undertake work in the reference week or in the following one.

From the point of view of the problems considered here the most important criterion for the classification of persons defined as jobless is lack of work. According to ILO recommendations this would mean that an unemployed person cannot carry out any work, for even 1 hour a week. This certainly is a very rigorous definition of an unemployed person, since in its light the unemployed person must really have no work to do (even occasional, seasonal or unregistered).

The methodological differences between the two sources of information on unemployment (records and the LFS), resulting from the different definitions of the unemployed person, served as the basis for the elaboration of the estimate of the number of unemployed who in fact work in the underground economy. This was possible as LFS also provides information on persons registered as unemployed in the labor offices.

The method was for the first time applied in August 1993 and since then the calculations have been performed every quarter of the year. In the present report we will limit ourselves to the outline of the method itself and the results of calculations for August 1993-1995.

In August 1993, the number of unemployed registered in labor offices was 2,830,000 persons. In that survey it was established that the number of unemployed registered in the labor offices and who meet the international criteria (i.e. do not have any work at all) was lower and amounted to 1,746,000 persons. Hence, the difference was quite important – 1,084,000 persons. It was this number that was treated as describing the hidden labor among the unemployed registered in labor offices. Such an interpretation does not necessarily have to be fully true, since some of the unemployed may work officially and therefore their work may be registered officially. In practice, however, such cases are rather sporadic, because the allowed income from work of the unemployed is very low, and one can hardly find an official job with such a wage. Thus, we wilt not commit a significant error if we assume that according to the second method the number of persons working in underground economy in August 1993 was 1,084,000, and was therefore almost three times higher than the one obtained with the first method. This certainly is a convincing evidence of the difficulties encountered in an estimation of the size of hidden labor.

Similar calculations were also performed for August in two consecutive years. The results were very similar. In August 1994 the number of employed in underground economy was 1,126,000 (7.5% of the total official employment), and so it was higher than in 1993. Then, in turn, for August 1995 the estimate gave the result of 1,011,000 persons working in the underground economy (6.6% of the officially employed) - more than 100,000 less than in the preceding year. For both years the number of persons involved in hidden labor was higher than when determined with the first method. In the following years, though, the differences were much smaller than in 1993.

It is worth emphasizing that both methods indicated an increase in unregistered employment (understood as main employment) in 1994, and, likewise, in 1995 both showed signs of stabilization or perhaps even a decrease in the size of this phenomenon. Depending upon the method of estimation, in August 1994 the number of persons employed mainly in the underground economy amounted to 800,000 or to more than 1.1 million persons, and in August 1995 to 755,000 or to more than 1 million. It seems that in the years 1994-1995 the most probable number of persons employed exclusively in the underground economy was between 800,000 and 1 million.

Methodology of the Survey on Unregistered Employment

The calculated estimates of the numbers of persons employed in the underground economy turned out to be very interesting from the point of view of the assessment of the scale of phenomenon. Still, the scope of the information gathered was limited to the total number of persons employed exclusively in the underground economy. The potential influence of the underground economy on the overall situation in the labor market and the high public interest in this subject made us look for additional sources of information on hidden labor. Eventually, the decision was made to go on with a special module survey carried out within the framework of the August LFS.

The choice of such a solution resulted from at least two causes. First, CSO has already had significant experience in carrying out module surveys, and had a trained staff of interviewers, who were capable of undertaking difficult tasks. Besides this, during the last four years the justified conviction was formed in the respondents that the results of the LFS are used exclusively for statistical purposes, this fact being of foremost importance for the reliability of the information acquired on hidden labor. Second, experience to date from surveys on the underground economy has shown that acquisition of information on unregistered employment mainly from the employer's side did not guarantee any success. It was therefore assumed that there are greater chances of getting the relevant data from the employees themselves.

In line with the assumption mentioned, the module survey of unregistered employment was carried out in August 1995. It was a separate questionnaire survey devoted entirely to problems of unregistered employment and incomes. Due to this, the scope of information on hidden labor was much broader than in the previous CSO estimates or in any such analysis performed in Poland. The study covered, at the national level, more than 11,000 households, equivalent to more than 25,600 persons of 15 and more years of age. This was a half of the population of households (and therefore also approximately a half of the number of persons) randomly selected for the quarterly LFS. Simultaneously, the principle was adopted according to which the module survey was applied to this subsample of persons, whose cooperation with CSO in the framework of LFS terminated at that time (they participated for the fourth time in the study), and to the subsample of households that had had a half year break in the survey. In this manner the present authors tried to minimize the potential negative consequences of this module survey for further collaboration between the respondents and the CSO. Contrary to our expectations we encountered a high degree of understanding and readiness to cooperate on the part of respondents. It is worth mentioning that only 546 persons refused to participate in the survey.

The advantages of the module survey of unregistered employment are not limited to a large survey population and its nation-wide character, but include a quite broad scope of information about the phenomenon. Let us first of all emphasize that for the first time the very same survey served to provide information on persons employed in the underground economy (labor supply) and on employers using unregistered employment (demand for hidden labor). In the first case information was gathered directly from the persons who declared working in unregistered jobs in 1995; in the second case, households and persons conducting some economic activity (private firms) were asked about the employment of third persons (including foreigners) without a formal contract.

For purposes of diagnosing the labor market and in particular for the comparison of the results of this study with previous estimates it was not unimportant to distinguish the persons who worked exclusively in the underground economy (main job) from those who treated unregistered jobs as additional employment. In this manner the possibility appeared of assessing in a general manner the phenomenon of hidden labor and its size with respect to persons who worked exclusively in this segment of national economy. If we add in the fact that information was gathered on the types of jobs performed in the underground economy and on the distribution of hidden labor over consecutive months of the year (seasonality), as well as the possibility of linking all the information from this study with the results of the standard quarterly LFS, then we see that the scope of data on the population employed in the underground economy is beyond all those obtained from other sources of information.

The data on households and firms employing people without formal contracts are not as comprehensive as in the case of employed persons. This results first of all from the essence of the LFS, which is primarily oriented towards the individual economic activities of the population. In spite of this, the questionnaire of the module survey accounted for several information items that made it possible to carry out the analysis of households taking advantage of unregistered employment, at least in terms of basic data.

A significant complement to the characteristics of the persons employed in the underground economy was constituted by the incomes gained from this work, and in the case of households providing unofficial employment also the expenditures on such work. Information of this type will be particularly helpful in computation of the national accounts.

In the framework of the study here considered information was gathered as well on the causes of taking unregistered employment and the work most frequently performed in the underground economy. Opinions on these subjects were expressed both by the persons who worked in the underground economy and by those who used such work or who knew the phenomenon from first-hand observation.

To close the methodological part let us note that the concept of the study on unregistered employment was elaborated in the Labor Statistics Division of CSO in cooperation with the Center for Economic and Statistical Studies of the Central Statistical Office and the Polish Academy of Sciences, with reference to the opinions of experts from outside the CSO.

Persons Having the Unregistered Jobs

Hidden labor can be looked at from the point of view of employers or employees. We will first try to describe the size of hidden labor on the basis of declarations of the persons employed in this segment of economy. This information is the most important from the point of view of the labor market, since it speaks both of the number of extra jobs actually existing in the national economy and of the actual number of persons employed, irrespective of the formal character of their employment.

In 1995 at least 2,199,000 persons were employed in the underground economy in Poland. In a breakdown by month, the highest employment in the underground economy was observed in July (1,151,000 persons), and then in June (959,000) and in August (909,000). Employment in the underground economy started to gain momentum in April (704,000), but it did not disappear totally in winter, though its scale would go obviously down (ranging from more than 300,000 in January to 491,000 in March).

For every third person who took an unregistered job in the year considered, this fact related only to one month, and in this group, for 20% of persons, such an occurrence was a rather singular event, for it lasted quite a short time - up to 5 days. There is, however, a rather large group of people (more than 450,000, that is - some 21% of all those employed in the underground economy), for whom unregistered employment is permanent (at least four months a year). The latter group of employees is certainly bigger over the whole year, for the analysis considered was carried out in August, i.e. in the peak period of performance of certain kinds of unregistered jobs.

Hidden labor more often involves men (more than 64%) than women (approximately 36%). If we consider that there are more women than men in Poland, then the indicator of employment of men in the underground economy (i.e. the ratio of the number of men employed in the underground economy to the total number of men aged IS and over), equal 10.2%, is almost twice as big as it is for women (5.2%).

The share of women who perform permanent unregistered employment is bigger than the corresponding share for men. During winter it is more often women who carry out unregistered employment, while with the coming of spring the professional activity of men in the underground economy starts to dominate. Consequently, the share of those who worked in the year in question during at least three months is higher among women, and therefore the average number of days of employment in the underground economy is higher for women (22 days) than for men (19 days).

Employment in the underground economy is higher among the urban population (1,147,000) than among the rural population (1,052,000), but this is partly connected with the level of demographic urbanization of the country. If we compare the numbers of people employed in the underground economy in towns and in the countryside with the relevant population aged 15 and over then we obtain an employment rate in the underground economy which is essentially higher for the rural population - 9.7% - than for the urban population - 6.3% . This difference remains valid both for men and women.

The August CSO survey provided the prerequisites for a more though not yet entirely complete answer to the question: who works in the underground economy? Two other characteristics of persons employed in the underground economy are especially important, namely age and education.

It turns out that representatives of virtually all the generations work in the underground economy. The biggest group is constituted by younger and middle-aged persons (25 to 44 years old), who make up more than 52% of all those employed in the underground economy. Still, both the younger people (up to 25 years of age) and persons near retirement (the age of so-called occupational stabilization) or even in the post-working age find employment in underground economy. It is also interesting to note that in the group of the young e (up to 24 years of age) and the elderly (60 and more years of age) who take up employment in the underground economy there are relatively more women than men.

If we refer the number of persons employed in the hidden labor to total population aged 15 and over (by calculating the employment rate by age) then it turns out that the previous conclusions gain an additional empirical justification. We can thereby make more precise certain observations, especially on the involvement of the population of various age groups in hidden labor. Thus, the largest share of persons employed in the underground economy are in the age bracket 25-34 years (more than 11% of persons in this age group). This concerns, in particular, men, of whom as many as 15.6% work in the underground economy, with the appropriate indicator for women being a mere 7%. Very similar values for involvement in the underground economy are observed for the age groups 35-44 years (9.4%) and up to 24 years (9.1%). In case of these two age groups the indicator of involvement in the underground economy is also decidedly higher for men than for women.

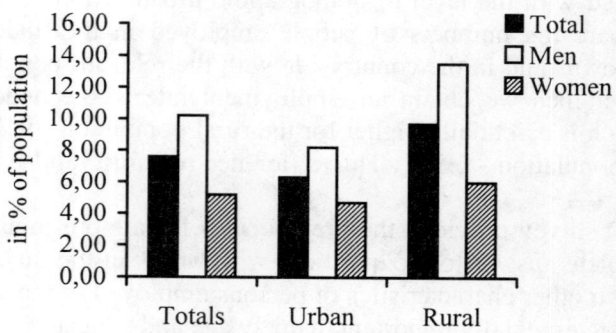

Figure 12.1 Persons employed in the hidden economy in 1995

Against the background of these numbers one can formulate a comment, which results from the general diagnosis of the situation in the Polish labor market. As is commonly known, one of the most difficult problems is constituted by the very high unemployment rate among young people, of up to 24 years of age. For several years the rate of unemployment among the youth in Poland has been at a very high level, in Western European terms, exceeding 30%. This also means that in our country young people are in relatively the most difficult situation on the labor market. On the other hand it turns out that every eleventh person from this age group (15-24 years) finds employment in the underground economy. In the population of young males this percentage is yet higher: every ninth man from the age group in question works in the underground economy. It can be roughly stated that the number of young people working in the underground economy is approximately equal to half of the number of unemployed in the same age group who are registered as such in the labor offices.

Work in the underground economy is commonly imagined to be associated with low skills and very simple jobs. Such an image of the informal work is certainly still true, but it does not apply any more to all types of such work. The underground economy no longer employs exclusively people with low levels of education and limited skill levels.

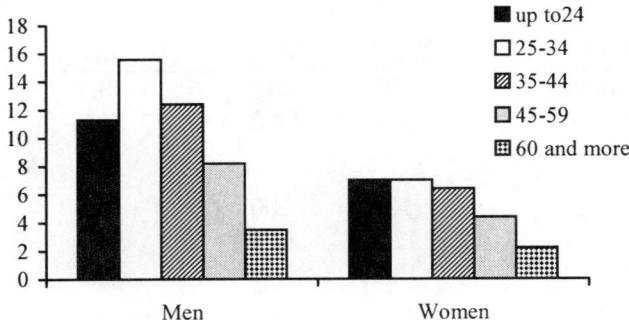

Figure 12.2 Persons employed in the hidden economy by age

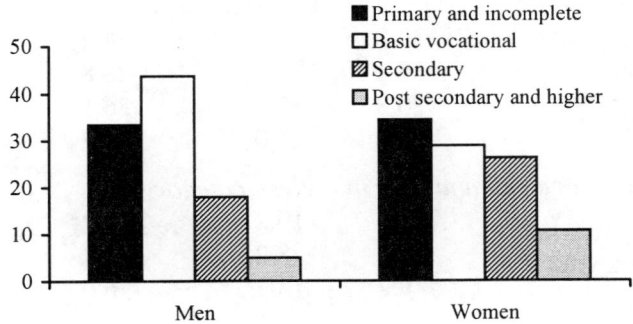

Figure 12.3 Persons employed in the hidden economy by education level

Table 12.1 Persons having an unregistered job in 1995

Population categories	Total	Men	Woman
Totals in thousands	2199	1412	787
in %	100	64.2	35.8
% shares			
Totals	100	100	100
Urban	52.2	48.9	58.1
Rural	47.8	51.3	41.9
Age groups			
up to 24	22.4	21.4	24.3
25-34	22.5	27.5	21.8
35-44	26.9	27.7	25.5
45-59	17.6	17.3	18.2
60 an over	7.6	6.1	10.2
Education			
Primary and incomplete	33.8	33.4	34.4
Basic vocational	38.4	43.7	28.8
Secondary	20.8	17.9	26.1
Post secondary and higher	7.0	5.0	10.7
In % of population aged 15 and over in a given category			
Totals	7.6	10.2	5.2
Urban	6.3	8.2	4.7
Rural	9.7	13.5	6.0
Age groups:			
up to 24	9.1	11.3	7.0
25-34	11.4	15.6	7.0
35-44	9.4	12.4	6.4
45-59	6.2	8.2	4.4
60 and more	2.7	3.5	2.2
Education:			
Primary and incomplete	6.7	10.1	4.3
Basic vocational	11.1	13.0	7.8
Secondary	6.9	8.1	4.7
Post secondary and higher	5.5	5.7	5.3

A confirmation to this proposition is provided by the results of studies carried out by CSO, which make it possible to characterize the structure of employment in underground economy in terms of education level.

More than 38% of all the people employed in the underground economy (844,000) are those with basic vocational education. The high number of skilled workers employed in the underground economy seems logical in Polish conditions. On the one hand, the greatest group within the adult population of Poles is constituted by persons with basic vocational schooling, and on the other hand it is them who have the greatest difficulties in getting a job on the official labor market. It is widely known that the highest unemployment rate is observed exactly in this group of people.

The underground economy traditionally offers quite an important number of jobs for persons with very low or no professional skills, with relatively low remuneration. This is the factor which motivates someemployers (private firms and households) to undertake the risk of employing people without a formal contract. Then, for a person with low skills taking up an unregistered job often constitutes the only opportunity for gaining any — or additional — income. Resulting from such a coincidence of circumstances the underground economy in 1995 employed very many persons with primary or incomplete primary education (743,000, i.e. 34% of all those employed in the underground economy).

Thus, we got a confirmation of the fact that the underground economy primarily generates jobs for unskilled workers, mainly for blue collar workers with basic schooling or no vocational schooling at all. In spite of the fact that the underground economy adds significantly to the volume of labor demand in Polish economy, therefore, it does not constitute an engine of socio-economic progress in our country. It constitutes, instead, a method of survival for some employers and for these job-takers who would otherwise have no chances in the official labor market.

Still, one should note that unregistered jobs are being performed currently by a significant number of persons with secondary general and vocational education (457,000, equivalent to 21% of the total employment in the underground economy). This group of persons is most probably involved in work requiring higher occupational skills.

Employment in the underground economy includes work requiring significant skills and knowledge in various fields. This is evidenced by the fact that 155,000 persons working in the underground economy (7% of all those working in the underground economy) possess higher or postsecondary education. Thus, the informal labor market broadens the employment offer for differing employee groups, though it is still dominated by the demand for semi-skilled workers and for those with minimum qualifications.

Thus, we run no risk when we state that unregistered work currently involves various groups of the population, irrespective of education level and skills. Still, the degree of this involvement, as measured by the employment rate, is essentially differentiated. The underground economy employs now — relatively — the largest share of persons with basic vocational training (more than 11% of persons of 15 years and more having this kind of education). The remaining population groups distinguished with respect to their education levels do not differ that much as to the rates of their employment in underground economy. Thus, although this rate is here the highest for persons with primary and incomplete primary education (6.7%), there are similar percentage shares for persons with secondary education (more than 6%) and with post-secondary education (5.5%) working in the underground economy.

At all the educational levels, the rates of employment in the underground economy are much higher for men than for women. Here, though, a kind of exception is provided by the highest education level group (post-secondary and higher): 5.7% of men and 5.3% of women, i.e. quite similar indicator values. It appears that the employment of women in the underground economy is more frequently related to their own qualifications and not — which is more often the case of the male population — with the seasonality of some work. In order to confirm this conclusion let us state that more than 3/4 of men employed in the underground economy possess basic vocational education, while among women this share falls to 63%. The proportions are reversed for persons with at least secondary education. The percentage share of women from this group involved in hidden labor (37%) is much higher than among the corresponding male population (23%). It is now hard to say whether this is caused by the more difficult situation of women in the labor market in Poland, or by the creation, within the confines of underground economy, of jobs requiring higher skills, these jobs being more often taken by women, just due to their greater labor market flexibility. In any case there is no doubt that the character of unregistered jobs taken up by men and women differs significantly with respect to skills required.

From the point of view of the labor market one of the basic pieces of information is connected with the distinction of main and additional work. It is also important in the analysis of demand for employment in the underground economy. That is why we will now turn to consideration of the numbers of persons working exclusively (or mainly) and additionally in the underground economy.

Table 12.2 Percentage of persons employed exclusively in the underground economy by age

Segments of the hidden labor market	Totals	Men	Woman
Totals in thousands	957	590	367
in %	43.5	41.8	46.6
Urban	49.7	49.8	49.6
Rural	36.8	34.2	42.4
Age groups			
up to 24	64.3	11.3	7.0
25-34	35.9	15.6	7.0
35-44	37.5	12.4	6.4
45-59	36.4	8.2	4.4
60 and more	45.5	3.5	2.2
Education			
Primary and incomplete	51.5	49.6	55.0
Basic vocational	43.2	41.2	48.9
Secondary	40.3	34.9	46.8
Post secondary and higher	16.1	19.7	13.1

The distinction between main and additional employment in the underground economy concerns recently performed jobs. In the majority of cases (approximately 57%) the relevant jobs were additional ones, though 957,000 persons declared that employment in the underground economy constituted for them the main job. This means that a large number of persons find no occupation outside the underground economy. For this portion of the population, unregistered labor is simultaneously the main source of income. Therefore, in spite of the fact that the majority of those employed in the underground economy treat these jobs as additional, there recently appeared a significant group of people for whom unregistered employment is the only opportunity to carry out economic activity.

It is worth recalling that in accord with the estimates of the CSO Statistics Division employment in the underground economy currently amounts in Poland to somewhere between 800,000 and 1 million, depending upon the method of estimation, with respect to persons for whom this is the sole job. In 1995 no broadening of the scope of underground economy was observed. This, however, means that the scale of the phenomenon remains important in Poland, as also indicated by the results of the module survey. Thus, it seems that the results obtained are quite reliable, though they should perhaps be treated as the lower bound on the size of hidden labor in Poland.

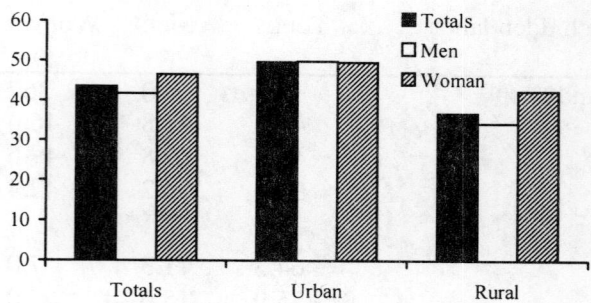

Figure 12.4 Percentage shares of persons working exclusively in the underground economy

Unregistered employment is carried out as the main (or exclusive) work more frequently by men (62%) and by the urban population (60%). On the other hand, more inhabitants of rural areas work additionally in the underground economy. Consequently, more or less the same number of inhabitants of urban areas work exclusively and additionally in underground economy, while in the rural population those for who it is an additional job decisively dominate (more than 63%).

For the majority of the young (up to 24 years of age) who work in the underground economy this job is the main one (more than 64% of persons in this age group state that their job in the underground economy is the only one). Similarly, almost a half of persons of 60 and more years of age (some 46%) declared that unregistered employment provides their main job. Then, in the age bracket 25-59 years the majority of those involved in hidden labor (63-64%) declare they treat their job there as an additional one.

Low skills, i.e. the characteristics of persons' with primary or incomplete primary education and basic vocational training, limit the capacity to take an unregistered job as an additional job. This portion of hidden labor is therefore dominated by persons working exclusively in it, while in the group of skilled workers there were more than 43% of those who worked exclusively in the underground economy. The higher the education level, the better the chances of finding an additional job in the underground economy. This is most visible in the group of persons with post-secondary and higher education. As many as 84% of those from this group involved in the underground economy worked there additionally, and only the remaining

16% treated this work as the main one. Hence, it can be concluded that exclusive employment in the underground economy applies primarily to semi-skilled workers, while additional employment is found there to a greater degree by persons with higher skills and education levels.

The observations presented confirm the earlier diagnosis of the labor market in Poland, stating that there is high demand for highly qualified personnel and a limited possibility of finding an official job by low skilled persons. For this latter group of people a 'black job' often constitutes the sole chance, while for the former — just an opportunity for extra income. It can anyway not be excluded that in this former case the possibility of tax evasion constitutes a motivation for taking up additional work in the underground economy.

Information on the nature of jobs performed within the underground economy undoubtedly provides an extension to the basis for drawing conclusions about the essence of unregistered employment. This report presents, out of necessity, only a synthetic view of the problems mentioned.

A kind of surprise is brought by the observation that the greatest number of persons employed in the underground economy was involved in gardening and farming jobs. To a certain extent such a state of affairs is, of course, related to the period of the survey, when the seasonal work of the kind mentioned is at its peak. Anyway, however, every fourth person in hidden labor was involved in this kind of activity. It is, naturally, more often performed by persons living in the countryside (38%) than in towns (12%). Most of this work had an additional nature, but 214,000 persons stated that gardening and farming jobs were their main job in the underground economy.

The second place as to the popularity was taken by work in the field of construction and installation of fittings (313,000 persons, i.e. more than 14% of total employment in the underground economy), followed by the so-called neighbourhood service (284,000, equivalent to approximately 13%). The latter are much more frequent in the countryside and tend to be additional in nature. The former, on the other hand, are equally frequent in towns and in rural areas, and are more or less equally distributed between main and additional jobs.

Table 12.3 Persons employed in the underground economy by type of activity, in % of total employment in the underground economy

Type of action	Totals	Urban	Rural	Type of job Main	Additional
Trade	8.2	10.4	5.8	10.6	5.1
Construction and installation	14.2	14.2	14.2	13.2	10.3
Construction and maintenance	11.4	14.2	8.3	11.2	8.1
Car repairs and maintenance	6.4	6.6	6.2	4.5	5.5
Transport service	5.2	4.5	6.0	3.0	4.9
Repairs of electrical and technical equipment	1.6	2.4	0.8	0.5	2.0
Health care service	2.2	3.1	1.2	0.2	3.7
Hairdressing and beauty service	1.0	0.9	1.3	1.1	0.9
Tourist and catering service	1.9	2.2	1.6	2.9	1.7
Bookkeeping and legal counseling	1.1	1.7	0.4	0.2	1.8
Private lessons	3.8	6.1	1.2	2.0	4.8
Translation	0.3	0.4	0.2	0.1	0.5
Tailor service	6.7	7.9	5.3	6.7	5.7
Housekeeping service	3.0	4.3	1.7	3.4	1.8
Babysitting and care of elderly	4.3	5.5	2.9	4.2	3.1
Property protection	0.7	1.0	0.3	0.7	0.2
Gardening and farming	24.7	12.4	38.1	22.4	21.7
Production activity	3.2	3.3	3.1	4.4	1.8
Neighbourhood service	12.9	7.8	18.5	5.4	14.1
Other work	2.6	3.2	2.0	2.7	2.0

Other popular activities in the underground economy include repairs and maintenance (above 11% of employment in the underground economy, more often a main job than an additional one, and more often in towns than in the rural areas), trade (above 8% - more often a main job and in towns), tailoring service (about 7%), car repairs and maintenance (more than 6%) and transport services (more than 5%).

The kinds of activities which were most often performed in the underground economy involve primarily persons with low or medium professional skills. The structure of these activities reflects therefore the structure of employment in terms of education level. It should be noted, though, that activities requiring high and very high professional qualifications are also performed as unregistered. Thus, significant numbers of persons are involved in such activities within the underground economy as the giving of private lessons (83,000), health care service (48,000) or bookkeeping and legal advice (24,000). It seems therefore that the unregistered labor market extends the scope of activities and offers a wide range of activities.

Quite common in Poland is the opinion that it is first of all the owners of private firms who are interested in providing jobs without an appropriate contract. The results of the module survey only partially confirm this supposition. According to the declarations of the surveyed persons, only in about 14% of cases were unregistered jobs performed for private firms (303,000 persons from the hidden labor pool). This situation most often concerns production activities (41,000 persons), construction and assembly service (40,000), building and installation repairs (36,000), gardening and farming activities (36,000), as well as trade (33,000) and tailoring (20,000). Let us emphasize, however, that if work is performed for a private firm it much more often constitutes the main job than an additional one.

Altogether, hidden labor is mostly (70%) performed for private persons, this work providing additional, and not primary, income. Private persons employ without a contract most often for work in the garden and in farming (424,000 persons employed), for construction and installation activities (200,000), repairs and maintenance (163,000) and neighborhood services (220,000).

In spite of expectations, there is quite a small group of employed in the underground economy for their own account (260,000, i.e. approximately 12% of total hidden labor). Working on one's own account in the underground economy usually constitutes an additional job (approximately 63% of persons working on their own account in the underground economy). Most frequently this activity is trade (90,000 persons) and tailoring service (36,000), but also gardening and farming activities (21,000), private lessons (17,000), car services (16,000), as well as construction and neighborhood services (14,000 each).

Households Offering Unofficial Employment

The issue of unregistered employment should be regarded also from the point of view of employers, not only from the point of view of the persons employed. This is indeed a very important element of the evaluation of this phenomenon on the Polish labor market. Such a viewpoint reflects the so called demand side of the unregistered employment, i.e. the demand for services offered without a formal contract. In Polish reality quite an important demand for unregistered labor is generated by households.

The results of the August survey showed that 1,922,000 households, i.e. 15.8% of the total, took advantage of unregistered service in 1995. This phenomenon was relatively more frequent in the rural areas (22.7% of the households) than in the towns (12.1%).

In 1995, between January and the middle of August, every household employing hidden labor did it on the average twice, with the respective frequency being higher in rural areas than in towns.

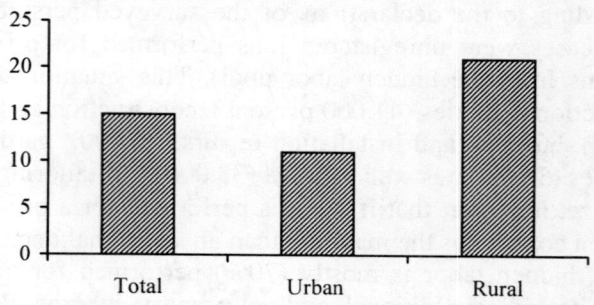

Figure 12.5 Households employing unregistered workforce

The largest number of households hired unregistered labor in August, and this result was observed in spite of the fact that not the whole of August was covered with the survey. Generally, the highest intensity of work done for the households took place in the summer months, in June through August, while the lowest intensity was in January of the given year. It should be noted that the seasonal intensity of work done for the households within the underground economy looks entirely differently in the rural and urban areas.

Thus, households in towns use unregistered labor more regularly than in the rural areas (in January 12.6% of urban households used unregistered labor, while in June - 33.2%), but seasonality appears here as well very clearly.

Table 12.4 Households using unregistered employment by month, per cent

Months	Total	Urban	Rural
January	9.5	12.6	6.3
February	12.9	18.1	7.6
March	18.6	23.6	13.7
April	29.2	30.4	27.9
May	26.8	28.4	25.3
June	31.9	33.2	30.7
July	34.6	27.9	41.2
August	36.9	21.4	52.3

Among the rural households the seasonality of providing unregistered employment is much higher - the shares range from 6.3% in January to 52.3% in August. The figures quoted imply the much more frequent performance of jobs of a distinctly seasonal nature in rural households.

During a month the majority of households use unregistered work just once (from approximately 90% of households in March and August to about 95% in February and April of 1995). In terms of this indicator the differences between urban and rural households are insignificant. It is worth explaining at this point that single-event jobs ('once a month') include also those that have a discontinuous character but are repeated systematically over the month, like private lessons, house cleaning etc. If, however, we consider the whole of 1995 until August then we observe that such single unregistered employment events applied to a mere 1.4% of households, while the remaining 98.6% of households employed workers repeatedly.

Work performed for households is usually of a short-time character. Some 65% of households used hidden labor for up to 3 days a month, a further 27% - for 4 to 10 days, and only approximately 8% for more than 10 days.

One can clearly see the differences in these proportions between the urban and rural households. There are far less urban than rural households taking advantage of the short-term unregistered work (57.2% compared to 71.8%), and consequently the percentage share of urban households giving longer-time hidden employment is almost twice as high as in rural areas (11.5% compared to 6.0%).

Table 12.5 Households hiring hidden labor according to the average number of workdays within a month

Location	Totals	Number of workdays in a month		
		up to 3	4 - 10	11 and over
Totals	100	64.5	26.7	8.8
Urban	100	57.2	31.3	11.5
Rural	100	71.8	22.2	6.0

In winter, demand of households for hidden labor decreases, but the employment offered is then more often of longer standing (several days a month). In summer, on the other hand, households generate a greater demand for short-term jobs. Thus, for example, in January only 57.1% of households employed hidden labor for short-term jobs, while in August this occurred in 66.0% of households considered. The opposite situation takes place, of course, in the domain of longer-term jobs - in January they concerned 17.2% of households, but in August - only 9.8%. These proportions result from the seasonal character of the majority of activities done within the underground economy, both in urban and rural areas, though in both cases the activities have a different character.

Table 12.6 Households by number of months in which they employed hidden labor

Length of employment	Totals	Urban	Rural
Total	100.0	100.0	100.0
1 months	50.4	60.1	40.7
2 months	26.3	19.7	32.9
3 months	11.8	7.6	15.9
4 months	4.9	3.9	6.0
5 months	2.4	2.2	2.6
6 months	1.4	2.0	0.7
7 months	0.6	0.8	0.3
8 months	2.2	3.7	0.9

Half of all the households employing hidden labor in 1995 did it only during one month, more than 1/4 - during two months, and only slightly more than 2% - during all the eight months considered.

Urban households did much more often employ hidden labor during just one month of 1995, and simultaneously - much more often provided unregistered employment during all the eight months considered. This, again, is the consequence of the differences in the character of jobs offered by urban and rural households.

One of the primary issues in the survey of the informal labor market is the character of work carried out most often in this labor sector, since it implies the answer to the question as to the degree of demand for individual types of informal jobs, and therefore the domain of economy which generates more jobs than shown in official statistics, and further — what kinds of activities could or even should be developed in the formal setting.

The August survey of the underground economy involved the questions on 19 types of activities and services, for which — in the opinion of the authors of the questionnaire — there existed demand generated by the households. It turned out that this list accounted for almost one hundred percent of the services actually rendered to the households.

Among all types of activities and services, a clear superiority was displayed by gardening and farming activities, provided by 53.0% of all the households using hidden labor. The work of this type concentrated timewise in June through August, when approximately 70% of it took place. The second rank was occupied by construction and installation repairs and maintenance, which were carried out in approximately 35% of all the households employing hidden labor. This type of activity intensified from March and peaked in June, with more than 22% of all service in this category. Then came the so-called neighborhood services, observed in every fifth household. This service got more intensive since April, with the highest intensity (more than half of employment events) occurring in July and August. The fourth position among the activities carried out informally was taken by construction and installation services (registered in 16.1% of households considered). In case of this service its seasonal character is also well seen, for although the relevant activities occur over the whole year, they tend to intensify from April and peak in June - July (43.5%). Quite significant positions among the types of activities performed for households are taken by health care services, transport services, babysitting and care of the elderly, housework (like cleaning), as well as private lessons and tailoring.

When we speak of the types of activities and services performed informally we should not neglect the differentiation which exists between the urban and the rural areas. Thus, in urban households the greatest demand exists for construction and installation repairs and maintenance (in 47% of all the households employing hidden labor). The second place is occupied by private lessons (19.2%), followed by babysitting and care of the elderly, housework (e.g. cleaning). On the other hand, the greatest demand generated by the rural households concerns gardening and farming activities (observed in 97% of rural households using unregistered labor). Subsequent ranks were taken by neighborhood services (approximately 30% of households) and construction and installation repairs and maintenance (22.5%).

Table 12.7 Households using unregistered labor by type of activity

Nature of work	Totals	Urban	Rural
	in % of all households		
Trade	3.0	5.2	0.8
Construction and installation	16.1	17.0	15.2
Construction and maintenance	34.7	46.9	22.5
Car repairs and maintenance	8.3	10.5	6.0
Transport service	10.8	7.7	13.7
Repairs of technical equipment	8.9	11.4	6.4
Health care service	11.2	13.8	8.6
Hairdressing and beauty service	7.5	7.8	7.3
Tourist and catering service	0.8	1.1	0.4
Bookkeeping and legal counseling	1.0	1.7	0.3
Private lessons	9.9	19.2	0.6
Translation	0.1	0.1	0.1
Tailor service	9.7	11.6	7.9
Housekeeping service	10.4	17.0	3.8
Babysitting and care of elderly	10.7	17.7	3.7
Property protection	0.4	0.7	-
Gardening and farming	53.0	8.3	97.4
Production activity	0.3	-	0.5
Neighborhood service	20.3	10.7	29.9
Other work	0.8	0.3	1.2

Urban households employed unregistered workers most often in June, and then in April, May and July (respectively: 33%, 30%, and 28% for the two latter months), and in each of these months construction and installation repairs and maintenance appeared most frequently. The second position in terms of type of activities was taken in April and May by private lessons, and in June and July by construction and installation services. Rural households, on the other hand, employed unregistered workers most often in August, and then in July and June (52%, 41% and 31% of all the rural households employing unregistered labor, respectively). First of all there were gardening and farming activities and neighborhood services in August and July and construction and installation repairs and maintenance in June.

In a commonly held opinion, activities in the underground economy are often associated with foreigners who are employed on Polish territory, also by households, without an appropriate labor permit on the one hand, and without a labor contract on the other. In accordance with the results of the August survey of unregistered employment the phenomenon mentioned is very limited. Only 1.1% of the households (21,000) from the group providing informal employment would state that they employed foreigners in this manner. Out of 10 such households 7 were urban and 3 rural. Among all the households employing foreigners informally, 45% employed 1 such person, a further 45% employed 2 foreigners, and 10% - 8 and more foreigners. If we calculate on this basis the number of foreigners finding employment in this way then we obtain for 1995 the number of 47,000 persons (or jobs). In this case the results of the survey differ significantly from the social opinion on the subject of employment of foreigners in the underground economy. It seems, though, that the majority of people coming from abroad, who do not have a permit to work in Poland, rather work on their own account than engage in work for households or for official firms.

A Sketch For the Balance of Hidden Labor in Polish Economy

The studies carried out confirm that hidden labor has already become quite a widespread phenomenon in our country and that it concerns a relatively differentiated group of persons. For an important part of them, especially for the semi-skilled and unskilled, an opportunity is thereby created of undertaking some job bringing income, often constituting the sole source of upkeep. For others, who make up the majority now, unregistered work has the character of extra work, and brings additional income. Against the background of conclusions drawn from the survey the question arises whether the results of this survey adequately reflect the state of things on the hidden labor market.

When attempting to answer this question we must first of all emphasize that approximately 2.2 million persons admitted performing such work and more than 1.9 million households as well as some 940,000 private firms conducted by natural persons admitted providing unregistered employment. These figures are doubtless evidence for the extraordinary type of pattern resulting from the survey. It is also significant that the results of the survey concerning exclusive employment in the underground economy are quite similar to the estimates of CSO. Still, the subject matter of the survey is so difficult and hard to observe that it is worth trying to make an assessment of the results obtained and subsequently to put together the balance of hidden labor.

The survey conducted provides such a possibility since the information was acquired from the two sides interested - the employers and the employees. Out of the total of 2,199,000 persons who admitted being employed in the underground economy more than 1.6 million indicated households as their employers. Then, the representatives of more than 1.9 million households included in the analysis confirmed that they hired unregistered labor. Hence, it can be concluded that more households than private persons declared their participation in underground economy. The difference may partly result from the fact that several households can employ the same person, which would decrease the number of job-takers. On the other hand, though, a household can also employ more than one person.

After appropriate estimates had been calculated it was assumed that the additional number of persons working in the underground economy - i.e. beyond the one resulting directly from the declarations of the job-takers themselves - was 306,000. Out of this number 146,000 persons work primarily in the underground economy, while for 160,000 persons their work in the underground economy has the character of extra work. Altogether, then, 2,505,000 persons found employment in the underground economy.

For the majority of these people (1,402,000) employment in the underground economy constitutes an additional job, but for 1,103,000 persons it is the main job (they work exclusively in the underground economy). This latter figure. is significant, for it constitutes 7.2% of the total official employment in Polish economy, though it is not as high as suggested by other estimates or surveys. It is also worth emphasizing that approximately 9.2% of Poles having formal (official) jobs do additionally perform unregistered work. Thus, these two groups together constitute 16.4% of the total number of persons officially employed in our country. The figures obtained constitute proof that hidden labor is not a marginal phenomenon in Poland.

Table 12.8 A sketch for the balance of employment in underground economy in 1995

Persons employed in the underground economy	Totals	Main job	Additional job
	in thousands		
According to declarations of respondents	2199	957	1242
Additionally in households	218	88	130
Additionally in private firms	88	58	30
Total employment	2505	1103	1402

Summary

One of the characteristic features of the contemporary labor market in Poland is widespread unregistered employment, often referred to as employment in the hidden or underground economy. Hidden labor is not directly statistically observable and so indirect methods must be used to estimate its size. In Poland it was not possible to provide such estimates until implementation of the labor force survey (LFS). In practice two methods of estimating hidden employment have been used in CSO.

The first method relies on comparison of the number of the employed taken from the LFS, which - according to the approach adopted - covers all the employed (including the underground economy) and the number of the employed reported from company statistics, which in turn covers - due to obvious reasons - only persons formally employed. The number of the employed, according to the LFS, should be higher by the number of those employed in the underground economy.

The second method of estimating hidden employment involves comparison of data on unemployment from the LFS and registered unemployment (from administrative registers). This method draws inspiration from a common belief that some of the unemployed registered in local labor offices have unregistered jobs. According to the regulations binding in Poland an unemployed person can work and remain on the register with full rights.

The data on unregistered employment provided by estimates were limited to the total number of employed exclusively in the underground economy so it was necessary to carry out a special single module survey under the LFS. The survey was conducted in August 1995 as a national-wide sample survey, covering people working not only exclusively but also additionally in the underground economy as well as employers using unregistered labor (supply and demand). The scope of the survey included the size of the phenomenon, the characteristics of the employed, the kind of unregistered jobs, the reasons for undertaking hidden jobs, revenues from unregistered jobs and household expenditures to cover the cost of unregistered workers.

The survey confirms that hidden labor has become quite widespread in Poland and it concerns a relatively differentiated group of persons. According to the results of the survey 1,103,000 persons work exclusively in the underground economy and 1,402,000 people were employed additionally in the underground economy. These two groups together constitute 16.4 percent of the total number of persons officially employed in Poland.

13 The Spatial Distribution of Informal Marketplaces and Informal Foreign Traders in Contemporary Hungary

ENDRE SIK*

Informal marketplaces are open-air, periodic marketplaces. In economic anthropology they are often called peasant markets or bazaars (Alexander and Alexander, 1987, 1991; Dewey, 1964; Geertz, 1978, 1979). In these markets, unlicensed traders mix with licensed ones, black labor characterizes the transactions and a large proportion of the goods are sold cheaply because of their low quality or due to their shady origins. Some goods are smuggled, counterfeited, or sold without tax or custom duties. Two types of informal marketplaces are analyzed, the so called 'slave markets'(SM) and the COMECON markets (CM).

The main characteristic of the 'slave market' is that it is a marketplace of labor transactions which are not observed statistically, and neither the employer nor the employee pays taxes or social security contributions. These open-air market places appear on squares or streets close to stations or marketplaces or in pubs. On a 'slave market', casual jobs are typically allocated, and they do not last more than one day. Normally the market functions only for some hours every morning. The typical types of jobs are construction and agriculture work.

SMs are known to exist traditionally for domestic servants, seasonal agricultural and construction workers. The traditional term for the SM is 'köpködő' (spitting place). According to the description of a Hungarian ethnographer these SMs originally were situated on the main marketplace.

The COMECON markets (CM), which according to Böröcz (1992) began in the 1970s, were marketplaces dominated by mainly Polish travelers. Many of them were guest workers in Hungary, intimately familiar with arrangements in the domestic second economy, as well as dynamics of mar-

---

* TARKI – (Social Science Informatics Centre), Budapest, Hungary, e-mail: sik@tarki.hu
The research was commissioned by the ILO/Japan Project and by ICCR - Budapest.

ket demand. They established themselves as a firm segment of discount consumer supplies in Hungary's second economy in commodities ranging from children's shoes to small machine tools. Yugoslav citizens ... along with Austrians ... of the regions next to the Hungarian border... specialized in large-scale 'private' food imports from Hungary. A similar form of regional cross-border integration emerged (under the umbrella of bilateral provisions called 'small-border-traffic') around the Hungarian-Slovakian and Hungarian-Romanian borders. By the late 1980s, the practitioners of these small-scale informal trade linkages were joined by residents of Western Ukraine shopping for all movable items in Eastern Hungary. In a similar vein, the Lake Balaton area had become, by the mid-70s, a relatively quiet meeting point for German families split by the 'inner-German' border... Early during this period, the Hungarian forint obtained the status of an overvalued, 'quasi-hard' currency in the second economy of COMECON consumer trade...' (pp. 199-200).

Due to their initial Polish domination, these marketplaces used to be called 'Polish markets'. However, by the mid-1980s ' ... these marketplaces were also referred as the 'Little Comecons', an ironic analogy with the international trading bloc that worked so imperfectly. The usual currency on these markets was the Hungarian forint, but barter was also common, and until 1990 western currencies (above all the Deutsche Mark) were increasingly influential. Most of the items supplied were for domestic consumption: Hungarians were fairly sure of getting goods from Poland on the 'polish' markets at a better prices than in the state shops, likewise shoes from Czechoslovakia, and various tools from Romania and the USSR. I also heard of teenagers who traveled to Hungary from East Germany and Czechoslovakia to buy denims originating in Istanbul from Polish middlemen. Others would go to these markets in search of some vital components for their car, a part perhaps not available in any country through official channels... these market-places have always been dominated by small dealers. There is a limit to the capacity of a Polski Fiat and trailer, even if by 1990 there was no limit to what amenable customs officials were prepared to wave through. At the extreme end of this petty trading were the efforts of ethnic Hungarians from the USSR to secure a few forints for local purchases... all they could bring with them were one or two bottles of vodka or cheap wine, so they would set out their stall, complete with a single glass, to provide market-goers with a tipple... In general, tolerance (of the authorities E.S.) increased over the decade, and (as in Poland in 1990) efforts were made to bring all forms of open-air trading under local council controls. .. the council allocated a suitable field on the outskirts of a major resort (by Lake Balaton E.S.), put up notices in Polish, and attempted to collect relatively small sums from traders as a daily levy.' (Hann, 1992).

The two questions most often raised in concern with informal marketplaces in Hungary refer to their number and whether foreigners dominate them. The first part of the paper tries to offer a tentative answer to the former, the second part to the latter question.

As to the source of data, in early 1995 we interviewed the mayors of the approximately 3100 Hungarian settlements to find out if there were informal markets on their settlements. We supposed that local authorities must have fresh and reliable information concerning the existence and (if there is any) the activity of informal markets within the boundaries of their settlements. There were no questions in the survey concerning their attitudes towards the informal markets; we only sought the best available information on the number and composition of informal markets for goods and labor. Approximately 800 mayors (about one fourth of all the mayors in Hungary) answered the postal questionnaire. The data was weighted by location (six territorial units of Hungary, Budapest excluded), size and status (county capital, city or village) using the HCSO settlement data from 1993. Finally, this database was merged with the HCSO data files to have settlement-wise information from 1988, 1990 and 1993 (more detailed information about the data and the questionnaire can be found in Sik, 1995).

The Spatial Distribution of Informal Marketplaces

In the following analysis we focus on two types of informal marketplaces, i.e. the COMECON and the 'slave markets'. The spatial distribution was operationalized in three forms, i.e. settlement size, administrative status and region. Settlement size was operationalized by the number of permanent residents in 1993. Administrative status has two forms in the text. I use it either as a three-category variable, making a distinction between county capitals (administrative centers of the nineteen counties of Hungary), cities without any administrative role and villages, or as a dummy variable in which case all cities are collapsed into the same category. Finally, the region variable splits Hungary (excluding Budapest) into six regions with a special emphasis on the East-West dimension.

The basic assumptions are as follows:

Hypothesis 1: CM and SM are more widespread in larger settlements than in smaller ones. This assumption does not need any further explanation since both urban sociology and the economics of consumption offer proper explanations why this hypothesis makes sense.

Hypothesis 2: CM and SM are more widespread in the North and East regions. This assumption follows from the assumption that a, informal activity is a means of coping (both in the course of consumption and production) for the worse off (Sik 1994) and b, from the fact that the Northern and Eastern parts of Hungary are the regions which contain worse-off households (lower income, higher unemployment rate, etc.).

Hypothesis 3: CM and SM can be found in the same settlements partly since the same social factor (demand for cheap goods and supply of cheap labor are both the consequences of poverty) generates them, partly since the latter is a useful addendum to the former, i.e. we assume that the operation of informal markets of goods is based on informal labor bought on SMs.

Hypothesis 4: Finally, we assume some sort of interrelation between the spreading of CM and SM and that of formal trade (formal markets (accommodating only licensed traders, having stable stalls and continuous control by local authorities) and retail shops). This correlation can be either negative or positive. In the former case informal markets are the substitutes for formal commerce while in the latter case both formal and informal trade form a symbiotic relationship in which they both compete for the customer and cooperate to make profit. The first assumption makes sense if impoverishment is so advanced that formal traders do not expect any profit and withdraw from the region and at the same time state authorities tolerate informal trade to avoid political instability. The second assumption conceptualizes formal and informal trade as complementing each other. They obviously compete for the consumer but also cooperate in cases in which it is profitable for them, i.e. forming cartels to buy wholesale goods cheaper. Formal and informal trade can exist at the same place in a peaceful way in cases in which both formal and informal trade have different types of consumers to do business with (Galasi-Kertesi, 1985). If both types of consumers (the quality sensitive, who can afford higher prices, and the price sensitive group of the poor) exist in the same region then the correlation between the formal and the informal trade will be positive.

Since there was no previous research on the spatial distribution of informal trade I cannot refer to any direct empirical findings concerning the preceding assumptions. However, research on consumption patterns including informal sources as well shows that

- Shopping on CM is common among Hungarian households. According to a large scale survey in 1993, 68% of Hungarian households used CM to cut their expenses, and 28% of them regularly bought basic items on these markets (Harcsa, 1995; Sik, 1995). These activities were slightly more widespread among town than among village dwellers.

- A survey concerning the volume of informal trade in the case of four types of goods (cigarette, beverages, coffee and cosmetics, Hungarian Household Panel Survey, 1995, N=2200 households) found that the proportion of informal sources are significantly higher among Budapest dwellers than among inhabitants of any other type of settlement, and lower among those living in Western Hungary compared to those living in any other region (Sik, 1996).

The spatial distribution of CM and SM

There is at least one CM in every seventh and at least on SM site in every fifth Hungarian settlement (Table 13.1). The spreading of CM is positively associated with settlement size and administrative status. To have a CM is uncommon in settlements with less than 2000 inhabitants and frequent in cities,[1] and while in 89% of the county capitals, and 69% of the cities in general there is at least one CM, in the villages the same figure is only 10%.

The association between size and status of the settlement and the spreading of CM and SM is even closer if we focus on 'large' CMs.[2]

There is at least one 'large' CM in every fifteenth settlement (6.9% of all settlements), and 0, 1, 12, 41 and 62% by settlement size categories, respectively, have 'large' CMs. The trend is the same as we saw in Table 13.1 but the deviation from the average is sharper. For example if we use the general CM definition, the proportion of informal markets in the cities is approximately five times bigger than on average, the same figure for 'large' CMs is close to nine.

The distribution of SMs (whether we measure it by their existence or by the number of their types) by settlement size is smooth, except that they are somewhat over represented in the settlements with more than 10 000 inhabitants (Table 13.1). SMs are more spread in cities (29% of them have at least one SM) than in county capitals (20%), and the same is true as far as the number of SM types are concerned. The average value of SM sites in county capitals is .42, in cities and in villages .56 and .26, respectively.

The distribution of CMs is less uneven among the regions than by settlement size (Table 13.2). The proportion of settlements with CM is the largest (approximately three times the average) in Southeast Hungary (here settlements are significantly larger than in general)[3] and is below average in the western regions. As to 'large' CMs, the distribution is almost the same as for CMs in general, the overrepresentation of the Southeast is about four times the average.

The regional distribution of SMs is again rather smooth with a slight overrepresentation among the southeastern settlements. In this case there seems to be some difference whether we use the nominal (there is at least one SM site or not) or the interval (the number of SM sites) measurement format. This latter variable indicates sharper difference between the Southeast and the rest of the country, and the settlements of the Central region are slightly above the average (while in the former case they are below it).

The variance analysis in Table 13.3 is a first step in analyzing the role two of the spatial dimensions play in explaining the distribution of CM and SM.[4] The F values and the eta squares show the strength of the two spatial variables (relative to each other and without controlling for any other dimension) and the regression coefficient gives an estimate regarding the strength these two spatial variables have in determining the distribution of CM and SM.

In the case of CM the role of settlement size is much stronger than that of the region and their combined influence is weak as well. The size-dominated role of the two spatial dimensions has had a substantial influence on the distribution of CM. The case of SMs is quite different. There is not much difference between the role of the two spatial variables and the overall influence of the spatial dimensions on the distribution of SMs is very small.[5]

When the analysis was repeated using regression technique (and incorporating administrative status into the model but still not controlling for any other social factor), the strength of the model remained almost the same for both CM and SM (Table 13.4). As to CM, the role of size variables is stronger than that of administrative status and region but the latter have their independent and significant strength as well. In the case of both CM and SM among the region variables it is the Southeast region that increases the probability of having informal trade the most. While in the case of CM larger settlement size (note that the smallest and the largest size categories have significantly less strength that the medium categories) and having city status of were somewhat stronger than the region variables, in case of SM the opposite is the case (Table 13.4).

The next step in analyzing the spatial distribution of CMs is to develop a multivariate model. Table 13.5 contains the variables we have used to control for the social composition of the settlements by settlement size. The six variables in the upper panel of the table are proxies for the social composition of the demand for informal consumption and the supply of informal labor. The following assumptions (in the order of rows) were developed:

- Decreasing population (measured as the changing number of inhabitants or as the rate of inflow and outflow of migrants) can both be negatively or positively associated with the spreading of CM and SM. If we consider these variables as proxies for the decrease of the demand for informal goods and labor and of the supply of informal labor and if we assume that all groups of the original population decrease proportionally, in that case we should assume negative association simply because the number of potential customers diminishes. But if we assume that there is a segregation process going on, i.e. the better off groups leave the settlement disproportionally in that case positive correlation will occur since the shrinking population will contain more and more poorer households which are more likely to be interested (both as customer and trader) in informal trade.

- Higher rate of aging and high proportion of older inhabitants are negatively correlated with SM since they indicate a shrinking supply of informal labor while they may or may not witness increasing demand for informal wage labor from the SM. Elderly households in case of need (lack of income to buy formal labor and lack of physical ability to do domestic labor) may rely more on reciprocal labor or charity than on informal wage labor from the SM. As to CM, the relation between aging and the spreading of CM is not obvious either. On the one hand we can assume negative correlation if the solvent demand of the elderly population is extremely low and their physical ability to go shopping to the CM (often far from the downtown area) is limited. On the other hand empirical evidence shows that pensioners (except the very old with limited ability to visit CMs) are active consumers of CMs (Sik, 1996).

- Unemployment and long term unemployment are positively associated with the spreading of CM and SM since they constitute both demand for cheap goods and supply the for informal labor market. The second panel in Table 13.5 contains variables which approach the demand for and the supply of informal marketing of goods and of labor through wealth.- Increasing and high level use of electricity in the household are positively correlated with the domestic production based elements of the informal economy (Lackó 1995). If we assume that these activities are positively correlated with informal trade and labor (and especially with the latter which is the major source of casual labor for seasonal small scale domestic production) then we can assume positive association between the trend and current level of domestic electricity consumption and the spreading of CM and SM.

- The relation between the spreading of CM and SM and the proportion of car and phone owners can be both negative and positive. Since the possession of durable goods is a form of wealth and since wealthy households can afford to buy in the formal trading system we assume a negative association between car/phone ownership and the spreading of CM and SM. However, since to have a car or a phone is not a luxury item anymore in Hungary, the possession of these durable goods does not exclude the possibility of income pressures. Households under such conditions are more mobile than those lacking a car or phone and may increase the level of involvement in informal production and consumption, i.e. the correlation may be positive between ownership and the spreading of informal trading activities.

- While the previous two variables were proxies for the wealth of the households the per capita budget expresses the wealth of the community. We assume negative association between the wealth of the community and the spreading of CM and SM since a better-off community can afford not to get fees from the informal traders and is more willing and able to control crime-prone informal activity. The last panel of Table 13.5 contains proxies for the size and trend of formal trade. In the introductory section we already argued that positive or negative association both make sense as far as the relation between informal and formal trade are concerned.

- In case of the first variable in this panel (the trend of the number of retail shops) a higher rate indicates the expansion of formal trade. The following two sets of variables (the existence of a formal market and at least one gas station in 1988 and in 1993) describes the shrinking of formal trade (market or gas station lost), the expansion of it (market or gas station won) or the stable presence of it (market or gas station always).

- Finally, we assume a positive association between the higher proportion of private formal trade and catering and the spreading of CM and SM. Partly since the spread of private formal trade is a sign of increasing demand, partly since small private firms are the most prone to be involved in informal activity.

Table 13.6 shows the results of the multiple regression analyses using all three spatial variables and the proxies of the social composition of the settlements and of the demand and the supply for CM and SM.[6]

The spreading of CMs is still strongly influenced by the three spatial factors. Compared to Table 13.4 we can see that while the strength of the model - due to the incorporation of the social composition variables - has slightly increased, the control for the demand and supply factors reduced the strength of settlement size, city status and region. Still all spatial factors have played a significant role in determining the spatial distribution of CMs and despite the control for the demand and supply dimensions their structures have remained unchanged . This indicates that these dimensions though connected with the spatial factors (as Table 13.5 indicated in case of settlement size) do not override the independent role of the spatial dimensions. The explanation is that the size, status and locality of the settlements cover dimensions relevant in understanding the spreading of CM and SM which are different from those we used as control variables in the regression models. Just to give some examples it is possible that

a in larger settlements the transaction costs of hiding, disguising informal activities (or in case of being caught that of damage control) is lower than in smaller settlements,

b in certain localities there are substantial differences concerning the regulation and law enforcement of inhibiting informal activity,

c the structure of informal production and consumption is different in the regions and this modifies the costs of informal activities, etc.

The stable presence of formal market between 1988 and 1993 and the increasing presence of it have a strong and positive association with the presence of CM. Besides the presence of formal market the spreading of gas stations, private ownership and increasing use of domestic electricity also significantly increases the likelihood of the presence of an CM. All these findings fit the assumptions we made previously,

a greater and increasing solvent demand for goods increases the chances of a growing formal and informal trade simultaneously,

b with private ownership and small scale production have positive influence on the spreading of informal trade.

The two cases in which our assumptions were not confirmed are the following: the rate of unemployment has no significant role in determining the spread of CM while long-term unemployment has a negative one. The wealth of the households has an ambiguous effect on the spreading of CM, i.e. car ownership decreases but phone ownership increases the spreading of CMs.

As far as SM is concerned, by adding the demand and supply proxies as control variables to the three spatial dimensions a model has been created which substantially differs from the original model in Table 13.4. The role of administrative status and size disappear. The region still has some influence though much weaker than in the original model. Interestingly, while previously only the Southeast region increased the probability of the presence of a 'slave market' in the extended model the Northern/Northeastern region has an equally strong but decreasing effect. It may indicate the migration of casual labor from the North/Northeast towards the Southeast. This may be interpreted as the revival of a traditional historical route of labor migration since for ages there were well organized labor groups (gangs, bands) which commuted during the most of the year from the North to the South to earn their living with casual work.[7]

According to our hypotheses private wealth decreases the probability of the presence of SM while the wealth of the community has no significant effect. The model also confirms that the more formal markets and private property are spread and the higher domestic electric consumption is, the more likely SM can also be found. This seems to fit the hypothesis that markets, private retail and restaurants and petty production need local supply of informal (casual, seasonal) labor. This assumption is supported also from the supply side, i.e. the higher rate of unemployed and the decreasing proportion of elderly increase the probability of having an SM in town.

Formal Trade, CM and SM

The extended regression models indicated a significant and positive association between the spreading of formal and informal markets. Table 13.7 contains the correlation coefficients between the number of CM and SM versus the existence of a formal market and the number of retail shops in 1988 and in 1993. The figures suggest that

- the assumption that CM and SM are present simultaneously was wrong, there is but a weak correlation between the spread of CM and SM, which in other words means that CMs and SMs are two different and not closely related parts of the informal economy,
- to have a CM in town is strongly associated with having a formal market in town, and the number of retail shops and the existence of a for-

mal market before the transition also positively correlates with the existence of CM today (while the two elements of formal trade are also positively correlated).[8]

If we slightly rephrase our original question and instead of the existence of CM we focus on the size of CM (using the proxy of the number of traders), we find a somewhat stronger correlation between the spreading of CM and SM and much stronger correlation between the size of informal market of goods and the number of retail shops (both in 1988 and in 1993).

These stronger associations may be the artifacts of the uncontrolled size of settlements. As the last row of the second part of Table 13.7 shows, if we select the subsample of settlements with 'large' CM (which are also large settlements), the correlation between the size of CM and SM drops significantly, which again implies that these two forms of the informal economy are spatially independent of each other. However, the strong correlation between the size of CM and retail trade remains strong.[9] This reinforces the validity of our assumption that formal trade and informal trade are spatially correlated.

The Spatial Distribution of Foreigners in the Informal Marketplaces

The role of foreigners in the informal economy is perhaps one of the hottest issues in contemporary Hungary but I assume Hungary is not an exception in this sense. Research on xenophobia showed that the increasing level of xenophobia (between 1989 and 1995) has been associated with 'welfare chauvinism' which is a modern form of nationalism, in which citizens are afraid of (and/or jealous and suspicious of) foreigners who they think are abusing their welfare rights, from jobs on the labor market to welfare benefits (Csepeli-Sik, 1995). From time to time in the media (and in the programs of some small but loudmouth right-wing parties) foreigners (as well as Gypsies) are the main scapegoats of every problem of contemporary Hungary. The following summary illustrates the view of a foreign anthropologist about this issue:

> '(In 1990 in the television E.S.)... there was footage at peak viewing times of chaotic market-place scenes, and interviews with concerned council officials, and long-suffering local residents who would bemoan the lack of any effective regulation by the council... In one television news bulletin the scandal focused on traffic in young

children, allegedly being routinely sold by their Gypsy parents... counterfeit currency disseminated on some large market-places in southern Hungary by powerful gangs with origins in Yugoslavia and Bulgaria... violent disputes between Syrian and Algerian gangs for control of the money-changing business on the streets of central Budapest... Soviet soldiers selling potentially lethal shells and rockets...' (Hann, 1992).

As is the case with every stereotype and prejudice, these anti-foreigner feelings are not without some well-founded truth. Just to give some hints of the scale and relevance of the issue, the first form of informal markets in Hungary as early as in the mid-seventies were called Polish-markets, since they were dominated by impoverished and adventurous Polish 'handlers'[10] while nowadays the most visible informal markets are dominated by Chinese. As far as tourism is concerned, the number of tourists coming annually to Hungary is approximately twice the size of the entire Hungarian population. Finally, as I argued in a previous paper, the opening up of the previously very well guarded borders was a major structural component of the increasing informal economy in post-communist Hungary (Sik, 1994).

This section focuses on two issues closely related to the preceding phenomena. First I give some figures concerning the volume of foreigners in the informal economy. Secondly I analyze which social factors increase the probability of foreign involvement in the informal markets.

The average number of traders in a CM is about 63 (Table 13.8). There is a significant deviation from this average depending on the size of the settlement (the size of the CM and of the settlement positively correlate) and only an insignificant difference by region (Table 13.8 and Table 13.9). The average number of permanent foreign traders is somewhat higher than the number of tourist traders and the two groups of foreign traders together constitute about a third of all traders at the CMs.

As to the spatial distribution of foreign traders, their number also increases with increasing settlement size but the deviation from the average if less sharp. This explains why the proportion of foreign traders is higher in the smaller settlements than in the bigger ones. More precisely the distribution of the proportion of foreign traders shows a U curve. The peak value is at the small (but not the smallest) settlement size type while the lowest point is at the two medium-range settlement size types. Regionally, foreign traders are overrepresented in the North/Northeast region while CM traders are more numerous in the Southeast and in the Central regions.

By origin the two most widespread groups of foreign traders are the Russians and the Romanians, present at half of the CMs (Table 13.8 and

Table 13.9, Panel 2). Their distribution by settlement size is rather flat with some overrepresentation in the smaller and biggest settlement categories. Regionally the spreading of the Russians is again rather flat; they are present all over Hungary but are over represented in the Northern/North-eastern region. The spatial distribution of the Romanians is more uneven. They are overrepresented in the Central region and underrepresented in Western Hungary and especially in the Southwest.[11]

Hungarians from abroad and Poles are present at every fourth CM. The spatial spreading of the Hungarians from abroad resembles that of the Romanians - not by chance since most of them are from Romania. The case of Poles is entirely different. Their spatial distribution is the most uneven which in itself indicates that at least in a spatial sense they have selective trading strategies. This strategy focuses on the larger settlements and the Western and Central regions of Hungary.

The spreading of Chinese and ex-Yugoslavian traders is small compared to the other groups of origin. The small group of Chinese traders is very unevenly distributed by settlement size; they are overrepresented in the highest settlement category while their regional distribution is similar to that of Poles.

The spreading of foreigners at the SMs is less significant than on the CMs (Table 13.8 and Table 13.9, Panel 3). The most widespread are the Romanians, followed by the Hungarians (mostly from Romania) and Russians and the ex-Yugoslavians. As to the characteristics of the spatial distribution, Romanians and Hungarians from abroad are concentrated in larger settlements mostly in the Southeast and Central regions. The Russians are overrepresented in the smaller and medium settlement categories and can be found all over the country. The ex-Yugoslavians are equally distributed by settlement size but are very much concentrated in the southwestern part of Hungary.

If we use a narrower definition of CM (considering as a large CM only those markets with more than 25 traders) the proportion of foreign traders compared to all traders falls to 25%, which is another indicator of the trend for foreign traders to act as mobile vendors for the population of smaller settlements. However, while the proportion of foreign traders is decreasing in the large markets their spread is more or less the same, i.e. the spread of foreign traders by origin is about the same in the large CMs as in CMs in general. Chinese and Romanians are present at large CMs more than at CMs in general, 27 and 57%, respectively.

Instead of the spatial factors focusing on the characteristics of CMs, Table 13.10 shows that the proportion of foreign traders is higher at smaller markets than on average. As to the spread of foreign traders by origin, there are basically two types. The ex-Yugoslavians and the Russians are spread rather evenly among the markets. In the latter case it is interesting to note that this is the only group of traders who are overrepresented in the mini-market category. All the other trader groups show a positive correlation between market size and their presence, the strongest being the Chinese.

The other three characteristics of CM we analyzed (the presence of impoverished quasi-traders (poor people selling their own possessions), whether the market contains stalls (or there areno built structure and traders sell their goods from the trunks of their cars or from their hands or tables), and whether the market operates seasonally (or is open during the whole year), did not indicate major differences in the spread of foreign traders. Their proportion is somewhat higher at CMs with poor traders (39%) and where there is no built infrastructure (36%) and lower all-year markets (31%). These associations of course could be the artifacts of the strong association between the size of the market and the presence of foreign traders. One would assume that the smaller the CM is, the more likely it is that there will be poor traders, built infrastructure will be missing and the market will operate seasonally only. However, while the last two assumptions are correct,[12] the first is wrong. Poor traders can be found at 78% of the largest markets and this value decreases continuously with decreasing market size (48%, 27%, 21%, and 19%, respectively). As a consequence the higher presence of foreign traders on informal markets where there are poor traders exists independently of the strong association between size of markets and the spread of foreign traders.

As to the spread of foreign traders by origin, the only difference compared to their presence at CMs in general is at markets with poor traders. In this case, the presence of all groups of foreign traders is somewhat higher than at CMs in general but Chinese and Romanian traders are significantly overrepresented at these markets (they are present on 29% and 63% of these CMs, respectively).

The Causes of the Spread of Informal Traders and of Foreign Traders

As a first step, the roles of settlement size and region uncontrolled for any other dimension are to be tested. Table 13.11 shows that at CMs in general settlement size has a strong influence on the spread of traders in general and on both types of foreign traders. The proportion of foreign traders among all traders is less strongly determined by settlement size and the role of region is somewhat stronger. This is especially the case if we focus on the large informal markets (Table 13.11, lower panel).

A more straightforward way to test the role of the spatial factors can be seen in Table 13.12. In this model beside the regional factor both the size of the market and of the settlement are incorporated into the analysis. The way these three factors influence the spread of permanent and tourist foreign traders and their proportion compared to all traders is entirely different.

The number of permanent traders is determined by the two size related factors independently, i.e. controlling for settlement size the influence of the size of the market remained significant. This means that permanent traders show up in larger settlements and within them at bigger markets.

The number of tourist traders is influenced only by the size of settlement. This means that this form of informal trade is seeking those places where products can be sold, and not necessarily on the informal markets but in streets, at workplaces, etc.

Finally, the proportion of foreign traders as less strongly influenced by spatial dimensions than the number of foreign traders and the role of regional differences is more visible in this approach.

Correlation coefficients confirm the proceeding (Table 13.13). The proportion of foreign traders has only an insignificant correlation with spatial and market variables. The number of permanent and tourist foreign traders shows s strong and positive correlation with market size, weaker positive and negative correlation with the presence of poor traders and the lack of built stalls on the market. However, the number of foreign traders is characterized also by s strong and positive association with settlement size and the number of market hours.[13]

The next step in analyzing the role social factors play in the spread of foreign traders is to build regression models which show the role spatial and market factors jointly plays in this process (Table 13.14).

As was supposed, settlement size and city status are the strongest components of this model. The number of permanent foreign workers is higher at larger informal markets, in the cities and in north(eastern) Hungary and decreases with settlement size. As to tourist trade, its magnitude increases with market and settlement size and with longer market hours but decreases in the cities.

The proportion of foreign traders rising with the presence of poor trade, with longer market hours and in the northern regions of Hungary.

Focusing on larger markets, the models showing the role of spatial and market forces are more or less unchanged in case of the number of all and of permanent foreign traders (Table 13.15). However, the models became more robust in the case of the number of tourist traders and the proportion of foreign traders. In the former case regional variables though weaker than the market and settlement size variables, became significant and show the spread of the tourist trade in Northern and Eastern Hungary (and in the Southwest). As to the proportion of foreign traders at large informal markets, beside the presence of poor traders and being situated in the North/North-eastern region it is having built stalls that increases the share of foreigners in informal marketing on large markets.

Table 13.5 contained the variables we have added to the spatial and market variables. Since we do not assume major differences, the social factors influence informal traders in general and foreign traders in particular, we consider the previous assumptions valid in the case of foreign traders as well.

Table 13.16 shows the results for all informal markets. The model explaining the number of traders is somewhat more robust that the basic model was (Table 13.14). The same spatial and market characteristics play identical roles in the extended model as they did in the basic one, which means that their influences were independent of the extended variables. In other words, having city status, many permanent inhabitants and poor informal traders increase the probability of informal trade.

The extended model shows no modification of the preceding influences but adds some other components. First of all, there are the proxies for the decreasing size of the formal trade. A diminishing formal retail sector, disappearing formal markets and the lack of private restaurants are all signs of a deteriorating formal trading sector. This association suggest that in contemporary Hungary informal trade substitutes for rather than co-exists with formal trade. Another factor that increases the spread of informal trade is the growing demand for informal goods. One sign of it may be the growing size of the population and at the same time the large proportion of the elderly population. These demographic factors increase the demand for goods but not for expensive, quality products since pensioners are not famous for being lavish and quality sensitive buyers.

The extended models of the number of permanent and tourist traders have the same robustness and elements as the basic models. This means that the new variables cannot give any further explanation above the already recognized spatial and market variables. The only exception is that the number of tourist traders increases if there are more migrants among the inhabitants, which can be interpreted in different ways (increasing population, more informal trade oriented demand, more involvement in the informal economy).

The extended model of the proportion of foreign traders is much more robust compared to the basic model and the newly added variables replaced those in the basic model (except the presence of poor traders). The high proportion of long-term unemployed is the strongest factor of the increasing proportion of foreign traders. The other variables that increase the spread of foreign trade are the collapse of formal trade and decreasing demand (i.e. diminishing population).

Focusing on large informal markets (Table 13.17), the number of informal traders is still a function of settlement size, city status and the presence of poor traders. In this sense there is no difference from the basic model (Table 13.15). But - as was the case for the models covering all informal markets - decreasing size of formal retail trade, diminishing electricity consumption and a high proportion of the elderly, i.e. increasing demand for informal goods, have a significant and positive influence and increase the robustness of the model as well.

There is much less change compared to the basic model in the case of the permanent and tourist foreign traders. In the former case the spread of private retail shops and phones increases the presence of permanent foreign traders which are signs that in special circumstances the coexistence between formal and informal trade is not out of the question. In the latter case, the regional variables are replaced by decreasing retail trade, more migrants among the inhabitants and more private restaurants

Finally, the proportion of foreign traders is much better explained by the extended than it was by the basic model. It is not that the factors which played significant roles in the basic model have lost their strength. The presence of poor traders, being situated in the Northern part of Hungary and having built stalls increase the chances of having more foreign trader in the extended model, as they did in the basic model, But the presence of formal markets, private restaurants and phones, and decreasing formal retail trade and electricity consumption significantly increase the proportion of foreign traders.

Summary

Informal marketplaces are open-air, periodic marketplaces. The paper analyzes two types of informal marketplaces, the so called 'slave markets'(SM) and the 'comecon markets' (CM). The 'slave market' is a marketplace of those labor transactions that are not observed statistically, and neither the employer nor the employee pays taxes or social security contributions. At a 'slave market' casual jobs are typically negotiated, and they commonly do not last more than one day. Normally the market functions only for some hours every morning. The typical types of jobs are construction and agriculture work. The 'comecon market' is the communist and post-communist version of bazaars or flea markets.

The two questions most often raised in connection with informal marketplaces in Hungary refer to their number and whether foreigners dominate them. The first part of the paper attempts to offer a tentative answer to the former, the second part to the latter question.

Table 13.1 The spread of informal markets by settlement size

	-500	501-2000	2001-5000	5001-10000	10000-	Total	Adj. Eta Square
N (all settlements)	947	1368	510	140	142	3107	
Informal market (%)[a]	2	5	34	53	69	13.7	0.29
'Large' informal market (%, settl. with CM, N=420)[b]	0	11	36	77	97	50	0.41
'Slave' market (%)[c]	18	16	21	21	31	19	0.01
Number of 'slave' markets[d]	0.20	0.25	0.38	0.42	0.51	0.28	0.01

a Dummy variable, 1= the settlement has an informal market.
b Dummy variable, 1= the settlement has a large informal market (number of traders above 25).
c Dummy variable, 1= the settlement has a 'slave' market.
d In the questionnaire there were seven sites mentioned which are wellknown to be associated with 'slave' market. These were the pub or bar, the coffee house, the main street or the main square, the bus terminal or the train station, a special place traditionally housing 'slave' market, the market or the informal market, and any other place. The variable shows the number of places 'slave' markets operate in the settlement (maximum 7).

Table 13.2 The spread of informal markets by region

	South West	South East	North/North East	North West	Central	Total	Adj. Eta Square
N (all settlements)	650	330	831	867	436	3107	
Informal market (%)	6	43	14	8	15	13.7	0.10
'Large' informal market (%, settl. with CM, N=420)	72	58	44	36	51	50	0.04
'Slave' market (%)	20	26	20	14	18	19	0.01
Number of 'slave' markets	0.24	0.54	0.27	0.20	0.31	0.28	0.02

Table 13.3 The influence of settlement size and region on the spread of informal market

	Settlement size		Region		Settlement size and region	Multiple regression square
	F value	Adj. eta square	F value	Adj. eta square	F value	
Total sample (N=3107)						
Has informal market	274.3	0.53	49	0.20	9.1	0.33
Number of 'slave' markets	3.8	0.08	8.3	0.11	5.7	0.02
Settlements with informal market (N=420)						
Number of 'slave' markets	5.1	0.20	3.6	0.18	5.8	0.08
Settlements with 'large' informal market (N=215)						
Number of 'slave' markets	0.9*	0.13	5.2	0.34	2.8	0.13

* Non significant parameter

Table 13.4 The basic spatial models of the spread of informal markets (N=3107, multiple regression models)

	Beta coefficient	T value	Level of significance
Has informal market, Adj. R square= 0.34			
Medium-large settlement[a]	0.32	17.5	0.0000
Medium settlement	0.22	12.3	0.0000
Southeast	0.24	13.0	0.0000
Large settlement	0.24	9.0	0.0000
City93[b]	0.20	7.2	0.0000
North-Northeast	0.13	6.1	0.0000
Northwest	0.18	5.6	0.0000
Southwest	0.10	3.8	0.0001
Small settlement	0.04	2.2	0.02
Number of 'slave' markets, Adj. R square= 0.03			
Southeast	0.10	4.3	0.0000
City93	0.09	2.8	0.006
Medium settlement	0.06	2.5	0.006

a The terms referring to the size of the settlement are as follows: small = 501-2000 inhabitants, medium= 2001-5000 inhabitants, medium-large= 5001-10 000 inhabitants, and large=10 001 and more inhabitants. Settlements with less than 500 inhabitants were omitted from the models to avoid multicollinearity.

b Dummy variable, 1= city status in 1993.

Table 13.5 Social characteristics of settlements by size[14] (Budapest excluded)

N	- 500	501-2000	2001-5000	5001-10000	10000 -	Total	Eta Square
N	947	1368	510	140	142	3107	
Inhabitants 1993/88[a]	0.91	0.96	0.98	1.01	1.00	0.96	0.13
Migrant/Inhabitants[b]	-3.4	-2.2	-1.5	-0.03	-0.02	-2.1	0.04
Elderly 1993/88[c]	1.05	1.05	1.04	1.05	1.07	1.05	0.00
Elderly 1993 (%)[d]	27	22	20	18	17	22	0.18
Unemployed/Actives (%)[e]	28.9	23.4	23.3	21.8	17.5	24.6	0.03
Long term unemp./Unemp.[f]	0.92	0.85	0.88	0.87	0.81	0.88	0.02
Electricity 1993/88[g]	1.4	1.4	1.3	1.3	1.2	1.4	0.03
Electricity/household 1993[h]	1.8	2.3	2.5	2.6	2.3	2.2	0.13
Car/household 1993 (%)	31	38	39	40	46	36	0.08
Phone/household 1993 (%)	12	13	17	21	25	14	0.05
Budget/Inhabitants[i]	57.7	45.4	41.2	47.6	24.5	47.6	0.06
Shop 1993/88[j]	1.9	2.7	2.8	3.9	4.4	2.6	0.10
Market lost 88/93 (%)[k]	10	9	13	2	6	10	0.01
Market won 88/93 (%)	0	2	15	27	38	6	0.18
Market always (%)	0	1	18	36	52	7	0.27
Gas station lost 88/93 (%)[l]	12	9	6	0	4	9	0.01
Gas station won 88/93 (%)	4	13	38	46	44	17	0.14
Gas station always (%)	1	3	20	50	52	9	0.26
Private shop 1993 (%)[m]	50	73	75	73	65	66	0.14
Private restaurant 1993 (%)[n]	78	86	84	78	71	83	0.03

a   The number of non-temporary residents in 1993 per those of 1988.
b   Net migration in 1988, 1990 and 1993 (inflow minus outflow in the three years) was added and divided by the number of permanent residents in 1993.
c   The proportion of residents above 60 among all residents in 1993 per that of 1988.
d   The proportion of residents above 60 among all residents in 1993.
e   The proportion of unemployed (including those who lost their eligibility but are still without job) among those in the active age cohort.
f   The number of long term unemployed (those above 180 days of unemployment and those who already lost eligibility) per registered unemployed.
g   The per household electricity consumption in 1993 per to that of in 1988.
h   The per household electricity consumption in 1993.
i   The per capita budget.
j   The number of retail shops in 1993 per those of 1988.
k   Comparing whether there was at least one retail shop in the settlement in 1988 and in 1993 I developed three types. Lost means there was retail shop(s) in 1988 but not in 1993. Won is just the opposite. Always refers to settlement with retail shop(s) both in 1988 and in 1993.
l   Comparing whether there was at least one gas station in the settlement in 1988 and in 1993 I developed three types. Lost means there was gas station in 1988 but not in 1993. Won is just the opposite. Always refers to settlement with gas station both in 1988 and in 1993.
m   The proportion of private retail shops among all shops in 1993.
n   The proportion of private restaurants (including snack bars, pubs and small kiosks) among all restaurants in 1993.

Table 13.6 The extended models of the spread of informal markets (N=3107, multiple regression models)

	Beta coefficient	T value	Level of significance
Has informal market, Adj. R square= 0.39			
Large settlement*	0.15	4.8	0.0000
Medium settlement	0.22	9.0	0.0000
Medium-large settlement	0.11	4.9	0.0000
Southeast	0.18	8.5	0.0000
North-northeast	0.14	5.6	0.0000
Northwest	0.15	6.2	0.0000
Market won 88/93	0.16	7.9	0.0000
Market always 88/93	0.25	11.0	0.0000
Gas station won 88/93	0.008	4.7	0.0000
City93	0.14	4.5	0.0000
Southwest	0.10	4.0	0.0001
Car/household	-0.10	-4.0	0.0001
Long unempl./Unempl.	-0.07	-3.3	0.0009
Phone/household	0.06	3.2	0.001
Elderly	-0.06	-3.0	0.002
Inhabitants 93/88	-0.06	-2.8	0.005
Electricity 93/88	0.04	2.6	0.009
Private restaurant	0.04	0.29	0.003
Migrants/Inhabitants	-0.04	-2.3	0.02
Small settlement	0.05	2.3	0.02
Number of 'slave' markets, Adj. R square= 0.08			
Car/household	-0.16	-5.3	0.0000
Electricity/household	0.12	4.4	0.0000
Market won 88/93	0.09	4.2	0.0000
Gas station always 88/93	0.11	3.9	0.0001
Market lost 88/93	-0.08	-2.8	0.0002
Unempl./Active	0.07	3.0	0.003
Phone/household	-0.06	-2.8	0.005
Private shop	0.06	2.7	0.007
Private restaurant	0.05	2.6	0.009
Elderly 93/88	-0.05	-2.4	0.02
Southeast	0.05	2.1	0.04
North/Northeast	-0.06	-2.1	0.04

* The terms referring to the size of the settlement are as follows: small = 501-2000 inhabitans, medium= 2001-5000 inhabitans, medium-large= 5001-10 000 inhabitans, and large=10 001 and more inhabitants. Settlements with less than 500 inhabitants were omitted from the models to avoid multicollinearity.

Table 13.7 Intercorrelation matrix among trading characteristics of the settlements[15] (total sample and settlements with 'large' markets)

	Number of informal markets*	Number of 'slave' markets	Had market in 1988	Had market in 1993	Number of retail shops in 1988	Number of retail shops in 1993
Total sample (N=3017)						
1	-	0.13	0.26	0.55	0.38	0.30
2		-	0.10	0.17	0.07	0.05
3			-	0.43	0.24	0.19
4				-	0.49	0.41
5					-	0.97
Number of traders (N=420)	0.22	0.24	0.42	0.69	0.60	
Settlement with 'large' markets (N=215)						
2		-	0.09	0.14	-0.11	-0.11
3			-	0.27	0.19	0.17
4				-	0.25	0.20
5					-	0.97
Number of traders	0.04	0.20	0.26	0.62	0.53	

* The interval version of the variable expressing the existence of informal market in the settlement. The difference, however, between this variable and the one I used before (informal market (%)) is negligible since to have more than on informal market is exceptional.

Table 13.8 The spread of foreign traders and workers at CMs and SMs by settlement size (Budapest excluded)

	-500	501-2000	2001-5000	5001-10000	10000 -	Total	Eta Square
N (market-settlements)	17	64	175	74	96	426	
Number of traders[a]	3.0	7.8	28.0	87.7	163.5	63.4	0.40
Numb. of permanent foreign traders	0	2.6	5.1	15.5	36.6	12.5	0.16
Number of tourist traders	1.4	1.0	3.1	3.5	28.7	8.6	0.10
Foreign trader/all trader (%)[b]	47	60	27	19	36	34	0.16
Foreign traders by origin[c] (N= CMs)	17	64	175	74	96	426	
Ex-Jugoslavians (%)	0	5	4	16	0	5	0.01
Chinese (%)	0	0	6	8	47	14	0.43
Poles (%)	0	22	23	20	45	26	0.20
Hungarians from abroad (%)	32	29	18	37	37	28	0.10
Russians(%)	64	61	42	33	67	50	0.02
Romanians(%)	64	51	44	51	56	50	0.03
Foreign workers by origin[d] (N= SMs)	154	203	105	29	42	534	
Ex-Jugoslavians(%)	0	4	7	8	6	4	0.12
Hungarians from abroad(%)	0	2	13	21	39	8	0.39
Russians(%)	11	2	10	15	0	7	0.04
Romanians(%)	0	10	28	48	34	15	0.37

a   An estimate of the number of traders on the informal market. If there were more than one the questionnaire asked information about the largest market. As to the changing number of traders on a market day, the question focused on the prime time of a market day.

b   The proportion of foreign traders among all traders on the informal market. The term foreign trader covers both foreigners' settled in Hungary and tourist traders.

c   Dummy variable, 1=foreigner (settled or tourist) of a certain ethnic group trades on the informal market.

d   Dummy variable, 1=foreign worker of a certain ethnic group seeks job on the 'slave' market.

Table 13.9 The spreading of foreign traders and workers at CMs and SMs by region (Budapest excluded)

	South West	South East	North/ North East	North West	Central	Total	Eta Square
N (market-settlements)	42	147	108	64	65	426	
Number of traders	64.3	78.3	52.1	45.4	68.3	63.3	0.02
Num. of permanent foreign traders	5.8	13.1	20.0	6.1	8.4	12.6	0.03
Number of tourist traders	4.7	7.1	11.8	9.8	7.9	8.6	0.00
Foreign trader/all trader (%)	16	27	48	38	27	34	0.08
Foreign traders by origin (N= CMs)	42	147	108	64	65	426	
Ex-Yugoslavs	0	11	0	11	0	5	0.07
Chinese	38	9	5	15	28	14	0.06
Poles	32	19	13	32	55	26	0.21
Hungarians from abroad	0	33	38	0	23	28	0.06
Russians	33	43	72	48	37	50	0.02
Romanians	6	55	55	40	67	50	0.16
Foreign workers by origin (N=SMs)	114	84	151	110	73	534	
Ex-Jugoslavians	15	0	0	0	3	4	0.21
Hungarians from abroad	0	20	6	5	11	8	0.05
Russians	4	13	8	4	5	7	0.02
Romanians	4	43	5	9	27	15	0.05

Table 13.10 The spread of foreign traders at CMs by the size of the informal market[16] (%)

	1-5	6-10	11-40	41-100	101 and more	All	Eta Square
N	80	101	72	91	75	420	
Foreign trader/all trader	43	39	26	26	32	34	0.04
Ex-Jugoslavs	14	4	7	4	9	5	0.02
Chinese	0	7	3	32	40	14	0.18
Poles	23	26	16	36	34	26	0.01
Hungarians from abroad	12	34	17	27	44	28	0.05
Russians	41	51	52	53	55	50	0.00
Romanians	37	51	34	63	67	50	0.07

Table 13.11 The influence of settlement size and region on the spread of foreign traders on CMs

	Settlement size F-value	Adj. eta square	Region F-value	Adj. eta square	Settlement size and region F value	Multiple regress. square
Settlements with informal market (N=420)						
Num. of traders	73.7	0.65	4.5	0.16	4.9	0.41
Num. of perm. foreign traders	25.3	0.46	7.8	0.26	4.8	0.23
Num. of tourist traders	11.8	0.35	1.3[b]	0.12	2.4	0.12
Foreigners' trade	19.2	0.40	9.4	0.27	7.3	0.24
Settlements with large[a] informal market (N=215)						
Num. of traders	20.5	0.47	1.6[b]	0.16	3.0	0.23
Foreigners' trade	12.9	0.39	12.5	0.45	7.6	0.27

a   The mean number of traders on the IMs was 25. We defined Ims as large in case the number of traders was above the means.
b   non significant parameter.

Table 13.12 The influence of market size and region on the spread of foreign traders on the informal markets controlling for settlement size (N=420)

	Market size F-value	Adj. eta square	Region F-value	Adj. eta square	Market size and region (covariance of settlement size) F value	Multiple regress. square
Num. of perm. foreign traders	36.5	0.55	4.0	0.16	3.9 (34.8)	0.32
Num. of tourist traders	0.04	0.00*	2.0	0.01*	3.9 (354.0)	0.45
Foreign trad./ all traders	2.3	0.16*	6.5	0.26	2.7 (0.19[a])	0.11

*   Non significant parameter.

Table 13.13 Intercorrelation between the spread of foreign traders and the characteristics of informal markets (N=420)

	Foreign trader/all trader	Num. of permanent traders	Number of tourist traders	Market size	Settlement size	Market hours open	Poor trade
Market size	−0.03*	0.51	0.57	–			
Settlement size	0.002*	0.22	0.67	0.68	–		
Market hours open	0.18	0.08*	0.44	0.23	0.39	–	
Poor trade	0.12*	0.36	0.23	0.43	0.27	0.09*	–
No-stall market	0.04*	−0.11*	−0.21	−0.28	−0.30	−0.16	−0.09*

* Non significant parameter.

Table 13.14 The basic spatial models of the spread of foreign traders at the informal markets (N= 420, multiple regression models)

	Beta coefficient	T value	Level of significance
Number of traders, Adj. R square=0.57			
City93	0.37	9.0	0.0000
Settlement size	0.43	10.3	0.0000
Poor trade	0.16	4.3	0.0000
Southeast	0.14	2.8	0.002
Number of permanent resident foreign traders, Adj. R square= 0.34			
Market size	0.46	6.6	0.0000
City93	0.22	3.7	0.0002
North-Northeast	0.22	3.3	0.001
Settlement size	−0.19	−3.0	0.003
Poor trade	0.12	2.4	0.02
Number of tourist traders, Adj. R square= 0.55			
Settlement size	0.43	8.3	0.0000
Market size	0.38	6.7	0.0000
Market open hours	0.25	5.8	0.0000
City93	−0.24	−5.0	0.0000
Proportion of foreigners, Adj. R square= 0.13			
Poor trade	0.21	3.5	0.0005
North-Northeast	0.25	3.2	0.002
Northwest	0.23	3.2	0.002
Market hours open	0.15	2.3	0.02

Table 13.15 The basic spatial models of the spread of foreign traders at large informal markets (N=215, multiple regression models)[17]

	Beta coefficient	T value	Level of significance
Number of traders, Adj. R square= 0.45			
Settlement size	0.43	6.3	0.0000
Poor trade	0.26	4.3	0.0000
City93	0.19	3.0	0.003
Number of permanent resident foreign traders, Adj. R square=0.29			
Market size	0.41	4.6	0.0000
North/Northeast	0.33	3.4	0.001
City93	0.27	3.4	0.001
Number of tourist traders, Adj. R square= 0.61			
Market hours open	0.48	7.3	0.0000
Settlement size	0.27	4.0	0.0000
City93	−0.23	−4.2	0.0000
Market size	0.33	5.1	0.0000
Southwest	0.21	3.2	0.001
North/Northeast	0.17	2.6	0.01
Proportion of foreigners, Adj. R square= 0.32			
Poor trade	0.36	4.3	0.0000
North-Northeast	0.37	3.8	0.0000
No-stall market	−0.23	−3.5	0.0000

Table 13.16 The extended models of the spread of foreign traders at informal markets (N= 420, multiple regression models)

	Beta coefficient	T value	Level of significance
Number of traders, Adj. R square= 0.63			
City93	0.42	8.3	0.0000
Poor trade	0.25	6.2	0.0000
Shop 93/88	−0.23	−5.0	0.0000
Elderly	0.18	3.5	0.0000
Settlement size	0.40	9.1	0.0000
Inhabitant 93/88	0.23	3.7	0.0003
Private restaurant	−0.14	−2.6	0.009
Market lost	−0.13	−2.8	0.005
Number of permanent resident foreign traders, Adj. R square= 0.34			
Market size	0.46	6.1	0.0000
Settlement size	−0.20	−2.8	0.0005
City93	0.24	3.2	0.002
Poor trade	0.17	2.8	0.006
Number of tourist traders, Adj. R square= 0.56			
Market size	0.35	5.6	0.0000
Settlement size	0.44	8.0	0.0000
City93	−0.27	−4.5	0.0000
Market hours open	0.33	7.0	0.0000
Migrant/Inhabitant	0.16	2.2	0.02
Proportion of foreigners, Adj. R square= 0.34			
Long unempl./unempl.	0.29	3.9	0.0000
Southwest	−0.20	−2.9	0.004
Market lost	−0.19	−3.0	0.003
Poor trade	0.17	2.8	0.006
Inhabitant 93/88	−0.28	−2.9	0.004
Gas station won	−0.22	−2.5	0.01
Market always	−0.19	−2.4	0.02

Table 13.17 The extended models of the spread of foreign traders at large informal markets (N= 215, multiple regression models)

	Beta coefficient	T value	Level of significance
Number of traders, Adj. R square= 0.59			
Poor market	0.37	6.4	0.0000
Shop 93/88	−0.39	−5.6	0.0000
Settlement size	0.43	5.7	0.0000
City93	0.27	3.8	0.0002
Electricity 93/88	−0.25	−3.4	0.0007
Elderly	0.24	3.0	0.003
Number of permanent resident foreign traders, Adj. R square= 0.33			
Market size	0.46	4.4	0.0000
Private shop	0.28	3.0	0.003
City93	0.28	2.8	0.006
Phone	0.28	2.9	0.005
Number of tourist traders, Adj. R square= 0.68			
Market size	0.27	3.9	0.0000
Settlement size	0.35	4.7	0.0000
City93	−0.27	−4.2	0.0000
Private restaurant	0.30	4.0	0.0000
Market hours open	0.50	7.3	0.0000
Shop 93/88	−0.17	−2.3	0.01
Proportion of foreigners, Adj. R square= 0.50			
Market always	0.54	3.6	0.0005
Phone	0.30	3.4	0.0009
Poor market	0.30	3.5	0.0005
Market won	0.54	4.0	0.0001
North/Northeast	0.37	3.3	0.001
Private restaurant	0.28	2.8	0.006
No-stall market	−0.21	−2.8	0.006
Shop 93/88	−0.28	−2.7	0.007
Electricity 93/88	−0.26	−2.8	0.006

Notes

1. The association between the size and administrative status of settlement is very close in Hungary. On the one hand only 8% of the settlements with more than 10 000 inhabitants have no city status. On the other hand, all county capitald (N=24) have more than 10 000 inhabitants and 62% of the cities in general (N= 171) have more than 10 000 inhabitants.
2. To avoid the danger that in a small settlement two traders were enough to be perceived by the local authorities as informal market in the questionnaire we asked the mayors to tell us whether there is a marketplace in their settlement where 'several traders sell their goods'. The distribution of IM shows that the median of the number of traders was 25, and 5 or less traders constituted 19% of all cases. We redefined IM as 'large' informal markets in case there were more than 25 traders, i.e. we consider an IM as 'large' if the number of traders is above the median. The aim with this more accurate definition is to test whether there is any difference between IM in general and 'large' informal markets as far as the four hypotheses are concerned.
3. In general 6% of all settlements are cities but in the Southeast and Central regions their proportion is 15% and 11%, respectively, and while the average size of the settlements was 2,724 inhabitants in 1993, in the Southeast and Central regions these figures were 6,401 and 4,743, respectively.
4. The administrative status dimension was excluded from the variance analysis since it is very strongly correlated to the size variable.
5. When we repeated the variance analysis of SMs on the sample of settlements having IM or 'large' IM, we experienced no major change, except that in the latter case the role of the region is much stronger(lower sections of Table 3).
6. In the next step of the analysis we should run logistic regression to test the role of spatial, demand and supply variables on IM.
7. Just as in case of a Northeastern informal market the analysis of the spatial distribution of foreign traders showed the revival of the mediavel trade routes (Kókai 1995).
8. The correlation between the number of retail shops and the existence of formal markets is much weaker in 1988 than in 1993. This may refer to the changing nature of retail shops (in 1988 state-run retail trade was more wide spread than in 1993 and that also meant a different pattern of spatial distribution.
9. The less significant figures of the lower panel of Table 7 are the consequence of the greater homogeneity of settlement in the smaller subsample. However, the negative correlation between the existence of SM and the number of retail shops in 1988 and in 1993 are the strongest proofs of the incompatibility between 'slave trade' and lively formal trade.
10. The term has Yiddish origins but is widely used in Poland to describe petty (and often part time) trade and also the attitude of constant screening the possibilities to buy for selling, speculation (Wedel 1992).

11   The correlation coefficients describing the joint presence of foreign traders of different origin are rather weak in general but there is a strong correlation between the presence of Russians and Romanians (.47), somewhat weaker between Poles and Chinese (.38) and even weaker but still significant between Hungarians from abroad and Romanians, Poles and Russians (.10, .12 and .11, respectively).
12   While on average 64% of the IMs do not have stalls at all 91% of the smallest but only 42% of the largest markets do not have stalls. While in general 79% of the informal markets operate on an annual basis 95% of the largest and only 63% of the smallest ones operates all year long.
13   Market and settlement size strongly correlates, while the number of market hours, presence of poor traders and the size of market and settlement are less strongly but positively correlated. No-stall markets have negative association to the other market characteristics.
14   The source is the Settlements' Data Bank of the Hungarian Central Statistical Office (CSO).
15   The source of columns 3 to 6 is the Settlements' Data Bank of the Hungarian Central Statistical Office (CSO).
16   The categories of the size of IMs was constructed taking into consideration the mean (25) and average (63) value of the number of traders. In the light of these two figures the first two categories can be considered as very small and small Ims, the third as around the mean value, the fourth around the average value, while the last category contains the big IMs.
17   To avoid multicollinearity the small settlement category was omitted from the models.

References

Alexander, J. and Alexander, P. (1987) 'Striking a bargain in Javanese markets', *Man*, no. 22, pp. 42-68.

Alexander, J. and Alexander, P. (1991) 'What is a Fair Price? Price Setting and Trading Partnerships in Javanese Markets', *Man*, no. 26, pp. 493-512.

Böröcz, J. (1992) 'Dual dependency and the informalization of external linkages: the Hungarian case', *Research in Social Movements, Conflict, and Change*, no. 14, pp. 189-209.

Csepeli, G. and Sik, E. (1995) 'Changing content of political xenophobia in Hungary - is the growth of xenophobia inevitable?' in Fullerton, M., Sik, E. and Tóth, J. (eds), *Refugees and Migrants: Hungary at a Crossroads*, Institute for Political Science, Budapest.

Dewey, A. G. (1964) 'Capital, Credit and Saving in Javanese Marketing' in Firth, R. and Yamey, B.S. (eds.), *'Capital, Saving and Credit in Peasant Societies'*, Allen and Unwin Ltd, London, pp. 230-256.

Galasi, P. and Kertesi, G. (1985) 'Second Economy, Competition, Inflation' *Acta Oeconomica*, vol. 35, no. 3-4, pp. 269-293.

Geertz, C. (1978) 'The Bazaar Economy: Information and Search in Peasant Marketing', *The American Economic Review*, no 4, May, pp. 28-32.

Geertz, C. (1979) 'Suq: The Bazaar Economy in Sefrou' in Rosen, Lawrence et all. (eds.) *'Meaning and Ordering Contemporary Morocco'*, New York.

Hann, Ch. (1992) 'Market Principle, Market-place and the Transition in Eastern Europe' in Dilley, R. (ed.) *'Contesting Markets'*, Edinburgh University Press, Edinburg, pp. 244-259.

Hann, C. and Hann, I. (1992) 'Samovars and sex on Turkey's Russian markets' *Anthropology Today*, vol. 8, no. 4, pp. 3-6.

Harcsa, I. (1994) 'Megélhetési és vásárlási szokások a háztartásokban', *Társadalomstatisztikai Füzetek*, 6 sz., KSH, Budapest.

Sik, E. (1994) 'From Multicoloured to Black and White Economy: The Hungarian Second Economy and the Transformation' *International Journal of Urban and Regional Research*, vol. 18, no. 1, pp. 46-70.

Sik, E. (1995) 'Measuring the Unregistered Economy in Post-Communist Transition' *EUROSOCIAL Report, 52*, European Centre: Vienna.

Sik, E. (1996) 'Fekete fogyasztós (Black Consumption)', Report of the 5th Wave of the Hungarian Household Panel Survey, (eds. Sik, E. and Tóoth, I. Gy.), TARKI, Budapest.

Subject Index

adjudicator, 99
administrative corruption, 67
Albania, 70
Algeria, 286
arbitrary discretion
    regime of, 19
Armenia, 145, 153, 154, 156
arrears, 21
Australia, 94, 98, 163
Austria, 49, 50, 51, 60, 163, 276
Azerbaijan, 144, 145, 153, 154, 156

Balkan stereotype, 212
Baltic countries, 107, 143, 145, 148, 151, 153, 154
behavior
    acquisitive, 24
    noncompliant, 15, 17
    predatory, 23
    protective, 23
Belarus, 73, 115, 145, 153, 154, 156
Belgium, 162, 163
big state, 35
black jobs, 245
black markets, 20
Bosnia and Herzegovina, 120
bribery, 12, 14, 22, 53, 56
Bulgaria, 49, 50, 60, 70, 103, 115, 145, 147, 153, 154, 156, 286
bureaucratic corruption
    model of, 70

Canada, 163
CEE, 1, 3, 102, 103, 104, 105, 107, 114, 115
CEMA, 196, 209
Central Bureau of Statistics, 171
central planning
    inefficiencies of, 19
Chechen, 107
China, 287

CIS, 73, 106, 143, 145, 151, 153, 154
Citizen's Charter Complaints Task Force, 98
cleptocracy thesis, 47
COMECON markets, 275–303
Commonwealth of Independent States. *See* CIS
complaints system, 98
Compliance Cost Assessments (CCAs), 98
contract enforcement, 21
controls
    price and production, 17
corporate governance structures, 23
corruption, 5, 12, 14, 21, 22, 36, 55, 56, 61, 67–86, 122
    administrative, 67
    bureaucratic, 71
    economic cost of, 22
    judicial, 72
    model of, 73–81
    of public servants, 55
    organization model of, 22
    police, 73
    political, 67
    political-administrative, 71
    political-legislative, 71
    taxonomy of, 70
    types of, 70
costs
    adjustment, 12, 23
    administration, 99
    compliance, 90
    of misallocation, 17
    operating, 90
    production, 13
    transaction, 12, 13, 24
crime
    antiques, 106
    illegal migrations, 106
    narcotics, 106
    organized, 12, 14, 21, 105–6

308 *Underground Economies in Transition*

criminal behavior, 73
criminal economy, 102, 105–7
Croatia, 49, 50, 51, 59, 60, 70, 119, 120, 121, 127, 170
Croatian Central Bureau of Statistics, 173, 175, 182, 192, 193, 209
cultural inertia, 49, 52, 58, 59
Czech Republic, 70, 103, 104, 114, 115, 143, 145, 153, 154, 156, 162, 163, 276

Denmark, 163
deregulation
  recommendations for, 31
developmental paradigm, 43, 44
Discriminant Index Function, 92
distrust in institutions
  socio-cultural profile of, 56
  spatial distribution of, 57–58

EBRD, 70, 143
economic crime
  punishments of, 18
economic development, 212, 242
economic growth, 30
  organic, 19
economic performance, 23
  and institutions, 11–12
economic policy
  and underground economy, 29–41
  goals of, 29
  influence of unrecorded economy on, 33
  measures against underground economy, 37
economic traditionalism, 47
economy
  fictitious, 102
  illegal, 16, 102, 217
  parallel systems of, 212
  unrecorded, 16
  unreported, 16
egalitarianism, 48, 50
electricity consumption
  cross-country comparison of, 149–60
electricity intensity, 141–65

employment, 226–31
  activity rate, 219–26
Estonia, 107, 115, 145, 153, 154, 156

fictitious economy, 108
Financial Times, 92
Finland, 148, 149, 159, 160, 163, 164
fiscal administration, 68–70
fiscal burden, 218
fiscal crisis, 69
Former Soviet Union (FSU), 1, 3, 4, 17, 63, 102, 103, 104, 105, 106, 107, 115, 137, 143, 145, 149, 164
France, 72, 163

Georgia, 144, 145, 153, 154, 156
Germany, 163, 276
government
  credibility of, 20
  distrust of, 20, 21, 23, 36, 54, 97–98
  failure, 22
  perception of, 97–98
  trust in, 97–98
Great Britain, 133
Greece, 162, 163
growth, 243
  organic, 19

hidden labor in Poland, 245–74
Hungary, 49, 50, 51, 60, 70, 104, 114, 115, 145, 147, 148, 153, 154, 156, 162, 163, 276

IMF, 41, 68, 182
income distribution, 243
individual behavioral patterns, 212
  Balkan stereotype, 212–13
  Swiss stereotype, 212–13
inflation, 21, 23, 33, 87, 94, 99, 179, 181
informal marketplaces
  Hungary, 275–303
  spatial distribution of, 277–79
informal traders
  Hungary, 275–303
informalization of privileges, 47

Inland Revenue, 92, 99
institutional economics
   and underground economics, 15–16
institutions, 59, 118
   and economic performance, 11–12
   building of, 70
   change of, 11–24
   distrust of, 36, 48, 54, 55, 57, 58, 59
   formal and informal, 14–15, 23
   incentive to comply, 13
   opportunism of, 58
Internal Revenue Service of the United States, 92
International Labor Organization, 213, 247
investment
   productive, 20
Ireland, 49, 50, 60, 162, 163
Italy, 45, 49, 50, 60, 162, 163

Japan, 163

Kazakhstan, 103, 115, 144, 145, 153, 154, 156
KGB, 107

labor market, 211–42
   definition of, 213–14
Latvia, 115, 144, 145, 153, 154, 156
law
   rule of, 19, 22–23
legal institutions
   confidence in, 51
   distrust of, 51
   trust in, 61
legal system
   distrust for, 54
legalization, 24
legislative framework, 212
liberalization, 20, 24, 118, 127
Lithuania, 107, 115, 145, 153, 154, 156

Mafia, 21, 107
market liberalization, 70
material production
   concept of, 168

material production system (MPS), 181
Moldavia, 103, 115, 144, 145, 153, 154, 156
money-laundering, 14
moonlighting, 245

national accounts, 7
National Bank of Croatia, 180
national income, 168
national income accounts, 16
nepotism, 35, 122
Netherlands, 163
new economic sociology, 45, 59
new independent states (NIS), 20, 22
New Institutional Economics (NIE), 2, 4, 11, 15
New Zealand, 97
nomenklatura, 18
noncompliance, 4, 11–24
   consequences of, 16–17
   legacy of, 17, 19–22, 23
Norway, 163

OECD, 149, 161, 165
opportunism, 36, 47, 51, 53, 59
   index of, 51, 57
   socio-cultural profile of, 56
   spatial distribution of, 57–58

parallel currency, 181
past
   legacy of, 58
paternalism, 124
paternalistic capitalism, 126
path dependency, 4, 11, 14, 20, 23, 57, 121
PAYE, 93
performance
   economic, 13, 14, 15, 16
planned economy
   collectivist legacy of, 57
   cultural legacy of, 50
Poland, 70, 104, 114, 115, 143, 145, 153, 154, 156, 162, 163, 245
Portugal, 49, 50, 60, 163
poverty, 47

line of, 218
perception of, 53
'social cost' of, 58
power consumption, 141–65
power system
   Columbia, 212
   Italy, 212
predation, 13–14
   incentives for, 24
   preference for, 20
predatory activity, 18
price controls, 21
prices
   black market, 18
   decontrol of, 69
   state-controlled, 18
privatization, 20, 24, 108, 127
   and unofficial economy, 122–24
   consequences of, 108–9
   different approaches to, 108
   in Russia, 110–11
   objects and methods, 110–11
   programs of, 23
   schemes of, 22
property theft, 14
protection, 13–14
public officials
   corruption and bribery of, 31

reform
   institutional, 15
   policy, 14, 15
regulation, 118
   Croatia, 124
   of market economy, 124
rents
   creating, 19
   exploiting, 19
   opportunities for, 112–13
rent-seeking, 13, 19, 24, 69, 111
   opportunities for, 112–13
residual property, 23
rights
   property, 12, 13, 20
Romania, 49, 50, 60, 104, 115, 145, 147, 153, 154, 156, 276, 287
rule of law, 19

rules
   formal, 15
   informal, 15, 19
   of behavior, 13
   of procedure, 13
   Russia, 23, 25, 68, 69, 68–69, 70, 72, 103, 105, 109, 110, 115, 144, 145, 149, 153, 154, 156, 287

sanctions, 14
second economy, 17, 18
services, 127
shortage economy, 18
slave markets, 275
Slovakia, 70, 145, 153, 154, 156, 162, 163, 276
Slovenia, 49, 50, 60, 114
small firms
   and underground economy, 126–27
   growth of, 126–27
smuggling, 14
SNA, 167–82
   concept of, 168
   methodology, 192
social embeddedness of social actions, 45
socio-cultural capital
   dynamics of, 52
socio-cultural factors
   cross-cultural comparison, 50
sources of work
   Croatia, 218–19
   South America, 218–19
South America, 218
Soviet Union. *See* Former Soviet Union
Spain, 49, 50, 60, 162, 163
spend to save initiative, 92
state
   and economy, 124–26
   and regulation, 117–31
   and underground economy, 124–26
   cost of, 124–26
   Croatia, 124–26
   the role of, 124–26
   wasteful and corrupt, 35
state paternalism, 48, 50, 52

state property
  personal appropriation of, 20
structure
  incentive, 12, 15, 24
  institutional, 14
Sweden, 163
Swiss stereotype, 212
Switzerland, 163
Syria, 286

tax administration, 67, 70, 99
  funding of, 89–92
  marginal cost, 90
  marginal revenue, 89–90, 89–92
  measurement of costs, 92
tax collection, 70
  measures to improve, 68
tax effectiveness, 87
tax evasion, 5, 12, 14, 21, 34, 51, 53, 59, 67–86, 87–100, 99
  measures against, 99
  minimising oportunities for, 93
  policies dealing with, 87–100
  reducing the net advantages, 94
  reducing willingnes to, 96
  reduction of, 93
tax gap, 87
tax laws
  Australia, 34
  Canada, 34
  complexity of, 34
  France, 34
  improvements of, 34
  Ireland, 34
  Netherlands, 34
  New Zealand, 34
tax officials
  corruption of, 67–86
tax policy, 67–86
tax system
  complexity of, 34
taxation, 69
  administrative and compliance costs of, 34, 88
  burden of, 34
  Great Britain, 34
  lowering of, 31

non-compliant behaviors, 35
  USA, 34
Taxpayer Compliance Measurement Program, 92
taxpayer identification number, 94
transaction costs, 243
transformation costs, 242
transition, 19
  and socio-cultural factors, 49
  fiscal administration, 70
  tax revenue structure, 70
  underground economy, 101–15
transition economies, 1, 11, 12, 14, 15, 23, 143, 147, 148

Ukraine, 103, 115, 144, 145, 146, 147, 148, 153, 154, 156, 276
underground economics
  and institutional economics, 15–16
underground economy
  and antropologists approach, 44–45
  and economic development, 44
  and economic policy, 4–5, 29–41
  and institutions, 117–31
  and new economic sociology, 45–46
  and noncompliance, 11–24
  and regulation, 117–31
  and sociologists approach, 44–45
  and state, 4–5
  and transition, 11–24
  assessment of, 191–208
  by labor force survey, 226–31
  couses of, 142
  definitions of, 101–2
  estimations of, 141–65
  financial activities in, 106–7
  government measures against, 32
  in agriculture, 191–208
  in Croatia, 29–41, 43–63, 59, 117–31, 7, 191–208, 211–42
  in Hungary, 275–303
  in industry, 191–208
  in labor market, 211–42, 245–74
  in Poland, 245–74
  in Russia, 101–15
  in trade, 191–208

in transition, 101–15
institutional aspect of, 11–24
measurement by SNA, 167–82
measurement of, 141–303, 167–82, 191–208
natural reproduction of, 59
non-economic influences, 43–63
paradoxes of, 45
path dependency of, 4–5
political economy of, 6, 117–31
positive and negative influences of, 44
power system, 212
reduction of, 125
role of government in, 33–35
situational dimension of, 59
size of, 142
social and cultural factors, 59
socio-cultural aspects of, 43–63
state economy of, 6
trends in transition, 103–14
United Kingdom, 72, 92, 93, 97, 98, 99, 163
unofficial economy, 102. *See also* underground economy
by sectors, 233–37
causes of, 35–37
Croatia, 36, 37
distortion of macroeconomic indicators, 39
economic policy measures against, 37, 40
estimates for transition countries, 103–4
in Croatia, 29–41
in the labor market, 211–42
in Yugoslavia, 35
methods of measuring, 169
paradoxes of, 59
political economy of, 117–31

relation with official economy, 215
role of government in, 33–35
role of privatization in, 122–24
role of state officials in, 35
socially acceptable size of, 32
socio-cultural aspects of, 120–21
socio-cultural factors, 59
sources of work, 218–19
suggestions for further research, 38
the role of the government in, 33, 35
unrecorded economy, 168. *See* underground economy
distortion of macroeconomic indicators, 33
unregistered economy, 217. *See* underground economy
unregistered employment
Poland, 1–8
unregistered labor
Croatia, 7
unregistered work, 246. *See* underground economy
unreported economy, 217. *See* underground economy
USA, 163
USSR, 276
Uzbekistan, 103, 115, 145, 147, 153, 154, 156

wealth
redistribution of, 13
wealth accumulation
illegal, 21
wealth acquisition
perception of, 52
World Bank, 20, 70, 82, 103, 105, 165

Yugoslavia, 45, 49, 120, 276, 286, 287

Author Index

Alexander, J. 275, 305
Alexander, P. 275, 305
Alexeev, M. 17, 25, 26, 146, 164
Allingham, M. G. 73, 82, 94, 95, 100
Anderson, A. 17, 25
Anušić, Z. 134
Arrow, K. J. 134

Árvay, J. 148, 164

Bagnasco, A. 60, 62
Barro, R. J. 40
Barthelemy, P. 220
Basanez, M. 60
Bawly, D. 40
Becker, G. S. 73, 82
Behrman, J. 134
Bejaković, P. 44, 46, 62, 120, 122, 134
Benham L. 24, 25
Benham, A. 24, 25
Benton, L. A. 46, 47, 60, 62, 118, 136
Besley, T. 134
Bićanić, I. 46, 47, 62, 118, 121, 134, 135, 219
Biljan-August, M. 126, 134
Blades, D. W. 209
Blasi, J. 23, 25
Böröcz, J. 275, 305
Bowles, R. A. 5, 70, 73, 82
Burić, I. 48, 62

Cadot, O. 73, 82
Carter, M. 101, 116
Castells, M. 44, 46, 47, 60, 62, 118, 136
Clark, G. 40
Coleman, C. 96, 100
Crnković-Pozaić S. 120, 131, 134

Csepeli, G. 285, 305

Čengić, D. 132, 135
Čučković, N. 40, 109, 116, 119, 135

De Soto, H. 16, 17, 25, 118, 134
Dean, P. 88
Dewey, A. G. 275, 305
Dietz, T. 46, 62
Dobozi, I. 142, 143, 144, 147, 149, 150, 160, 163, 164
Dornbusch, R. 30, 40
Dublin, J. A. 92, 100

Eggertsson, T. 14, 25

Ékes, I. 148, 165

Feige, E. L. 4, 16, 22, 23, 25, 26, 40, 43, 44, 62, 101, 116, 128, 135, 192, 209, 213, 214, 215
Feldbrugge, F. J. M. 18, 25, 47, 62
Filkin, E. 99, 100
Franičević, V. 6, 35, 39, 40, 117, 120, 121, 123, 125, 127, 131, 133, 135
Frank, R. H. 119, 135
Franz, A. 198, 209, 214
Freeman, C. 165
Freeman, L. 96, 100
Fullerton, M. 305

Galasi, P. 278, 305
Garoupa, N. 73, 82
Gatarić, Lj. 132, 135
Geertz, C. 275, 305, 306
Giovannini, A. 40
Glas, M. 118, 135
Glinkina, S. 5

Graetz, M. J. 92, 100
Granovetter, M. 45, 62, 121, 135
Greenfield, H. I. 118, 135
Grossman, G. 4, 17, 18, 26, 164

Handleman, S. 26
Hann, C. 277, 286, 306
Hann, I. 306
Harcsa, I. 279, 306
Henry, S. 119, 135
Hodgson, G. M. 121, 135
Huntington, S. 24, 26

Ingham, G. 60, 62
Inglehart, R. 60
Ivandić, N. 131, 136

Jankov, Lj. 40, 131, 135

Kalaska, M. 7
Kalogjera, D. 132, 135
Kaštelan-Mrak, M. 126, 133, 135
Kertesi, G. 278, 305
Kesner-Škreb, M. 32, 40, 124, 135
Klein, E. 117, 118, 128, 137
Klitgaard, R. 17, 22, 26
Knežević, D. 132, 136
Kornai, J. 141, 142, 165
Kraft, E. 120, 123, 125, 135
Kregar, J. 132, 134, 136
Kroumova, M. 25
Kruse, D. 25
Kukar, S. 167, 192, 209
Kuzenkov, A. 111, 116
Kuznetsov, Y. 26

Lacko, M. 6, 24, 26, 101, 116, 148, 163, 164, 165, 281
Laffont, J. J. 80, 82
LaPalombara, J. 136
Leff, N. H. 24, 26
Leitzel, J. 16, 17, 26
Lotspeich, R. 17, 26
Lovrić, Lj. 126, 134
Lyman, S. 45, 62

Macaulay, S. 26

Madžarević, Sanja 7, 40, 41, 125, 131, 136, 203, 206, 209
Madžarević, Saša 7, 32, 41, 126, 131, 136
Malyshev, N. 164
Mateša, Z. 120, 136
Mauro, P. 17, 26
Meier, A. 68, 82
Mihalyi, P. 108, 116
Mikulić, D. 7, 32, 41, 126, 131, 136, 203, 206, 209
Miljenović, Ž. 209
Moreno, A. 60
Mueller, D. C. 136

Nellis, J. 25, 26
Nelson, J. 26
North, D. C. 11, 12, 26, 45, 62, 121, 136

Obradović, J. 45, 62
Ott, K. 4, 5, 26
Owens, J. 34, 41

Pardo, I. 47, 62
Peattieau, L. 41
Pohl, G. 142, 143, 147, 149, 150, 160, 163, 164
Polishchuk, L. 19, 23, 26
Popović, J. 126, 133, 136
Portes, A. 43, 44, 46, 47, 60, 62, 63, 118, 121, 136, 213, 214
Powell, W. W. 121, 136
Primorac, Ž. 136
Pusić, E. 123, 125, 136
Putman, R. 45, 60, 63
Pyle, D. 81, 82

Radnić, A. 131, 136
Ramljak, O. 125, 136
Reljac, B. 41, 136
Rose-Ackerman, S. 133, 136
Rosen, H. S. 41, 306
Ross, J. 111, 116
Roth, J. A. 92, 96, 100
Roxburgh, I. 149, 165

Sabine, E. E. V. 93, 100
Sandford, C. 5, 34, 82, 100
Sandmo, A. 73, 82, 94, 95, 100
Santini, G. 136
Sassen-Koob, S. 43, 44, 46, 63
Savas, E. S. 116
Sayer, A. 164
Scholz, J. T. 92, 96, 100
Sekulić, D 47, 63
Shapiro, J. 149, 165
Shelley, L. 17, 26, 47, 63
Shleifer, A. 22, 27
Siegelbaum, P. 26
Sík, E. 8, 148, 165, 277, 278, 279, 281, 285, 286, 305, 306
Simončič, M. 135
Skolka, J. 219
Skorupan, V. 37, 41, 119
Smith, S. 169
Soete, L. 165
Srinivasan, T. N. 134
Standing, J. 149, 165
Stern, P. 46, 62
Stiglitz, J. E. 41
Swedberg, R. 45, 63, 136

Šajatović, M. 136
Štulhofer, A. 4, 5, 36, 41, 45, 63, 120, 121, 131, 137

Tanzi, V. 17, 27, 31, 41, 116, 137
Thomas, J. J. 118, 137
Tilly, C. 26
Tirole, J. 80, 82
Tokman, V. E. 117, 118, 124, 128, 137
Tóth, J. 305
Trang, D. V. 17, 27, 136, 137
Treml, V. 164

Vehovec, M. 126, 133, 135
Vértes, A. 148, 164
Vishny, R. 22, 27

Walker, L. 26
Wallschutzky, I. 93, 100
Whitehouse, E. 34, 41
Wied-Nebbelin, S. 169
Wilde, L. L. 92, 100
Wiles, P. 43, 44, 45, 46, 63, 218
Witkowski, J. 7
Witte, A. D. 92, 96, 100